Currency Competition and
Foreign Exchange Markets

The Dollar, the Yen and the Euro

Currency Competition and Foreign Exchange markets by Philipp Hartmann is a major new theoretical and empirical study of international currencies, which focuses on the role which the euro (the future single European currency) will play, along with the US dollar and the Japanese yen, in the international monetary and financial system.

In contrast with much of the existing literature, which approaches the subject from a macroeconomic perspective, Hartmann develops theoretical and empirical models which use game theory, time series and panel econometrics, and link financial market micro-structure analysis with transaction cost economics. The results of *Currency Competition and Foreign Exchange Markets* are presented with reference to political, historical and institutional considerations, and provide accessible answers for policy-makers, business people and scholars world-wide. The sections on spread estimation and multiple vehicles with inter-dealer price and entry competition will be of particular use for finance professionals.

PHILIPP HARTMANN is an economist at the European Central Bank in Frankfurt. He formerly worked in the Financial Markets Group at the London School of Economics. He is widely regarded as one of the leading young economists in Europe, and his work has been featured on BBC Radio 4 (UK) and in publications including *Le Figaro* (France), *The Wall Street Journal* and the *Frankfurter Allgemeine Zeitung – Blick durch die Wirtschaft* (Germany). His previous writings include the monograph *Financial Regulation: Why, How and Where Now?* (with Professor Charles Goodhart *et al.*) and numerous articles published in leading academic and policy journals.

Currency Competition and Foreign Exchange Markets

The Dollar, the Yen and the Euro

Philipp Hartmann

CAMBRIDGE
UNIVERSITY PRESS

PUBLISHED BY THE PRESS SYNDICATE OF THE UNIVERSITY OF CAMBRIDGE
The Pitt Building, Trumpington Street, Cambridge, United Kingdom

CAMBRIDGE UNIVERSITY PRESS
The Edinburgh Building, Cambridge CB2 2RU, UK   www.cup.cam.ac.uk
40 West 20th Street, New York, NY 10011–4211, USA   www.cup.org
10 Stamford Road, Oakleigh, Melbourne 3166, Australia
Ruiz de Alarcón 13, 28014 Madrid, Spain

First published 1998
Reprinted 1999 (twice)

Printed in the United Kingdom at the University Press, Cambridge

Typeset in 10/12pt Times   [CE]

A catalogue record for this book is available from the British Library

Library of Congress Cataloguing in Publication data
Hartmann, Philipp.
Currency competition and foreign exchange markets: the dollar, the yen and the
future international role of the Euro / Philipp Hartmann.
     p.   cm.
Includes bibliographical references.
ISBN 0 521 63273 0 (hbk.)
1. European currency unit.   2. Euro-dollar market.   3. Currency question.
4. Monetary unions – European Union countries.   I. Title.
HG925.H367   1998
332.4′56–dc21   98–36046   CIP

ISBN 0 521 63273 0 hardback

Contents

Figures

Tables

Preface and acknowledgements

When I started working on international currencies in 1992 the Maastricht Treaty, establishing a concrete timetable for the completion of European Economic and Monetary Union (EMU), had just been signed. Many citizens, economists, journalists and politicians, in particular in the United States but also in Europe, remained sceptical whether such an ambitious project would ever go ahead, and most people pondered what the internal consequences for Europe would be and whether EMU was really such a good idea. In this situation, only a limited number of people, most of them within or close to the European Commission, found it worthwhile to think about 'great ideas', such as the external role of the single currency and its future competition with the US dollar. Fascinated by the idea of 'getting under the skin' of the workings of the world monetary and financial system, I began to wonder whether I could tackle this issue with modern economic analysis.

It was at that time that I met Richard Portes, who was one of the few academics recognizing the political determination in Europe to bring EMU into being and who was prepared to make 'the great leap forward' necessary to think about the implications for the international monetary order. He encouraged me to start a long-horizon theoretical and empirical research programme on the determinants of international currencies in general, which could alleviate the lack of rigorous analysis in this field and also satisfy a great deal of demand once the introduction of the single currency was imminent. The time has now come; when this book is available in bookstores the introduction of the euro will only be a couple of months away. The book is the synthesis of my work in this area over the last couple of years: however speculative the predictions in the applied parts may sound to some readers, I hope that it helps reduce the uncertainty and confusion about what the likely consequences of EMU will be for the international monetary and financial system.

The first person I would like to thank is Richard Portes, who – since Summer 1992 in Paris – followed my work in this area closely and did not spare suggestions, criticism and support for my projects. Most of the work was done while I was on the staff of DELTA (Ecole Normale Supérieure, Paris) and of the London School of Economics' Financial Markets Group (FMG). I would like to express my gratitude to Roger Guesnerie and François Bourguignon, and David Webb and Charles Goodhart as well as to my other colleagues from DELTA and the FMG for the stimulating research environments they provided. Financial support by the EU Commission's Human Capital and Mobility Programme and by the UK's Economic and Social Research Council (ESRC) is gratefully acknowledged.

Among the other researchers who have expressed an interest in the various projects contained in this book I would like to mention explicitly Christian de Boissieu (Université Paris I, Panthéon–Sorbonne), Bernard Dumas (HEC), Jürgen von Hagen (Bonn University), Torsten Hens (Bielefeld University) and Charles Wyplosz (University of Geneva), who with their suggestions and criticism have helped improve substantially some of the more technical aspects. I have also greatly benefited from discussions with Roel Beetsma and Peter Schotman at Limburg University; Stanley Black at the University of North Carolina; Marc Flandreau at OFCE; Rüdiger Frey at ETH, Zurich; Paul de Grauwe at Leuven University; Dominique Guillaume at Oxford University; Nobuhiro Kiyotaki at the University of Minnesota; Michael Leahy and Shang-Jin Wei at Harvard University; Ward Brown, Charles Goodhart, Asbjørn Hansen and Richard Payne at LSE; Guillermo Larraín, Thierry Magnac, Mathilde Maurel, Georges de Ménil, Nathalie Picard, Gilles St Paul and Bertrand Villeneuve at DELTA; Alvaro Almeida, Peter Clarke, Peter Quirk, George Tavlas and Jens Weidmann at the IMF; Michel Dacorogna, Rakhal Davé, Ueli Müller and Richard Olsen at Olsen & Associates; Ann Fremault-Vila and Dirk Schoenmaker at the Bank of England. Another indispensible input were the discussions I had with market economists and traders, in particular Francis Breedon of Lehman Brothers, Jean-Christophe Doittau of Compagnie Bancaire, Michael Feeney of Sumitomo and Dirk Wegener of Citibank.

Some sections of chapter 4 were first presented at the Centre for European Policy Studies' (CEPS) working party on 'The Passage to the Euro' (May 1996); I am grateful to the Chairman, Helmut Schlesinger, and the two Rapporteurs, Daniel Gros and Karel Lannoo, for having given me this opportunity and to all the working party members for a lively debate on this occasion. Parts of the book have also been presented at academic conferences and seminars too numerous to list in this Preface.

For the empirical parts of the book I had to gather a substantial amount of very specific data. Without the extraordinary cooperation of

Olsen & Associates and a large number of central banks this would never have been possible. It is therefore a pleasure to mention the hospitality of Olsen & Associates in Zurich, where I spent one month in the research group. In particular, Rakhal Davé assisted me generously in the use of Olsen & Associates' high-frequency foreign exchange data bases. Thanks go also to Ashwin Rattan of Cambridge University Press, who has taken so much care of the manuscript. Last but not least, my readers and I owe a lot to the anonymous subway driver who found my notebook and diskette with the complete manuscript of the book.

The manuscript was finalized while I was on the staff of the London School of Economics' Financial Markets Group. Any views expressed are solely my own.

London, September 1997   PHILIPP HARTMANN

1 Introduction

> The world today is dominated by the US dollar ... This structural imbalance in the international monetary system is a factor of instability. I see advantages in not living in a dollar-dominated world.
>
> *(Yves-Thibault de Silguy, 1997)*

> The international role of the euro is the hidden agenda of Europe's long-planned adoption of a single currency. *(Charles Wyplosz, 1997)*

This book studies the phenomenon of international currencies, from both a theoretical and an empirical perspective, and applies the results in order to give an answer to the question: 'what role will the euro, the future single European currency, play in the international monetary and financial system *when competing with the US dollar and the Japanese yen* after its introduction, scheduled for January 1999?' An 'international currency' is a currency which fulfils one or several of the classical money functions – medium of exchange, store of value and unit of account – for non-nationals or non-residents of the issuing country, be they private or public agents. 'International currency competition' refers to the process determining to what extent various national currencies are employed by non-residents. With respect to the euro, the issuing 'country' is the sum of all European Union (EU) countries joining European Monetary Union (EMU). 'Euro internationalization' refers only to the acceptance of the single European currency by non-EMU-area residents, since there will not be any genuinely competing alternative currency within the EMU zone.

The intention of my project is twofold: on the one hand, I hope to make an academic contribution to an area which, in my view, has been considerably under-researched. Two out of six chapters (chapters 3 and 5) are analytical, using the quantitative theoretical and empirical tools of modern economics and finance – game theory, time series and panel econometrics – to throw some light on the key mechanisms at work determining which national currencies achieve an important international role. In contrast to most of the previous analytical academic literature, which usually takes a macroeconomic perspective, my approach links financial market – in particular foreign exchange (forex) market – microstructure analysis with transaction cost economics. In chapters 2 and 4 I apply the analytical results and provide an additional empirical, historical and institutional dimension in order to answer more practical and policy-relevant questions of international currency use. Now that EMU is imminent, there is tremendous demand by government officials and business men and women to know the impact the euro will have on the international monetary and financial system. For the purpose of motivating what follows in the main body of the book I proceed in reverse order, starting with the policy questions.

1.1   Importance of currency internationalization and European Monetary Union

The extent with which national currencies in general and the euro in particular are used in the international sphere after 1999 is of major importance, for both the global community and for the specific issuing country. The more important is a country's national currency for cross-border or completely foreign transactions the stronger the impact of exogenous domestic shocks as well as the monetary and exchange rate policies of that country on other countries. The issuer of a large international currency will therefore have to be a major player in international policy coordination: in other words, a large international currency gives a country a lot of political power in international monetary relations, with substantial geopolitical consequences. In modern history a dominant international currency has often been the expression of, or even one of the driving forces behind, political and/or economic world leadership, as was the case for the British pound during the nineteenth century and for the US dollar after the Second World War.

Beyond the political sphere the internationalization of a currency has substantial consequences for internationally active businesses, which are the transmitters of this internationalization. Transnational corporations, for example, may find it more cost-effective to base their internal accounting on the dominant international currency instead of their home currency at headquarters. Banks and non-bank financial institutions offering financial services internationally will face increased demand for products in internationalized currencies, requiring them to develop expertise and operations in the respective financial markets (be they domestic or off-shore ('euro') markets). Of course, this increased demand will also feed back into domestic financial markets of the country issuing an international currency, enhancing their size and liquidity. In case of a virtual regime shift – say, from one dominant international currency to another or from a one-currency to a two-currency system – private payments and settlements systems will have to be adjusted to the new monetary order. Similarly, the pricing practices and hedging needs of international traders of homogeneous primary goods, which are usually priced and settled in the dominant international currency, may change substantially.

It can also be argued that banks and other financial institutions have an advantage in dealing with products denominated in their home currency, be it through more experience with domestic macroeconomic policies, the legal and regulatory environment, better knowledge of the functioning and organization of the local securities and banking markets, long-standing relationships with an important domestic end-investor base, or easier access to the domestic payments and settlements systems. In this sense, banks from a country issuing a dominant international currency start with an advantage *vis-à-vis* their foreign competitors. While it might be objected that these competitive advantages should not play an important role among the truly global players operating in practically all important financial centres, the evidence is in favour of home currency advantage.[1]

Since the Second World War the US dollar has been the dominant international currency, a situation ratified rather than caused by the Bretton Woods system of fixed exchange rates – built around it. A gradual diversification out of dollar into mainly Deutsche mark and Japanese yen since the unravelling of the post-war monetary order in the early 1970s came to a halt since the early 1990s and, in any case, never seriously threatened the dollar's dominance (see chapter 2). EMU is certainly the most important event in the international monetary and financial system since the end of the Bretton Woods system in the early 1970s (Bergsten, 1997). Depending on the number of countries qualifying for the European currency union the size of the domestic monetary habitat of the new common European currency, the euro, will become comparable to that of the dollar and larger than that of the yen or that of the mark, the most important European currency at present (see chapter 4).

Will this 'shock' to the international monetary system cause further diversification out of the dollar? Will the euro become as important as the size of Europe in the world economy suggests and challenge the current dollar dominance, maybe even replace the US currency as the world leader? Any of these scenarios has important implications for world

---

[1] For example, McCauley and White (1997) show that bookrunners in the primary eurobond markets have dominant market shares in issues denominated in their home currency.

monetary and financial affairs, for both the European common policy institutions as well as for the distribution of power on a global level.

With respect to the European level a quick and far-reaching internationalization of the euro has implications for the domestic monetary policy approach chosen. Large foreign short-term euro holdings are likely to render European money aggregates more unstable and therefore a pure monetary targeting strategy (as opposed to, say, an inflation targeting strategy) more difficult.[2] Moreover, strong euro internationalization will reinforce the case for a structure of EU-internal monetary institutions which allows Europe to speak with one voice to the outside world for the purposes of world monetary policy and exchange rate coordination. The Maastricht Treaty says in article 109 that the EU EcoFin Council can decide unanimously on formal fixed exchange rate agreements or give by qualified majority 'general orientations for exchange rate policies', whereas the European Central Bank (ECB) is in charge of the remaining exchange rate decisions. In fact, the EU summit in Mondorf-les-Bains in September 1997 seems to have confirmed that in normal times the operational responsibility for exchange rate policies would be with the ECB. It remains to be seen how a comparatively large group of national finance ministers, such as represented in the EU EcoFin Council, can effectively decide on formulating coherent policies in times of misalignment or crisis and coordinate them with the ECB.

On the world level, US influence on international monetary affairs will decline and EU influence increase, further strengthening the case for tightening of EMU-internal institutions. When a common EMU-external policy of European monetary institutions is fully accomplished, the composition of cooperative bodies such as the G-7 (currently comprising the USA, Canada and Japan on the one hand, and Germany, France, Italy and the UK on the other), and the refinancing and governance structures of the major international organisations, in particular that of the International Monetary Fund (IMF), will have to be reformed in order to reflect the new balance of power.[3] Other issues concerning the impact of EMU on the international monetary system, relate to reforms

---

[2] Internationalization is not the only factor which can make monetary aggregates less reliable intermediate targets for monetary policy. Another major factor which plays a role is financial market development and, in particular, financial innovations resulting in more volatile money demand behaviour. Of course, these two factors are not independent: deep, broad and sophisticated financial markets make a currency more attractive for international traders and investors and internationalization itself will produce competitive pressures and incentives accelerating domestic financial market development.

[3] See Alogoskoufis and Portes (1991) and Bergsten and Henning (1996) on these issues. The present share of the USA in total IMF quotas is about 18 per cent, while the cumulative share of all fifteen EU countries amounts to about 30 per cent (Henning, 1997).

of IMF macroeconomic policy surveillance (EMU-wide surveillance versus single-country surveillance), to potential access of EMU countries to IMF liquidity assistance and to the redefinition of currency weights for the Special Drawing Right (SDR), the IMF's artificial basket currency.[4]

The international competitive edge which the European banking industry could gain through euro internationalization and EMU-internal consolidation is likely to lead to more truly global financial players and fiercer international competition, raising the question: how will the related potential systemic risks be matched by financial regulators and supervisors? Although a large part of regulation for the foreseeable future is likely to remain fundamentally national, even within Europe more pressure will build up to improve international coordination in banking supervision and financial crisis management.[5]

1.2   Pivotal role of forex markets

Several parts of this book focus on forex markets and media of exchange in currency trading, which I denote as *vehicle currencies in the forex market*. Although there are also some purely academic reasons, this choice has been mainly made because of the key role forex markets play in the international monetary and financial system in general and in the internationalization of currencies in particular. First, for any (non-forex) international transaction, at least one of the parties involved has to enter the forex market at some point to either purchase or sell foreign currency balances. Conditions in this market thus considerably influence the denomination of the underlying transaction.[6]

Second, since the abolition of capital controls among industrial countries, forex markets are among the freest and most competitive markets in the world. Charles Goodhart (1997) has argued strongly that, on the national level, governments at most times in the past effectively determined which money their citizens had to use, with no (or very little) scope for true currency competition. The phenomenon of forex market vehicle currencies is an excellent example, maybe even the only example, of the truly spontaneous emergence of money on a large scale in modern times.

---

[4] Many of these issues are discussed in Polak (1997) and Thygesen (1997). The future of the SDR has even been the focus of a separate book (see Mussa *et al.*, 1996).

[5] This also raises the question whether European regulators will increasingly come to the Basle Committee on Banking Supervision (the G-10 coordinating body for banking regulatory affairs) speaking with a single voice (McCauley and White, 1997).

[6] While these conditions depend on fundamental trade and investment flows, the market micro-structure analysis below shows that exchange structures, trading volumes, volatilities and so on in forex markets can develop considerable 'autonomy' from these fundamentals.

Table 1.1   *Turnover comparison of different markets, 1995 (bn USD)*

	Global USD spot forex trading	Global US treasury securities trading[a]	US stock market trading[b]	Real-world GDP[c]	World merchandise trade[d]
Total volume per business day	351	125	24	130	20

Notes: [a] 1994 data, all maturities.
[b] On all recognized exchanges and NASDAQ.
[c] At purchasing-power-parity (PPP) exchange rates, assuming 255 business days per year.
[d] At market exchange rates, assuming 255 business days per year.
Sources: BIS (1996); Fleming (1997); IMF (1997b); OECD (1997); WTO (1996).

Last, but not least, the forex market is particularly important because of its huge size. As reported in table 1.1, total spot US dollar forex turnover alone is almost three times the size of total US Treasury securities trading (for all maturities) world-wide or global GDP. Even total US stock market trading and the overall volume of world trade are negligible compared to forex trading. For all these reasons, I fully agree with Peter Kenen (1995, p. 110) that 'the international role of the ECU [euro] will be affected crucially by the impact of EMU on the foreign exchange market'.

Another motivation for the emphasis on forex markets in the analytical chapters of this book has to do with the substantial interest which the micro-structure of these markets has recently attracted in the academic profession. It is all the more surprising, then, that until now the forex micro-structure literature has completely ignored the phenomenon of vehicle currencies and the quite peculiar structure of open and closed interbank currency markets. For example, the 300-page volume, *The Microstructure of Foreign Exchange Markets* (Frankel *et al.*, 1996) does not make a single reference to the dollar's or the mark's special roles as vehicle currencies.[7] One of the aims of this book, in chapter 3, is therefore to fill the gap and explain this phenomenon, in the hope that this might – in addition to the present applications to the internationalization of currencies – stimulate more research working out further implications, such as for information transmission through forex prices and volatilities, for example, or for optimal official intervention strategies.

---

[7] The same applies to the booming forex high-frequency data literature (see for example the survey by Goodhart and O'Hara, 1998) – with a single notable exception (de Jong *et al.*, 1996).

However, the relevance of the results go beyond the areas of currency trading and forex vehicle currencies. The hypothesis of a negative relationship between the use of a medium of exchange (its turnover or trading volume) and the transaction costs encountered by its users is at the very basis of the theory of money, but has hardly ever been rigorously tested. It can be traced at least as far back as to the writings of Karl Menger (1892) and it still plays a prominent role in modern search models of monetary exchange (Kiyotaki and Wright, 1989). These *network externalities* or economies of scale in the use of exchange media, are at the heart of a certain tendency towards centralization to a single or only a few monies. It has led to the interpretation of a medium of exchange as a public good (Tobin, 1980).[8] While the volume–transaction–cost relationship is hard to test in relation to fiat government money and goods exchange, the observability of bid–ask spreads – as a measure of transaction costs – and newly available data on trading volumes in the foreign exchange markets permit such a test. Forex market data therefore provide a unique opportunity to test for network externalities in monetary exchange in general, which is exploited in chapter 5, dealing with the empirical spread–volume relationship.

1.3   Overview of the book

The book is organized in six chapters. Following this Introduction, chapter 2 surveys the available literature about international currencies. The starting point is a restatement of the classical money functions in an international context. The following survey of the theoretical literature reveals that – without exception – existing theories of international currency can explain only a small part of the functions of international money. One of the most neglected international monetary functions appears to be that of a forex vehicle currency. This and other medium of exchange functions are characterized by the presence of network externalities, which imply forces driving towards concentration to one or a few dominant international currencies. In contrast, investment currency theory predicts that optimal international portfolio choice will be geared towards reaping the benefits of diversification. Currency competition may thus imply a friction between the store of value and medium of exchange functions, providing a new explanation for biases in international investment.

In a brief historical survey of international currencies since the Middle

---

[8] For differences between money and traditional public goods, however, see de Grauwe (1989).

Ages, I then argue that – in accordance with network effects and vehicle-currency theories – there has in most times been a hierarchy of several competing international 'key' currencies with one clearly dominating all the others in practically all dimensions. Moreover, the available historical evidence suggests that transitions from one dominant international currency to another have been slow: earlier this century, for example, the dollar needed at least thirty years to overtake sterling. The switch to a floating exchange rate environment in 1973 led to a gradual diversification out of the dollar into the Deutsche mark and the Japanese yen, which came to a halt at the beginning of the 1990s, without seriously challenging the US currency's post-war leadership.

In response to the gap in the theoretical literature, chapter 3 develops a theory of forex vehicle currencies which is based on micro-structure theory and exchange costs. First steps in this direction were taken by Black (1991). Chapter 3 builds on this paper, but goes beyond it in many respects. A forex-dealer model, integrating inventory and order processing costs, is used to derive the (long-run) relationship between transaction costs (bid–ask spreads), expected trading volume and expected exchange rate volatility. Inter-dealer and inter-market competition will cause a currency with high (predictable) turnover and low volatility to emerge as a forex vehicle. However, it is also shown that generally high volatility can completely demonetize the forex market (the 'barter' situation).

The theory explains the scope for multiple equilibria with respect to a single vehicle currency and the possible coexistence of multiple vehicle currencies in a forex market equilibrium. Some equilibria with multiple vehicle currencies exhibit a hierarchical structure, as has been observed so frequently in the history of international currencies. It is also demonstrated that the network externality in the use of media of exchange in the forex market can, in some cases, be negative (exchange cost increasing) instead of positive, at least in theory. Transitions from one dominant vehicle currency to another can be both gradual or dramatic, but – within the theoretical structure developed – multiple vehicle exchange structures need not be more unstable than single vehicle structures. An appendix extends the analysis to a Bertrand game of inter-dealer, inter-market price competition.

The multiplicity of forex vehicles is particularly relevant with regard to the recent emergence of the Deutsche mark as a second vehicle currency in addition to the US dollar (chapter 2, section 2.3). Chapter 4, in a first step, explains the mark's emergence and describes the current exchange structure in the global forex market. It appears that the mark benefited from the volatility-reduction effect of the European Monetary System

(EMS) and volume-enlargement effects through financial liberalization and EMU convergence trading. However, the German currency's new role is strictly limited to trading among European currencies and the dollar remains dominant on the global level.

The rest of the chapter discusses the impact of EMU on international currency use in general and the potential future role of the euro in particular. Forex trading, international trade denomination, official reserve holdings and private investments in the euro, dollar and yen are studied in depth. On all these levels, a distinction is made between initial 'arithmetic' effects and dynamic follow-up effects. The former effects – the 'simple arithmetics' of EMU – originate from the removal of intra-European flows and stocks from the 'international' sphere. The latter effects are driven by EMU-internal and EMU-external size effects as well as changes in price level/exchange rate volatilities and international financial market return correlations.

The 'arithmetic' effects push the starting level of the euro well below the current aggregate share of EU currencies in international trade and investment. However, the size jump in the 'domestic monetary habitat' and to a somewhat lesser extent in external relations will lead to a gradual extension of the euro's role. Decelerating forces in this dynamic process will be network externalities and inertia favouring the incumbent dominant currency, the US dollar. Accelerating forces may include the ability of modern financial markets to adjust more quickly than earlier in history. Whether these latter forces can develop will depend on the speed and the extent with which intra-EMU financial markets integrate further.[9] A study of the evolution of world trade flows suggests that the euro will expand its role more quickly in regions closer to the EU. The future of the Japanese yen, which is likely to fall behind the euro, will depend to a large extent on the new monetary and financial system which emerges in Asia as soon as banking and currency crises in the region are resolved.

As pointed out above, a recurrent feature in the theories of (national and) international media of exchange, surveyed in chapter 2, is the assumption or derivation of a positive externality or economies of scale in use. More use of an international medium of exchange makes it even more attractive for further use (see, for example, chapter 3; Krugman, 1980; Chrystal, 1984; Matsuyama *et al.*, 1993; Rey, 1997). In chapter 5 of the book a natural test for this is performed in two very different ways. This test involves the estimation of the impact of trading volumes in the

---

[9] Portes *et al.* (1997) argue that these forces alone could raise the euro to the level of sharing world power with the US dollar, or even beyond.

forex market on transaction costs, as measured by bid–ask spreads, and thus goes deeper into the testing of forex market micro-structure theory. If the network-externality hypothesis is true, increasing volumes in a currency market should decrease transaction costs, at least in the long run. (If this were not the case, a vehicle currency would incorporate a certain tendency to auto-destroy its role, because vehicle transactions increase trading volume.) One major challenge for these estimations is the general lack of volume data, due to the fragmented (over-the-counter or OTC) character of forex trading.

Chapter 5 first surveys spread theory and empirics, highlighting the quality of different measures for forex trading volumes. It then goes on to integrate high-frequency exchange rate data and different measures of trading volume (including Reuters 'ticks') into two new datasets, one an eight-year long daily time-series for dollar/yen and the other a short panel over many currency pairs. The former dataset is used to estimate the *short*-run relationship between trading volumes and transaction costs, further developing an idea by Bessembinder (1994), who suggests that predictable trading volumes in the forex market should decrease transaction costs, while unpredictable volumes should increase them. Building on these results, I then apply a random-effects specification to the monthly panel data in order to test for the *long*-run relationship between volumes and spreads. Taken together, the results of chapter 5 provide strong evidence in favour of a negative long-run effect of trading volumes on transaction costs and, therefore, also in favour of the presence of positive network externalities and economies of scale in the use of international currencies. Reuters ticks are successfully applied as proxies for unpredictable and predictable turnovers.

The final chapter 6 assembles the main results from the different parts of the book and draws some general conclusions for international monetary and financial policies as well as for desirable future research efforts in the areas of currency internationalization and forex market micro-structure analysis.

2 National and international money: a survey

Déjà, avant la révolution du XIIIe siècle, on usait sur un même marché de deniers provenant de multiples ateliers et qui, étant de teneur métallique différente, ne pouvaient s'échanger les uns contre les autres que moyennant de délicats calculs d'équivalence; en outre, se rencontraient fréquemment des *marabotins* ou des *millares* islamiques et des *besants* de Constantinople. – Après le XIIIe siècle, non seulement les ateliers du lieu vont procéder à l'émission de pièces de type désormais divers, mais les pièces étrangères, elles-mêmes beaucoup plus variées que par le passé, vont continuer à circuler en grand nombre. Jusqu'au XIXe siècle, aucun pays ou presque ne pourra, sur son propre territoire, se suffire avec sa propre monnaie ... Il faut donc concevoir la pratique monétaire de ces temps comme fondée sur un perpétuel système de change.   *(Marc Bloch, 1954, emphases in the original)*[1]

Some of the oldest questions in theoretical and empirical economics ask: why do people use money and what goods are chosen to become money? Many of the founding fathers of modern economic thinking have already addressed the question why goods destined for ultimate consumption are rarely directly exchanged against each other. And the answers provided by Adam Smith (1776) – pointing to the division of labour – and by William Jevons (1875) – claiming that money removes the costly necessity of 'double coincidence of wants' – still have a massive impact on contemporary theories of money (Kiyotaki and Wright, 1989; Ostroy and Starr, 1990). A similar statement may be appropriate regarding the choice of which goods can become money, where Karl Menger

---

[1] Already before the thirteenth century revolution coins from numerous mints were usually used on the same market and these coins, whose metallic content differed, could be exchanged against each other only with the help of delicate calculations to ensure equivalence. In addition, islamic *marabotins* or *millares* and *bezants* from Constantinople were often found. After the thirteenth century, not only local mints began issuing different types of coins but also foreign coins, which now were much more diverse than had been the case before, continued circulating in large numbers. Until the nineteenth century, no country (or almost none) could limit the circulation of coins on its own territory to the local currency ... hence, one has to interpret monetary practices of these times as having been founded on a perpetual system of exchange.

(1892) emphasized their 'saleableness' – meaning among other things their general availability, divisibility, transportability, storability and durability.

However, in the complex modern world economy the phenomenon of money has gained many more dimensions, sharing *some* of the general principles of primitive monetary goods exchange while requiring different theoretical and empirical considerations. This book focuses on *international* money and, thus, international currency competition. In this chapter I provide a comprehensive but focused survey of the academic literature on the various functions (section 2.1), the existing theories (section 2.2) and the historical experience (section 2.3) of international currencies to bring the reader up to date with the intellectual discussion of the subject.

2.1   Functions of international money

It has proved useful for developing monetary theories to identify three functions performed by money. Money serves as a medium of exchange, as a store of value and as a unit of account. These three functions are not independent. Any medium of exchange must be a store of value – or temporary abode of purchasing power (Friedman, 1971) – and also implies a unit of account – or standard of value.[2] In contrast many stores of value, like ten-year Treasury bonds or real estate, do not circulate as media of exchange (Fama, 1980) and other value standards than implied by the circulating medium of exchange can be published and used for the denomination of goods or asset prices as long as there is some (possibly floating) exchange rate relating the former to the latter (Cohen, 1971).

One might conclude that – from a *theoretical* perspective – the medium of exchange function is the single function characterizing money alone, although it was argued to be too narrow for *empirical* definitions of money, in particular to delimit aggregates for the purposes of monetary policy (Laidler, 1969; Osborne, 1984, 1985). Moreover, separating the unit of account from the medium of exchange imposes additional computational costs on the exchanging agents and will have little benefit, except in special circumstances such as a hyperinflation or the replacement of an old currency by a new one. From this perspective, there is a tendency of all three functions to stay together in one medium; they exhibit synergies with each other. However, as will be argued further

---

[2] Kindleberger (1973b) coins the term 'standard of deferred payment' for the denomination of claims and liabilities which are not due immediately.

below, currency competition can loosen these links through the benefits of diversifying between different stores of value.

In the case of international money the functional definition becomes much more complex and the relations between the different functions are less sharp. Today it is a political reality that sovereign states issue a single national currency and give it an important competitive advantage on their own territory by requiring taxes to be paid in this currency, granting it legal tender (so that government purchases can be paid with it) and discouraging the use of other currencies within the private sector.[3] Strictly speaking though, the domestic government 'monopoly' for money is limited to base money and the major part of the national money supply is endogenously determined by the private banking sector (creating deposits). Nonetheless, private banks do not issue competing domestic currencies, even though this is often not explicitly forbidden.[4] The domestic money market is dominated by a single ultimate supplier or 'lender of last resort', the central bank.

However, if there is more than one country and if the national currencies are not completely inconvertible through capital controls, then some currency competition enters through the ability of residents of different countries to substitute their home currency for foreign currencies (see the discussion of currency and asset substitution below). The national supply dominance still ensures that in *normal* circumstances most transactions between residents are conducted in domestic currency. But for cross-border transactions at least one of the transactors has to acquire or accept a foreign currency. This has led, Krugman (1984), de Grauwe (1989), Alogoskoufis and Portes (1992) and Matsuyama *et al.* (1993), for example, to claim that the main difference between national and international money is that the former is supply-dominated, while the latter is demand-dominated and therefore more competitive.

What are the dimensions of international money? Again a functional definition of international money starting from the traditional money functions, as first worked out systematically by Cohen (1971) and taken up with slight variations by later writers on the topic (Magee and Rao, 1980; Kenen, 1983; Krugman, 1984; Bourguinat, 1985; Klump, 1986; Tavlas, 1991; Alogoskoufis and Portes, 1992; Tavlas and Ozeki, 1992) has proved to be a good starting point to delineate the research field. In Table 2.1 I present another typology of international money functions, which apart from some minor terminological deviations from those

---

[3] Vaubel (1986) gives a list of barriers to national and international currency competition through government intervention.

[4] Financial institutions may, however, develop new *means of payments* based on the national money standard, such as cheques, debit or credit cards, etc.

Table 2.1   *Functions of international money*

Money function (1)	Private use (2)	Official use (3)
Medium of exchange	Vehicle currency (i) In goods exchange: – foreign trade vehicle – domestic trade vehicle (direct currency substitution) (ii) In currency exchange: – forex vehicle	Intervention currency
Unit of account	Quotation currency	Pegging currency
Store of value	Investment currency (including indirect currency substitution)	Reserve currency

formerly employed, explicitly integrates vehicle currencies and currency substitution in one general concept of international currency. Although these two phenomena have some strong links, they have mostly been treated separately in two branches of the economic literature – the former in the more theoretical (microeconomic) monetary exchange literature and the latter in the more empirical (macroeconomic) money-demand literature.[5] Moreover, I introduce the distinction between trade and foreign exchange vehicles, which is essential for an important part of this book, and was rarely clarified – except perhaps by Magee and Rao (1980) – in the earlier literature on international currencies.

The internationalization of a currency begins when an individual agent or institution residing in a country other than that of this currency accepts or uses it as a medium of exchange, unit of account or store of value.[6] The first distinction made in table 2.1 refers to the type of the

---

[5] One exception is Thomas and Wickens (1991), who integrate hypotheses from the exchange literature in empirical money demand equations.

[6] Some might argue that this definition of currency internationalization is too broad. Consider a world with three countries, each one issuing a domestic currency. Assume that all exports of all countries are invoiced in the exporter's currency ('symmetric' trade denomination). Then international currency use (for foreign trade) is completely analogous to the international trade flows and differences in international currency use reflect nothing more than differences in countries' international trade activities. If these were symmetric as well, then the definition of internationalization becomes void, because every currency is as international as any other. Notice however that there are huge differences in the foreign trade activities of various countries and that symmetry in trade invoicing is far from being complete and also varies between pairs of countries (the currency of invoice is a matter of negotiation between the exporter and the importer). On this basis I consider that the alternative definition of internationalization, restricting the term to the use of *third* currencies alone (currencies of countries not involved in the respective trade transaction, 'asymmetric' trade denomination), is definitely too narrow.

agent using this currency. Column (3) describes actions initiated by institutions forming part of the public sector of a country (official use). These are usually the central bank or sometimes the finance ministry or Treasury department. Column (2) concerns uses by private agents.[7]

Consider first the functions of international money in official use. Most of the expressions in the three cells are self-explanatory. Governments try to influence their country's exchange rates by intervening in the foreign exchange market (Roosa, 1965; Mussa, 1981; Dominguez and Frankel, 1993). However, their domestic currency can be traded against many foreign currencies. Hence, they have to decide in which of the bilateral markets to intervene determining the *intervention currency* (or currencies). Immediately related to intervention currencies are *reserve currencies* (Polak, 1992; Saville, 1992). Central banks can intervene only in those currencies in which they hold some reserves.[8] Even if they intervened in only one foreign currency, in a floating exchange rate environment they would usually hold a portfolio of reserve currencies in order to diversify against exchange rate risk (Dooley *et al.*, 1989). Finally, *pegging currencies* are those currencies against which some country's exchange rate has to be maintained at some fixed level (or within some interval) as specified in an exchange rate arrangement (Williamson, 1971, 1982). Notice that these three official functions establish another difference between purely national and international money (Cohen, 1971).

The delineation of international currency functions in private use is a more complex matter. I start with international media of exchange, which I denote as *vehicle currencies*.[9] There are two types of vehicle currencies – those which serve as media of exchange in goods exchange and those which serve as media of exchange in currency exchange. Before turning to the question of forex vehicles, let me introduce an additional distinction between domestic and foreign trade vehicle transactions. The phenomenon that residents of the same country use a foreign currency as medium of exchange for their *local* transactions is known as *direct currency substitution* (McKinnon, 1985). Direct currency substitution is mainly

---

[7] The distinction between private and official uses of international currencies goes back at least to Klopstock (1957) (who applied it to the store of value function of international money) and Aliber (1966).

[8] In practice, central banks often borrow reserves from other central banks to enhance their capacity to intervene. However, borrowed reserves usually have to be repaid quite quickly (Roosa, 1965; Giavazzi and Giovannini, 1989) and, hence, do not remove the need for holding own reserves.

[9] I traced the term 'vehicle currency' back to Roosa (1965). My definition of a vehicle currency is largely analogous to his. For a narrower definition, see Magee and Rao (1980); for a wider definition, see Tavlas (1991, 1992).

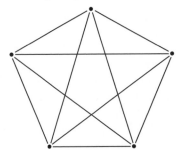

Figure 2.1 'Forex barter' in the interbank market

observed in developing or transition economies with completely destabilized monetary systems and therefore *asymmetric* (Calvo and Végh, 1992; Brand, 1993). In industrial countries foreign media of exchange are usually not accepted for domestic transactions (hence the asymmetry).

What is the difference between trade and forex vehicles? Take the typical case for most industrial countries where an international trade transaction is invoiced and *settled* in the exporter's currency ('Grassman's Law', 1973). The exporter need not accept a foreign currency, but the importer will usually not have balances in the exporter's currency available and will have to convert domestic cash into the foreign currency through a bank, which he or she then transfers to the exporter to settle the trade transaction. In this sense the importer is using the exporter's currency as a medium of exchange, implying its internationalization. Similar cases can be constructed for different invoicing practices. If, for example, settlement is agreed in the importer's currency (Japan) – the exception 'confirming' Grassman's Law (Tavlas and Ozeki, 1992; Dominguez, 1997) – the exporter has the burden of converting the foreign cash balances he or she receives into the domestic currency. The internationalization is even clearer when, as is often the case for trade in primary goods involving developing countries (Page, 1977, 1981), the invoicing (and settlement) is neither in the exporter's nor in the importer's currency. Some authors have considered this the genuine case of a vehicle transaction (Magee and Rao, 1980). I like to think of it as trade-vehicle use in the *narrow* sense.

Since banks provide the foreign currencies to the trading firms, and firms usually do not exchange currencies among each other, there is interbank currency trading so that the banks can quickly acquire the currencies required by goods traders as well as by international borrowers, lenders and securities traders. This interbank trading can be organized in different ways. In one extreme case, which might be called

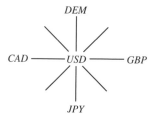

Figure 2.2 'Full monetization' of the forex market through a single forex vehicle (the US dollar)

'forex barter' (no vehicle currency), there exists a liquid interbank market for all bilateral markets between currencies. This case is illustrated in figure 2.1, where dots or 'nodes' represent currencies and arcs represent active interbank markets. Here a bank, which needs a certain foreign currency for a customer, converts its local currency directly into the foreign one with another bank.

In another extreme case there is only one currency, which has a liquid market with all the other currencies, while all the other 'cross-currency' markets are illiquid. This case is sketched in figure 2.2, where the US dollar (*USD*) was chosen to have this special position. It is one with 'full monetization' through a single *foreign exchange vehicle*, a bank which has cash balances in one non-vehicle currency – say pounds sterling (*GBP*) – and has to provide foreign cash to a customer in another non-vehicle currency – say, Japanese yen (*JPY*) – will actually make two transactions (with one or two other banks) to convert first the non-vehicle currency (*GBP*), which it has available, into the vehicle currency (*USD*) and then the vehicle currency into the ultimately desired foreign currency (*JPY*), which it transfers then to the customer.[10]

The vehicle currency enters into a currency exchange very much like a conventional medium of exchange enters into goods exchange – except, perhaps, that the period between demand and supply of the vehicle is almost always very short. This phenomenon is the basic subject of chapter 3, which develops a theory of forex vehicles based on endogenous transaction costs, which can explain different exchange structures in this market with one or several competing vehicle currencies. In chapter 1

---

[10] In order to ensure uniformity in currency abbreviations throughout this book I am using the United Nations ISO Codes (UNDP, 1994). In this system, which is widely used in forex markets, a currency is denoted by three capital letters, where the first two stand for the country of origin (often but not always the first two letters of the respective country's name) and the third for the initial of the currency's name. For example, United States dollar=USD, Deutsche mark=DEM, French franc=FRF, etc.

(pp. 5ff.), I have argued that it is particularly important, for example because of the sheer size of the forex market and the latter's pivotal role in currency internationalization.

In order to complete the description of table 2.1 I finally turn to the unit of account and store of value functions. *Quotation currencies* are those currencies in whose units prices of goods or assets are expressed when they are different from the currency of the respective supplier of the goods or issuer of the asset. There is almost no systematic theoretical or empirical analysis of quotation behaviour, as opposed to trade invoicing and asset denomination, in the literature.

Investment currencies are those currencies in which asset contracts are *settled*. In the case of asset contracts settlement includes disbursement as well as the whole redemption – for example repayment and interest payments in the case of euro-market bond issues. Financial innovations might even entail redemption in currencies different from that of disbursement (or of the original bond denomination). One example is double currency loans, where disbursement and coupon payments are in one currency while the remaining redemption is in another. Convertible bonds may include an option to redeem in another currency. As in the case of foreign trade invoicing, the decision by real investors in which currencies to issue equity or debt and the decision by savers in which currencies to put their money is distinct, but not independent, of the vehicle phenomenon in forex markets, in which those agents may have to convert the related cash flows into their home currency.

Of course investment currencies also include currencies used for international short-term asset substitution, or *indirect currency substitution* (McKinnon, 1982, 1985). Residents of industrial countries, for example, reciprocally take foreign currency deposits to get a better risk–return combination than with domestic deposits, while hardly losing liquidity for their local currency transactions (Filosa, 1995). Hence among these countries indirect currency substitution tends to be *symmetric*. Of course, foreign currency deposit substitution is also prevalent in developing countries (with or without direct currency substitution), but there disinvesting in domestic currency leads to investment in one or, maybe, two-industrial country currencies, and residents of industrial countries hardly invest in deposits in developing country currencies.[11]

---

[11] This indirect currency substitution must not be in deposits alone. A large part of all 100-dollar notes, the largest denomination issued by the US Federal Reserve, is actually held as a safer store of value than the respective national banknotes in developing and transition countries. For a recent survey of evaluations of this phenomenon and for comparisons of the US experience with those of other OECD countries, see Rogoff (1997).

Indirect currency substitution in developing countries is therefore usually *asymmetric*, like the direct currency substitution discussed above under the medium of exchange function. Exceptions to this rule may be observed with some emerging market currencies which have recently attracted the interest of international investors.

Generally speaking, there are, as in the domestic-money case, synergetic forces at work implying some tendency towards keeping the different functions together in one currency.[12] However, because of the multiplicity of currencies competing on the international level this tendency is much weaker. One reason is that under currency competition a friction between the medium of exchange and the store of value function may emerge. As explained in greater depth in the theoretical section below, media of exchange show a tendency towards concentration due to thick-market (or network) externalities, while stores of value show a tendency towards multiplicity due to risk-reducing diversification. In the international sphere, the scope for a separation of the unit of account and the other money functions is also enhanced. The now famous example in the area of foreign trade is the practice of some Persian Gulf countries before December 1974 quoting their oil prices in US dollars but requiring payment in pounds sterling, since they were still part of the sterling zone (McKinnon, 1979).[13]

Regarding the typology of international money discussed above, it appears that nowadays – in a world with relatively integrated international goods and capital markets – most industrial-countries' currencies are to some extent internationalized. However, there is a hierarchy among those currencies. Only a few perform *many* of the functions to a non-negligible extent: these may be named *key currencies*. And there may be a single currency performing most of the functions to a much larger extent than even the (other) key currencies – the *dominant* international *currency* (Fratianni, 1992) – the US dollar for most of the time after the Second World War (see section 2.3).

2.2   Theories of international money

In this section I do not intend to provide a completely balanced discussion of theoretical explanations for *all* the international money

---

[12] For a more elaborated discussion of the relations between some of the different functions, see Cohen (1971).

[13] A much less recent example of the separation of unit of account and medium of exchange is that of the so-called 'ghost monies' in the Middle Ages (Cipolla, 1956), which had practically stopped circulating but continued to be used as value standards in commerce. See also Bloch (1954).

functions. I rather made a decision to concentrate on *formal* explanations for the different *medium of exchange functions in private use*. Models of private international asset diversification are treated more briefly and non-formalized theoretical considerations for private international money are enumerated only at the end of this section. Rigorous theoretical explanations for international-money functions in official use are scarce, and are not surveyed.

The formal theory of vehicle currencies can be decomposed into four branches of models: branch 1, transaction cost/exchange models; branch 2, individual firm models of international trade invoicing; branch 3, money-in-utility and cash-in-advance models; branch 4, ad hoc models of aggregate money demand. The main characteristic of branch 1, is the *endogenous emergence of media of exchange* through the problem of exchange coordination. Three different methodological approaches have been used within this branch.

In the first, which still is rather macroeconomic in spirit, transaction costs are largely unexplained or exogenous. Niehans (1969) assumes exogenously determined transaction cost rates for (international) exchange of four goods, which can vary for different pairs of goods exchanged as well as for different countries exchanging, so that exchange costs increase proportionally with the quantities of goods transferred. Niehans then numerically derives the transaction cost minimizing intermediate flows of goods, which ensure that all exchange desires are satisfied under bilateral balance between each pair of countries. Depending on the assumptions on the exogenous transaction costs a universal medium of exchange or multiple media of exchange are socially optimal.[14] Krugman (1980) relaxes the assumption of bilateral balance between countries for the three-currency case. He assumes that value-proportional transaction costs are monotonically decreasing in the overall trading volume of a bilateral currency market and derives the currency-exchange structure, which is transaction-cost-minimizing for traders, from the inter-country payments structure. The endogenous structure of exchange can be partial or total indirect exchange through a *single* vehicle currency, the currency of a country which is important in payments of this three-country world.

Rey (1997) replicates Krugman's results in a three-country general equilibrium model without capital mobility, integrating international goods and currency exchange. Each country is assumed to be fully specialized in production and to invoice all exports in home currency ('Grassman's Law'). Foreign funds needed to pay for imports are

---

[14] Niehans presents numerical solutions for the case with four goods.

acquired through bilateral currency markets, where intermediaries charge for transaction services in units of their own home currency. These transaction costs are determined by a transaction technology, analogous to those often used in endogenous growth theory (Romer, 1986), which is competitive on the individual intermediary level but exhibits increasing returns in the aggregate. Consumers are cash-in-advance-constrained but the exchange structure in the currency markets is endogenously determined by the transaction costs.

Due to the thick-market externalities there can be multiple steady-state equilibria. As a consequence of the assumption of a Cobb–Douglas utility function, the emergence of a vehicle currency is determined by the goods preferences of the countries, not by their relative size. The more a country's good is desired, the higher its exports and the international demand for the domestic currency, the more liquid the respective foreign exchange markets, and the lower the related transaction costs. However, only a single exchange structure is welfare-maximizing. Whether this is total indirect exchange through a single vehicle currency depends on the exogenous size of the externality parameter in the transaction technology.

The second exchange model approach derives transaction costs from search costs alone. Chrystal (1984) reinterprets the model of Jones (1976) for commodity exchange in terms of the interbank foreign exchange market. A dealer who wants to exchange currency i against currency j forms an expectation about the share of other dealers wanting to buy i and the share of dealers wanting to sell j. This determines the expected search time of this dealer – say, the number of expected telephone calls – to carry out the desired transaction. Depending on the relative import-ance of certain currencies in forex trading, undertaking a desired transaction directly might imply longer 'shopping around' than under-taking it indirectly through a vehicle currency. With an adaptive updating of dealer beliefs about the distribution of exchange desires full monetization (with any currency as a vehicle) is always a locally stable (search-cost-minimizing) equilibrium. However, additional equilibria with partial vehicle use or even 'forex barter' may coexist and be reached depending on the initial conditions, while multiple vehicles are impos-sible.[15] Starting from a situation of 'forex barter' the currency with the most important original exchange desires by dealers would naturally evolve as the vehicle.

A more recent search-cost approach, which originates in the monetary

---

[15] Oh (1989) generalizes Jones' theory, so that exchange chains longer than two transactions are no longer excluded, but he does not explicitly derive equilibria with multiple media of exchange.

random-matching literature (Kiyotaki and Wright, 1989), looks at goods-trade vehicle currencies (Matsuyama *et al.*, 1993). Two countries are considered, and agents of the same country meet with equal likelihood, while domestic residents and foreigners meet with lower likelihood. The use of *some* fiat money to carry out goods exchanges is enforced by a cash-in-advance constraint, but the choice *which* currency is used in trade – the foreign or the local one – is endogenous. Exchange patterns are described by a Markov process in the inventory holdings of domestic and foreign agents (restricted to one unit of either the good produced or one of the currencies). A multiplicity of steady-state, symmetric, pure Nash equilibria may exist, depending, *inter alia*, on the relative size of the two economies (the likelihood of meeting a resident, if I am a resident), the economic integration (the likelihood of meeting a foreigner, if I am a resident), the degree of international specialization in production and the time preferences.

In one equilibrium (denoted as a currency union), both currencies are perfect substitutes and circulate freely in both countries. This is symmetric currency substitution *together with* two foreign trade vehicles. In another equilibrium, local agents trade their production good against the home *and* the foreign currency and also trade both currencies for their consumption good, while foreign agents use only their own currency. This is partial direct asymmetric currency substitution *together* with a single foreign trade vehicle. Currency exchanges occur only in the curious case where the locally produced good is a perfect substitute for the foreign currency and where mixed strategies are permitted.

The third exchange-cost approach employs financial market microstructure theory and is particularly designed to explain the functioning of the forex market and its role in the internationalization of currencies. In a first paper, Black (1991) employs a dealer model in order to explain transaction costs in any bilateral currency market. A representative dealer's bid–ask spread increases with exchange rate volatility and decreases with trading volume, where the latter can vary endogenously depending on vehicle-currency use. Black does not derive equilibria of vehicle use from a microeconomic currency exchange model, but determines the extent of the use of a single vehicle currency with the help of an index, measuring the relative transaction costs of vehicle use compared to no-vehicle use for the whole forex market. An important advance compared to the other two exchange-cost approaches is the identification of potential detrimental effects of exchange rate variability on vehicle-currency use, although – in this model – volatility is still assumed to be exogenous.

The basic notion that the world structure of currency exchanges depends not only on the fundamental structure of world trade and capital flows but also on the micro-structure of the forex market is substantially developed in chapter 3 of this book, which further extends the work in Hartmann (1994, 1997a). Forex dealers receive order flows from international traders and investors in the retail market and trade open positions with speculators in the wholesale market. The larger the open positions the more volatile the exchange rate has to be in order to equilibrate the wholesale market and the costlier the closing out of the positions for the intermediaries. However, the larger the predictable trading volume the smaller the revenues each currency unit exchange has to generate so that the dealer breaks even. Transaction costs of currency exchange can thus decrease with trading volume (thick-market externality) and will always increase with exchange rate volatility as well as dealers' fixed costs.

A forex market equilibrium is defined as a vector of currency exchanges given dealer spreads in all bilateral markets such that retail customers minimize transaction costs and a vector of spreads given currency exchange patterns such that profitable dealer market entry is no longer possible. Owing to network externalities in conjunction with inertia in the exchange structure a multiplicity of equilibria can exist. However, with the new framework not only a single but also several vehicle currencies can emerge, depending on the fundamental payments flows, the initial structure of exchange and dealer expectations about it, the market-specific volume–volatility relation and the structures of fixed costs for making markets and for opening formerly inactive markets. Moreover, both trading volumes as well as exchange rate volatilities are endogenous to the optimal exchange pattern. Those currencies with high fundamentals-based trading volume and/or low exchange rate volatility with respect to all or a subset of currencies can emerge as vehicles.

Most of these endogenous exchange-cost models suggest that thick-market or network externalities imply substantial self-fulfilling forces, giving the incumbent dominant vehicle currency a considerable competitive advantage over its potential rivals. Since it is most used, its transaction costs are the lowest and there is little incentive for an individual agent to deviate and use another vehicle currency, unless everybody else decides to do the same. In the case of strong price and entry competition among intermediaries, as described in the previous paragraph, set-up costs of re-opening inactive markets may also impose such a strong degree of inertia. Hence, even if the fundamental trade and capital flows begin to favour another currency, the incumbent dominating currency in such a framework may prevail for a long time.

However, if very large shocks (on fundamentals or expectations) hit the system, producing a lock-out from the prevailing equilibrium, there can be a dramatic transition to a new vehicle currency, since once the lock-out has taken place the network externalities will result, at least in theory, in a dynamic favouring the rising currency and discriminating at increasing speed against the declining currency. If shocks are more moderate (in size or in geographical scope), then the transition from one dominant vehicle to another in a world with many currencies can also occur in a more gradual fashion, because there can be many intermediate equilibria (chapter 3). In sum, which type of transition actually occurs – a 'catastrophic' or a gradual one – is an empirical question, which will be addressed in the historical section further below and in chapter 4.

The second branch of vehicle-currency theory focuses on which currencies individual firms will optimally choose for their foreign trade invoicing. In a first modelling attempt Baron (1976) analyses the optimal invoice-currency choice of an exporter, when the importer does not face any price risk. Bilson (1983) develops a model of bilateral bargaining between an importer and an exporter over price and invoicing practice, which highlights incentives for exporters *and* importers to seek or accept invoicing in the exporter's currency. This emphasis is motivated by the basic 'symmetry' in foreign trade denomination among industrial countries – that most contracts (usually much more than 50 per cent of a country's exports) are invoiced in the exporter's currency – first discovered by Grassman (1973) and subsequently often referred to as 'Grassman's Law'. If the importer's price risk in the domestic market is more highly correlated with the exchange rate (through approximations of purchasing power parity or PPP) than the exporter's cost risk, then the former will have a natural hedge when accepting invoicing in the latter's currency. This asymmetry in 'exchange-risk hedging' can be justified with the evidence that importers' exposures to exchange rate risk seems to be clearly longer than exporters' exposures to it (Magee, 1974). In this model a high *variability* of the domestic inflation rate also increases the incentive for any side to accept the other's currency.

In opposition to Bilson, Viaene and de Vries (1992) derive the dominance of invoicing in the exporters' currencies' from a bilateral bargaining model with random matching of exporters and importers, with complete forward cover but without referral to PPP. Based on the observation that import companies usually outnumber export companies, they infer that higher bargaining power of the exporters should lead to more invoicing in their currencies. Rao and Magee (1980) establish an irrelevance proposition in foreign trade invoicing. They argue that in equilibrium trade prices should incorporate exchange risk premia because of the absence of arbitrage possibilities between goods and bond markets together with covered interest rate parity. Risk-neutral agents should therefore be indifferent with respect to currency invoicing and differences in invoicing behaviour (in equilibrium) can reflect only differences in attitudes towards risk. However, this result and the assumptions about arbitrage possibilities between asset and goods markets on which it relies are controversial (Goeltz, 1980). Even this formalized literature pays little attention to general market equilibrium for the type of good considered or balance of payments equilibrium among countries.

Most of the foreign trade vehicle-currency literature tries to explain empirical regularities in invoicing with non-formal tools. McKinnon (1979) introduces a distinction between trade invoicing in strongly differentiated manufacturing goods (tradables I, like cars, for example) and relatively homogeneous primary goods (tradables II, like copper, for example). While in McKinnon's view each international trader's 'preferred monetary habitat' should in general be her home currency, no more than one party can get her will. In the case of tradables I the producers (exporters) have some market power to keep prices fixed. Demand shocks can be absorbed with inventory changes at constant sales prices. This 'pricing to the market' policy can be completed with international trade denomination in the exporter's home currency. If most inputs are paid in local currency as well, the exporter can in this way eliminate additional price risk from exchange rate fluctuations, another explanation for 'Grassman's Law'.[16] In the case of tradables II, single producers are rather price-takers and efficiency gains in price comparisons for customers lead to a tendency to quote (and settle) in a single international currency. These views are refined and extended by Carse and Wood (1979), Magee and Rao (1980).[17]

The third branch of vehicle currency theory ignores explicit specifications of exchange-coordination problems, as particularly highlighted in branch 1, and *assumes* the usefulness of money by putting it as an argument in the utility (Sidrauski, 1967) or the production function (Fischer, 1974) or *imposes* monetary exchange, for example through a cash-in-advance constraint (Clower, 1968). These two types are considered together here, because they are similarly ad hoc as a microfoundation of money and usually lead to quite similar results (Feenstra, 1986).

---

[16] Here a slight theoretical puzzle emerges from the convexity of the neoclassical profit function in price. By Jensen's Inequality expected profits will be larger for uncertain sales prices than for certain sales prices. From this point of view a neoclassical firm would prefer only to eliminate exchange rate risk (through home currency invoicing), if its aversion against risk exceeds a certain threshold.

[17] See the summary in Tavlas (1991) for more detail.

Four types of models may be distinguished. The first type is a money-in-utility approach to asymmetric currency substitution, where a domestic representative agent maximizes an intertemporal utility function with a consumption good, domestic and foreign cash balances entering as arguments. Such a model has been simulated by Bufman and Leiderman (1992) in order to estimate elasticities of substitution between domestic and foreign currency 'liquidity services'.[18] Notice that a simple money-in-utility approach does not distinguish the medium of exchange from other money functions.[19]

The second type of model exploits the literature on network externalities in product markets in order to study international monetary phenomena. Transaction-cost effects are mimicked by putting the *number* of the users of a currency as an argument in individual agents' utility (or production) functions. Positive network externalities in money use are *assumed* by postulating that the marginal utility (or marginal product) of an additional user of a currency is positive, because it saves resources for search and exchange. Vaubel (1984) applies the model of Rohlfs (1974), originally designed for telephone networks. Dowd and Greenaway (1993) use the model of Farrel and Saloner (1986) for product compatibility, while Allen (1993) elaborates on the model by Katz and Shapiro (1986) for technology adoption to analyse the potential of a new currency to be adopted in a game of foreign trade invoicing. Notice that, in contrast to this money-in-utility approach, most papers in the first branch of the vehicle-currency literature above derive network externalities *endogenously*.[20]

A third model type, which is somewhat related to the cash-in-advance approach, builds on Baumol's inventory-cost approach to the optimal average amount of cash-balance holdings when revenues and expenditures for goods purchases arrive at different points in time (Baumol, 1952; Tobin, 1956). Swoboda (1968) applies the original idea to the demand for a single currency in the euro-currency markets and uses the classical square root formula as an argument for economies of scale in euro-dollar deposit holdings. Poloz (1984) generalizes the Baumol model by requiring a continous overall expenditure flow to be met with

---

[18] See also the model in Obstfeld and Rogoff (1996, pp. 551–3). For more detailed survey of the currency substitution literature alone, see Giovannini and Turtelboom (1994).

[19] This is a general dilemma for the empirically oriented currency-substitution literature. See McKinnon (1985) as well as Giovannini and Turtelboom (1994) for discussions of this problem.

[20] A different approach to exploit network economics is undertaken by Deusy-Fournier (1995), who simulates a model with a double fixed cost of currency exchange, a national and an international one.

domestic *and* foreign currency at fixed shares. Revenues are in domestic money, which can be converted into domestic bonds at a brokerage fee or into foreign cash balances at a (different) foreign exchange dealing fee. However, apart from the relative importance of conversion fees the variable determining average foreign currency holdings is the expected rate of depreciation against the domestic currency. Poloz had asymmetric currency substitution as an application for this model in mind.

Finally, I mention in passing simple money-demand models, where exchange rate expectations enter in an ad hoc manner in order to determine the currency composition of the aggregated world money demand and to illustrate problems of indirect symmetric currency substitution for national monetary policies and international monetary policy coordination (McKinnon, 1982). Here, again, the distinction between the medium of exchange and the store of value function is not made explicit in the theory. One interpretation for these money demand equations is, of course, provided by the Poloz model.

The theory of quotation currencies is not nearly as developed as that for vehicle currencies or investment currencies. Kindleberger (1972, 1973b, 1986) emphasizes the public good aspect of measurement standards in general and applies it to domestic and international units of account. Often it is simply assumed that the quotation currency is the same as the invoicing or settlement currency and trade-vehicle theory applied. Again, medium of exchange and unit of account are closely related but not inseparable.

Investment currency theory and international capital flows enjoy some prominence in international monetary and financial economics and have been subject to two recent detailed surveys by Dumas (1994) and Lewis (1995). Both these surveys contrast partial equilibrium models with general equilibrium models of international portfolio choice. The international capital asset pricing model (CAPM) was developed by Solnik (1974) and Adler and Dumas (1983), adding inflation or exchange rate risk premia as explanatory variables for asset returns. General equilibrium models go back to Lucas (1982), Dornbusch (1983), Stockman and Dellas (1989), among others. Optimal international asset holdings can be derived directly from the international CAPM (Dumas, 1994), but not directly from general equilibrium models (Lewis, 1995).

A general result of international asset-pricing theory is that efficient (and expected utility-maximizing) portfolios – i.e. those which are not dominated by any other portfolio, having either the same risk but a higher expected return or the same expected return but a lower risk – will usually be diversified over many currencies. This illustrates the main difference between vehicle-currency theory and investment-currency theory. While the former predicts a limited number of important international media of exchange the latter predicts a larger number of important international stores of value. In practice, however, these two functions of international currencies are not completely disconnected. Large countries which are important in international trade and credit are more likely to develop deeper and broader financial markets in which it is attractive for foreigners to put their savings. Or, countries with large and sophisticated financial markets are more likely to experience an increased demand of their currencies for international payments.[21] It is not surprising then that the actually observed international diversification of most financial portfolios is much less than the optimal one as predicted by the CAPM, for example.

A second dimension of international 'under-diversification' is home bias, the fact that the share of the domestic currency in most countries' asset holdings seems to be too large from an optimal risk-sharing perspective (French and Poterba, 1991; Tesar and Werner, 1992). Theoretical analyses identified hedging of domestic price uncertainty (Branson and Hendersen, 1984; Eldor *et al.*, 1988) or consumption of non-tradeable goods (Stockman and Dellas, 1989), taxes (Stulz, 1981) and capital flow restrictions (Errunza and Losq, 1989) as factors producing this phenomenon. Asymmetric information can also lead to such capital market segmentation (Dumas, 1994, p. 313).

For monetary theory in general it is important (the observed biases in portfolio shares towards the home currency and dominant international currencies notwithstanding) to bear in mind that currency competition results in a friction between the medium of exchange and the store of value functions of money, the former implying centripetal forces driving towards centralization and the latter implying centrifugal forces driving towards diversification and multiplicity. This friction opposes the synergetic forces between money functions described further above.

Both Dumas and Lewis above shun attempts by Chrystal (1977), Kouri and de Macedo (1978) as well as de Macedo *et al.* (1984) to also develop theories of international asset diversification. Arguments against these approaches are given in Dumas (1984). Tobin's (1958) portfolio-balance approach is nonetheless used in the asymmetric asset-substitution literature (Cuddington, 1983). Solutions to the dominated-asset problem of money as a substitutable international asset are presented and discussed in Giovannini and Turtelboom (1994).[22]

A final approach to the international store of value function of money

---

[21] See, for example, Portes *et al.* (1997).
[22] Rother (1994) discusses the differences between the portfolio-balance and the cash-in-advance models.

is Niehans' (1984) application of the principle of comparative advantage in foreign trade to international financial services. In this framework it can be shown that some countries serve as an *international bank* or *world banker* (Despres *et al.*, 1966; Kindleberger, 1966), issuing short-term deposits and lending long-term to non-residents, if there are international differences in liquidity preferences, which makes for interest rate differentials under autarky even when the different assets are completely homogeneous between countries.

The non-formalized literature on explanations for the emergence of international currencies is vast and cannot be surveyed in depth here. The main arguments can be found in Aliber (1966); Cohen (1971); von Hayek (1977); Vaubel (1978); McKinnon (1979); Kindleberger (1981); Klein and Melvin (1982); Krugman (1984); Klump (1986); de Grauwe (1989); Kindleberger (1993); Iwami (1994); and, in particular, the three essays by Tavlas (1991, 1992) and Tavlas and Ozeki (1992).

In a very short summary, the following factors are emphasized to foster a country's currency's use in external transactions in this literature: the country should be big, in the sense of accounting for an important part of world exports and foreign direct investment; it should have a comparative advantage in the production of manufactured goods (tradeables I); financial markets should be free, deep and well developed, inflation low and exchange rate variability not excessive; the country should also be politically stable. Last, but not least, the already widespread use of a currency increases its chances to maintain or extend its position as an international money. Once the internationalization of a currency is at an advanced stage, enough liquid reserves or international lender-of-last-resort facilities should be available to avoid confidence crises, which may result in runs on the world banker. Most of these points – except maybe political stability – are also made in one form or another in the different formal approaches for international currencies surveyed above. However, there is no single mathematical theory of international currency which can explain all dimensions of international money at once. This illustrates the fact well that single analytical models can never deliver the overall picture as well as a comprehensive institutional and historical study can.

2.3   A brief history of international money

The emphasis put on economies of scale in the use of money by many of the theories surveyed in section 2.2 encourages the thought of money as a natural monopoly, which should imply a strong tendency towards concentration to a single money. And, in fact, many monetary theories are formulated in a way that only a single medium of exchange can evolve, or singularity is even assumed at the outset (Niehans, 1971; Ostroy and Starr, 1974; Jones, 1976; Ostroy and Starr, 1990). This factor is reflected in several historical, but also theoretical, analyses of international money (Krugman, 1980; Black, 1991), which tend to *over-state* the positions of dominant currencies in history. This has occurred in descriptions of sterling before the First World War (for example, Williams, 1968, or Yeager, 1976, qualified by Lindert, 1969) and with the role of the dollar after the Second World War (for example, Cooper, 1972), qualified by Grassman, 1973).[23]

There seems to have never been a currency which came close to being the *single* international currency for a large part of the globe. Nevertheless the structure of the international monetary systems showed a strongly hierarchical pattern for most of the time. Within a limited number of international key currencies, most often a single one quantitatively dominated by performing the international money functions to a larger extent than all the others (Fratianni, 1992). The chronology of *dominant* international currencies, as reported by economic historians (Lopez, 1951; Bloch, 1954; Cipolla, 1956; Klump, 1986; Kindleberger, 1993), begins with the Byzantine gold *nomisma* (also called *bezant*, fifth–seventh century), later joined by the Arab dinar (also *mancus* or *marabotin*, eighth–twelfth century), the Florentine *fiorino* (thirteenth and fourteenth century), and the Venetian *ducato* (fifteenth century). Bloch (1954) claims that the *bezant* and *dinar* played the role of the two 'supermonies' in the High Middle Ages, similar – in his view – to the US dollar and UK pound sterling after the Second World War.

After the Middle Ages the centre of economic activity shifted north and payment practices in international trade evolved more and more from gold coins to bills of exchange. A transitional period was followed by Amsterdam's growth into the role of the world banker and with it the growth of the bank guilder into that of the dominant currency (seventeenth and eighteenth century; Neal, 1990). For all these examples of early dominant international currencies hardly any quantitative data have been reported.

This changes only slightly for the sterling era, which began somewhere at the turn of the eighteenth and the nineteenth century, when Britain led other countries in industrialization, its foreign trade expanded rapidly and London took over as the leading financial centre, and was confirmed with Britain's return to gold convertibility in 1819–44 after the Napo-

---

[23] For example Walters (1992) writes that 'sterling developed into the *unchallenged* international currency of the 19th century' (emphasis my own).

leonic wars (Cohen, 1971; Klump, 1986). However, the little hard evidence on currency use available indicates that the dominance of sterling was not as unrivalled as is often suggested. For the period from 1900–13, for example, Lindert (1969) shows that private and official currency holdings outside Europe were in fact predominantly in sterling, but among continental European and Scandinavian countries the shares of Deutsche mark or French franc holdings were more important.[24] One primary force behind the evolution of the mark during the same period was its increased use in trade invoicing and finance (Klump, 1986).

Although sterling begins to lose its dominant role with the First World War, it continued to be an important international currency until the early 1970s (Roosa, 1965; Cohen, 1971; Klump, 1986; Eichengreen, 1997), well illustrating (similar to preceding cases of dominant monies) the scope for inertia in the use of international currencies, as predicted by the endogenous exchange cost theories described in section 2.2. In this regard, it is instructive to look at the few available numbers concerning the decline of the UK currency, for example as presented by Cohen (1971, pp. 71ff.) for foreign trade vehicle use. According to his sources, notably Williams (1968) and others, sterling peaked in the decades before the First World War at a share of 'at least 60 per cent of world trade' and declined rather gently until shortly after the Second World War to about 'half of all trade'.[25] For the 1950s the estimates become more numerous, but also more variable; a share between 30 and 40 per cent of world trade invoiced in sterling might be considered a conservative estimate. During the 1960s contemporaneous observers estimated a decline from 27 to 23 per cent. (By 1980 sterling's share was down to 6 per cent of world trade – ECU Institute, 1995.)

It is reassuring that this rather slow dethronement of sterling as the dominant international currency is also visible from other money functions. For example, Lindert (1969) finds that the share of sterling balances in the total official foreign exchange reserve holdings of thirty-five major central banks was 43 per cent in 1899 (French franc 11 per cent, Reichsmark 10 per cent, US dollar below 4 per cent) and 38 per cent in 1913 (franc 24 per cent, mark 12 per cent, dollar below 5 per cent). From the data provided by Eichengreen (1997, p. 9, quoting Triffin, 1964), one can deduce that by 1928 official reserves in sterling were probably not much lower than 40 per cent of the total (dollar 19 per

---

[24] The franc falls back, though, when the data are corrected for the large Russian debts denominated in French currency (Lindert, 1969). Flandreau (1995) disputes the strict dominance of sterling even before 1870.

[25] This number might be slightly too high, but it nevertheless shows that clear dollar dominance was not yet established immediately after the Second World War.

cent).[26] Further quoting Triffin (1964) Eichengreen then reports sterling shares in reserves of 55 per cent for 1949 (dollar 27 per cent),[27] 36 per cent for 1957 (dollar 49 per cent) and 28 per cent for 1962 (dollar 57 per cent).[28] From Polak (1992) one sees that sterling's decline continued thereafter, reaching 10 per cent in 1970 (dollar 77 per cent) and 3 per cent in 1980 (dollar 69 per cent). Overall, it turns out that sterling did not become less important than the dollar as an official reserve currency before the 1950s, which is compatible with the foreign trade invoicing figures reported above.

The emerging picture is also matched very well by Klopstock's (1957) account of the evolution of (private and official) foreign short-term asset holdings in the USA between 1921 and 1956. From this perspective, the use of the dollar as a short-term investment and reserve currency increased substantially during the 1920s but then declined sharply back to former levels in the early 1930s, mainly as a consequence of the unravelling of the Gold Standard and of the Great Depression. Only from 1934 onwards did a strong and continuous recovery of dollar investments set in, which by-passed the levels of the late 1920s in 1939 on a continuing trend. However, 'as late as 1940, the level of foreign-owned liquid sterling assets was still double the level of foreign-owned liquid dollar assets' (Frankel, 1992, p. 699). On the basis of all this evidence

---

[26] Notice that during the Gold Standard and the Gold Exchange Standard the figures on the currency distribution of pure foreign exchange reserve holdings may be distorted by shifts in and out of gold as an alternative reserve medium. After the 1922 Genoa Conference, which recommended the increased use of foreign exchange reserves, the role of sterling was strengthened by related shifts of central banks out of gold (Harrod, 1952).

[27] Eichengreen (1997, p. 11) cautions that while the 1949 figures give 'the appearance of impressive reliance on sterling reserves, ... the reality was different, since these balances were to a considerable extent blocked and inconvertible', as a consequence of special arrangements for Britain's wartime purchases of inputs paid in sterling. These wartime expenditures had substantially increased the so-called 'sterling balances' held in sterling-area countries but also in the USA and other war-ally countries (Harrod, 1952). Outside the sterling area there was some convertibility of these balances for current account transactions, but inside the area the use of most of these assets was strongly restricted for at least a decade after the end of the war. It is quite plausible that these provisions delayed the decline of sterling in official reserve holdings until *de facto* convertibility was established in 1955.

[28] Alternative estimates have been provided by Klump (1986, p. 314), who quotes IMF sources. He reckons that as late as 1951 the reserve share of sterling was still up to about 60 per cent of world forex reserves, with the US dollar at only 31 per cent and that this picture is reversed only by 1960 (sterling 36 per cent, dollar 63 per cent). Although there are some non-negligible differences between these numbers and those provided by Eichengreen (1997), at least for 1949–51, they can certainly not put in any doubt the overall picture of the dollar by-passing sterling not earlier than the 1950s. Interestingly, sterling continued to maintain a considerable – though further declining – share of world forex reserves for quite a long time even after convertibility of sterling balances had been re-established.

claims that the dollar quickly overtook sterling during the 1930s must be characterized as pure myth. The transition from sterling dominance to dollar dominance took, at the minimum, thirty years (starting around 1918 and being accomplished somewhere in the late 1950s).[29]

One important factor in the UK currency's long endurance was the creation of the sterling area before the Second World War (Cohen, 1992; Eichengreen, 1997). The intense regional use of sterling within this area for private trade, currency pegging and official reserves after the war ensured the coexistence of two leading international currencies for an extended period, even though the dollar became slowly more important than sterling on the overall global level.

After the rise of US industrial power at the beginning of the twentieth century the dollar emerged for the first time as an important international currency after the First World War, which impaired the financial flows through London, but it did not reach a really *dominant* position before the end of the Second World War (see above). By this time the USA, whose production capacity had not been as negatively affected by the war as that of many European countries, had become the leading country in national production and international trade, war finance and post-war reconstruction, so that governments attached to it a quasi-pivotal function in the Bretton Woods system of fixed exchange rates established in 1944. All countries participating in the system effectively pegged their currencies to the dollar, whose convertibility remained unrestricted (in contrast to many other currencies, notably sterling), so that by 1960 it had clearly also become the leading reserve and intervention currency (see above).[30] The important official role of the dollar should not disguise the fact that this rather accompanied or confirmed its emerging dominance in non-official transactions as the most important vehicle and investment currency (Klopstock, 1957; Aliber, 1966; McKinnon, 1969; Krugman, 1984). However, at least until the end of the Bretton Woods system, hard evidence on international currency use, except concerning data on official reserves still remains extremely patchy.

As indicated above, post-war dominance of the dollar was not complete. The British currency continued to be more important in the sterling zone. Moreover, the establishment of a franc zone between France and its former colonies in 1939 and the issue of the franc CFA

---

[29] Since these long transitions from one dominant international currency to another, long after the fundamental economic power of the issuing country has ceased, seem to be a *general* feature of world economic history, the theoretical chapter 4 offers explanations for this phenomenon.

[30] The number of IMF members participating in the Bretton Woods system during the 1960s was over 100 (Klump, 1986).

(Colonies Françaises d'Afrique) and the franc CFP (Colonies Françaises du Pacifique) and their peg to the French franc in 1945 created another geographical limit to dollar dominance (Roosa, 1965; Vizy, 1989). The franc zone was economically less important than the sterling zone, but it did not vanish with the breakdown of Bretton Woods. The increase in diversification in international currency use after the breakdown of the post-war monetary system (and after the dissolution of the sterling zone) is much better documented than the use of international currencies before 1973, and will now be summarized in order to complete this historical overview.

In spite of the breakdown of the Bretton Woods system the dollar could conserve its role as the most important pegging currency in the world until the present day (Kenen, 1983; Klump, 1986; Emerson *et al.*, 1991; Frankel, 1992; Bénassy and Deusy-Fournier, 1994; van de Koolwijk, 1994; Eichengreen and Frankel, 1996). However, the number of currencies pegged to the dollar declined from sixty-five in 1974 to twenty-three in 1995, and the weight of these twenty-three countries in world GDP was extremely low (less than 2 per cent). While the franc zone remained stable (fourteen currencies), the sterling zone disappeared (ten pegs to sterling in 1974, none in 1995). Interestingly, the Deutsche mark plays only a limited role as an official pegging currency to date and the Japanese yen hardly any role at all.[31]

However, these numbers are probably distorted by an accompanying move towards more flexible exchange rate arrangements, notably basket pegs and floating regimes. For example, the dollar's decline as an official international unit of account may be over-stated because many developing and transition countries now peg their currencies to a basket of foreign monies, such as the Special Drawing Right (SDR), for example, in which the dollar usually plays a prominent role. For similar reasons, the mark's and also the yen's current roles are likely to be somewhat under-stated, to the extent that they are represented in those baskets as well.[32] Finally, although exchange rates are fixed bilaterally among members of the European Monetary System (EMS), the EMS functions in several respects like a mark zone (maybe less so since the widening of bands in 1993).

The most complete information on international currency use is traditionally available for the official reserve function, provided in the International Monetary Fund's *Annual Reports* (IMF, 1997a, for

---

[31] Estonia, for a number of years now, and Bulgaria, since early 1997, are running currency boards with *explicit* pegs to the Deutsche mark.

[32] McCauley (1997, table 6) reports the DEM shares in the baskets of several Central and Eastern European pegs.

example). As has been pointed out above, the dollar had by-passed sterling in terms of shares of total global foreign exchange reserve holdings by central banks some time during the 1950s, and it has since never lost its status as the most important reserve currency. However, after the switch to general floating among industrial countries in 1973 a decline of the dollar share in official reserve holdings from around 79 per cent in 1975 to around 56 per cent in 1990 has been observed (Polak, 1992). In parallel with the decline of dollar reserves, Deutsche mark holdings picked up from almost nothing in 1970 to about 20 per cent of all reserves in 1990, while yen reserves increased from only 2 per cent in 1977 to almost 10 per cent. These developments are widely interpreted as central banks' diversification of reserve holdings in reaction to the upward jump in exchange rate volatility after 1973.[33] By 1990, though, this reserve diversification trend had come to a halt (IMF, 1995). And Eichengreen (1997, quoting IMF, 1997a data), observes that the US currency has effectively grown at the expense of the mark and the yen in the course of the 1990s, so that (including ECU–dollar swaps) 64 per cent of world reserves were in dollars by 1996, compared to 14 and 6 per cent for mark and yen.

Because of the high degree of confidentiality kept by central bankers about their official interventions, still relatively little hard evidence is available about the quantitative importance of intervention currencies. Nonetheless, there is a strong causal link between pegging and intervention currencies, and there does not seem to be any doubt about the overwhelming role of the dollar as the major intervention medium during Bretton Woods and several years after its disappearance (Aliber, 1969; Group of Thirty, 1982). Since then though, interventions in third currencies against mark or against yen have increased (Dominguez and Frankel, 1993). For example, within the EMS the dollar was still the most important intervention currency for the period from 1979 to 1982 (72 per cent of total EMS intervention volume, mark 24 per cent), but by 1986–7 the situation was reversed with the mark clearly dominating intervention volume (59 per cent, as compared to 26 per cent for the

---

[33] It is important to notice that the percentages reported are distorted, for example, by exchange rate fluctuations and changes in the number of reporting countries and the currencies covered. Therefore, they give an imprecise picture of the changes in the importance of reserve currencies (Kenen, 1983). However, it is now accepted that the *direction* of the long-run trends since 1973 – a rise in mark and yen holdings to the detriment of dollar holdings – are generally robust against these imprecisions, while the *extent* of changes may be over- or under-estimated depending on the period considered. For a decomposition of changes in official reserve holdings during the last ten years in quantity as well as price components, see IMF (1995). Of course, the problem of the distortion of shares of currency use also applies to the other international money functions reviewed in the following paragraphs.

Table 2.2   *Estimated shares of trade invoicing in world trade, 1980–92 (per cent)*

Year	USD	JPY	DEM	FRF	GBP	ITL	NLG	Total
1980	56.1	2.1	13.6	6.2	6.5	2.2	2.6	100.0
1987	47.9	4.0	16.1	6.5	5.5	3.2	2.8	100.0
1992	47.6	4.8	15.3	6.3	5.7	3.4	2.8	100.0

Source: ECU Institute (1995); van de Koolwijk (1994).

dollar; Tavlas, 1991). Similarly strong changes have not been reported for the yen however (Tavlas and Ozeki, 1992).

The evolution of the US dollar as a vehicle currency in foreign trade during the 1970s follows something like a U-shaped trajectory. While trade invoicing in the US currency first decreased after the switch to floating exchange rates, later in the decade it returned to former levels (Page, 1977, 1981; Kenen, 1983; Bourguinat, 1985). Estimates of invoicing shares for the 1980s and the early 1990s, based on data collected by the European Commission, are summarized in table 2.2. It has been reckoned that in 1980 55–56 per cent of world trade was invoiced in dollars (Page, 1981; table I.2). By 1987 the dollar share was down to about 48 per cent and remained almost stable at this level until 1992.[34] Mark invoicing advanced from 14 per cent in 1977 (Scharrer, 1981) to 16 per cent in 1980 and 19 per cent in 1987 and remained roughly at this level until 1992. Dollar-trade invoicing is much more important than the US share in world trade (roughly 11 per cent during the 1980s), while mark invoicing is only slightly more important than Germany's share in trade (10–12 per cent during the 1980s). In contrast yen invoicing, although increasing from about 2 per cent to 5 per cent during the 1980s, is still relatively unimportant and remains even lower than sterling invoicing or Japan's share in world trade.

As regards forex vehicle use, the evidence provided so far has been largely anecdotal and indirect, in particular because the infrequent turnover surveys undertaken by central banks cannot distinguish between vehicle and non-vehicle transactions (BIS, 1990, 1993, 1996; but see chapter 4). Observations made by foreign exchange dealers and central bankers, though, confirm that the US dollar has been the single vehicle currency at least until the early 1980s (Aliber, 1969; Swoboda, 1969;

---

[34] The reduction of the dollar's importance in world trade between 1980 and 1987 is also reported by Tavlas (1991). The drop in dollar invoicing between 1980 and 1987 can be explained to a large extent by a drop in export value from OPEC countries, whose exports are denominated more than 90 per cent in dollars (ECU Institute, 1995).

Kenen, 1983; see figure 2.2, p. 17). Kenen (1983) estimates that 90–99 per cent of wholesale trading went through the dollar at this time.

As first reported by market participants, this changed quite importantly in the late 1980s–early 1990s raising the Deutsche mark to the status of a vehicle currency within Europe (Andersen, 1992; Pineau, 1993; Hartmann, 1994; Menkhoff, 1995). This observation is supported by the April 1992 Bank for International Settlements (BIS) foreign exchange turnover survey (BIS, 1993). It reports that 71 per cent of global spot inter-dealer trading had dollar and 57 per cent mark on one side of the transaction (yen 20 per cent). (In the 1989 BIS survey, BIS, 1990, the dollar stood still at around 90 per cent.) However, there is hardly any vehicle role for the mark in forex derivatives trading, where the dollar still dominates. In contrast to the mark's emergence in Europe, there are no signs of the Japanese yen replacing the dollar as the dominant vehicle currency in Asian foreign exchange trading. The general picture was largely unchanged at the time of the 1995 BIS turnover survey (dollar 69 per cent, mark 57 per cent, yen 22 per cent; BIS, 1996). The emergence of the current exchange structure of world forex markets is addressed in greater detail in chapter 4, section 4.2.

Although a number of international organizations, notably the BIS and the Organization for Economic Cooperation and Development (OECD), do their best to provide currency breakdowns of various international financial instruments, the general structure of investment-currency use in world financial markets is somewhat more opaque, for at least three reasons. First, complete information on all the intra-day transactions on a gross basis can be very costly to provide. Second, private investment and borrowing practices may change much more quickly than, for example, trade practices or official reserve-holding practices. Third, currency denominations may differ considerably for different instruments, but coverage of instruments or reporting institutions is incomplete and varies over time. However, summarizing the information presented in von Whitman (1974); Kenen (1983); Tavlas (1991); Frankel (1992); Tavlas and Ozeki (1992); Maehara (1993); Bénassy and Deusy-Fournier (1994); Iwami (1994); van de Koolwijk (1994); Deutsche Bundesbank (1997); and Funke and Kennedy (1997), the following broad picture emerges.

1970s

Overall the dollar share of euro-currency deposits (starting at 77 per cent of total deposits) and euro-bonds outstanding (starting at 66 per cent) slightly increased after correction for the devaluation of the American currency. Deutsche mark euro-deposits grew slower than dollar deposits and mark bond issues (starting at 20 per cent) rather declined.

1980s

There seems to have been some pre-1985 reduction of dollar shares in euro-currency deposits, euro-bond issues and external bank loans, but further reductions after 1985 appear to have been driven by the dollar depreciation following the Plaza Agreement. By the end of 1989 the US currency accounts for roughly half of all international investments reported to BIS (outstanding amounts of euro-deposits, euro-bond issues, euro-notes, foreign currency loans to residents, at current exchange rates). Yen investments seem to have increased more significantly than mark investments but they did not exceed half the mark share of 12 per cent at the end of the decade. (The Swiss franc became less important.)

First half of the 1990s

By the same measures the dollar slides further down. The German mark continues to expand slowly, while the yen's strongly extended share is partly due to its appreciation with respect to the other major currencies during this period. McCauley (1997, table 13) reports shares of about 40 per cent for the dollar and 12 per cent for the yen on the latest available figures. The mark stands slightly above the yen.[35] The Deutsche Bundesbank (1997, p. 29) points to differences between financial instruments (in 1996): whereas the yen dominates the mark in international bonds outstanding (yen 17 per cent, mark 11 per cent, dollar 27 per cent), the situation is the reverse for international bank deposits in industrial countries (yen 8 per cent, mark 15 per cent, dollar 44 per cent).[36] Overall,

---

[35] Funke and Kennedy (1997, table 6) further report the portfolio compositions of ten internationally diversified investment funds polled by *The Economist* magazine in 1996. Taking the simple average these ten institutions hold 32 per cent of their total equity investments in the USA as well as 22 per cent and 7 per cent in Japan and Germany, respectively. For their bond holdings the currency composition is 33 per cent USD, 13 per cent JPY and 17 per cent DEM. However, given the substantial home bias observed in the investments of most other institutions, these ten funds may not be representative for global investment-currency use. Moreover, these figures are not adjusted for the institutions' domestic holdings, so that (for example) a Japanese fund's investments in yen assets are put on the same footing as its dollar or mark investments.

[36] The larger share of the Japanese currency in bonds than in interbank deposits suggests that the comparatively strong role of the yen as an investment currency is *not* due to transactions between home offices and overseas branches of Japanese banks, as suggested by Maehara (1993, pp. 157ff.), at least not in the mid-1990s.

the yen is stronger in international private investment than in foreign trade.

Summarizing this post-1973 overview of international currency use, it can be maintained that the world has moved somewhat towards a tripolar international monetary and financial system during the last twenty years without reaching anything close to symmetric tripolarity. There are three main key currencies – the US dollar, the Deutsche mark and the Japanese yen – but they differ quite considerably in their order of importance. The dollar still remains the most important international currency on a global level with respect to practically all money functions. The mark and the yen challenge the dollar on a regional level, not on the level of global leadership. However, while a clear mark zone has emerged in Europe during the 1980s, the increase in the use of the yen in Asia – though notable – is not nearly as important as that of the mark in Europe. The yen's weakness in international trade transactions contrasts with a more important role in financial investment. Whether Asia is actually moving towards a real yen zone is a still widely debated issue (Black, 1990; Tavlas, 1992; Tavlas and Ozeki, 1992; Frankel, 1993; Maehara, 1993; Frankel and Wei, 1994; Iwami, 1994; Kwan, 1994; Bénassy-Quéré, 1996; Dawkins, 1996; Eichengreen and Bayoumi, 1996; Garber, 1996; *Bloomberg News*, 1997; Dominguez, 1997; chapter 4). Whether the introduction of a Single European currency, the euro, at the end of this millenium will create a global challenger of the dollar (Alogoskoufis and Portes, 1992) and what the role of the yen could be in this competition will be addressed in chapter 4.

3   A theory of vehicle currencies

Aber der Aberglaube, es sei für die Regierung (im allgemeinen 'Staat' genannt, damit es besser klingt) notwendig zu erklären, was Geld sein soll, als ob sie das Geld erschaffen hätte und es ohne sie nicht existieren könnte, entspringt wahrscheinlich der naiven Vorstellung, so ein Werkzeug wie das Geld müsse 'erfunden' und uns von irgendeinem ursprünglichen Erfinder überlassen worden sein. Dieser Glaube wurde völlig durch unser Verständnis der spontanen Entstehung derartig ungeplanter Einrichtungen im Wege eines sozialen Evolutionsprozesses ersetzt, wofür das Geld seitdem zum Musterbeispiel geworden ist (während Recht, Sprache und Sitten die anderen wesentlichen Beispiele sind).'

(Friedrich August von Hayek, 1977)[1]

3.1   Introduction

One facet of the phenomenon of an international currency is its function as a vehicle in the foreign exchange (forex) market. This function is particularly important because of the pivotal role forex markets play in the internationalization of currencies in general (see chapter 1, section 1.2). In principle, a forex vehicle currency is nothing other than a medium of exchange. Analogous to a barter economy in goods markets, the necessity of 'double coincidence of wants' in a decentralized forex market may be overcome by using indirect exchange, through a generally acceptable medium of exchange instead of direct exchange of currencies (Swoboda, 1969). As will be shown below, even in an intermediated market (i.e. one where dealers stand ready to match all currency exchanges desired) international traders and investors can, in certain

---

[1] But the superstition that it would be necessary for the government (generally called 'state', to make it sound better) to declare what should be money, as if it had invented the money and it could not exist without the government, probably originates from the naive idea that such a tool like money needs to be 'invented' and must be inherited from some original inventor. This belief was entirely replaced by our understanding of the spontaneous emergence of such unplanned arrangements via a social evolutionary process, for which money has now become the prime example (whereas law, language and customs are the other essential examples).

circumstances, realize savings in transaction costs by vehicle use. This phenomenon leads to a very specific *network* of open and closed interbank currency markets, the structure of currency exchange.

Since the Second World War the US dollar has widely performed the vehicle function in the increasingly integrated markets for foreign exchange (Aliber, 1969; Kenen, 1983). However, during the 1980s a certain decline in its role was noticed (Black, 1991). And, in fact, since the late 1980s/early 1990s the Deutsche mark has emerged as second vehicle for trading among European currencies, while the dollar continues to 'intermediate' among practically all the other monies in the world (chapter 4; Hartmann, 1997a).

The present chapter aims to characterize the vehicle function in a particular theoretical setting, to identify the basic factors determining the extent to which vehicle currencies are used in overall forex transactions and to show how exogenous shocks can change this use. Since the theoretical survey in chapter 2 has shown that most of the previous authors on international currencies limited their attention to single media of exchange, one major focus is on the possibility of having multiple vehicle currencies. The partial equilibrium model developed here explains the degree of vehicle-currency use in an intermediated forex market by transaction cost advantages. The fundamental approach is market microstructure analysis.

Integrating a static currency exchange model and a dealer model of forex bid–ask spreads with market entry and exit decisions I find the following. First, one can confirm for an I-currency market Krugman's (1980) result that, due to economies of scale in the use of media of exchange, there can be multiple equilibria for the use of a single vehicle. However, this multiplicity occurs only if, for given values of the exogenous variables, set-up costs for forex dealers opening formerly closed bilateral markets introduce inertia in the exchange structure. Second, natural candidates for the vehicle function are those currencies with high trading volumes and low exchange rate volatilies, which result in low transaction costs. Third, and again in contrast to the existing literature, I prove under what circumstances equilibria with more than one vehicle currency can exist as well,[2] and I argue that these need not be characterized by instability in the exchange structure. Fourth, I show a case where high and widespread exchange rate instability can lead to the complete de-monetization of the forex market, the disappearance of vehicle currencies altogether.

Finally, the model provides a means to assess the effects which shocks

[2] This was already conjectured by Krugman (1984).

hitting the international monetary system may have on international currency use. In particular, the emergence or disappearance of a vehicle currency can occur slowly in several, rather gradual steps or quickly in a single dramatic restructuring of the exchange structure. Which type of scenario actually happens depends on the kind and the size of shocks on the fundamental trade and investment flows as well as forex dealers' expectations about order flows. In this way, the model can offer explanations for the recent emergence of the German mark as a competing vehicle to the dollar and it can help us understand what effect European Monetary Union (EMU) will have on the overall exchange structure in forex markets. These practical applications are undertaken in chapter 4.

In order to derive the main theoretical results, I proceed as follows. First I discuss transaction costs in the forex market and describe a model of the bid–ask spread, which further elaborates on the one proposed by Black (1991). In the third section, I first outline a currency-exchange model with opening (market entry by a dealer) and closing of bilateral markets. Then I discuss the types of equilibria which may occur, in particular those with multiple vehicles, and how they can change. The final section draws some conclusions. An appendix further elaborates on the concept of dealer and market competition and illustrates more cases of multiple vehicle exchange structures.

3.2   Transaction costs in the forex market

Three types of agents act in our forex market: liquidity traders or customers, intermediaries or forex dealers and position-taking traders or speculators. The first group randomly demands and supplies currencies, resulting from their activities in international trade and investment. Dealers offer markets to liquidity traders, and set bid and ask prices around the expected equilibrium exchange rate at which they can at any time satisfy their currency-exchange desires. The last group, the speculators, 'refinance' the stochastically appearing open positions of the dealers by taking positions in particular currencies themselves. Liquidity traders transact with dealers on the retail market and speculators transact with the dealers on the wholesale market. However, liquidity traders do not transact directly with speculators since access to the wholesale market is available only at some fixed costs, which are prohibitive for low-transaction volumes (banking authorization, foreign exchange know-how, 'good name' in the market, electronic trading equipment).

What are 'transaction costs' in this framework? Most generally, and in principle following Demsetz (1960, p. 15; 1968, p. 35), transaction costs can be defined as the costs of exchange of goods or assets. These usually include the costs involved in searching for potential exchange partners and costs for both the negotiation and control of contracts. In our context, costs of bargaining and control are neglected and no search takes place, since customers know for sure that they can exchange what they want through a dealer. The latter can quickly match compensating orders, but has to look for refinance if demand for a currency deviates from supply. In fact, the dealer can reduce this search dramatically by incurring some costs for access to electronic information and trading systems in the interbank market, where counterparties are readily available. On the other hand, if the dealer wants to close customer-induced positions at the end of the trading day – this seems to be roughly the case for many forex dealers (Goodhart, 1988) – he or she has to make concessions with respect to the refinancing price. Of course the dealer has to be remunerated for these two sources of production costs for exchange services and the bid and ask mark-ups serve precisely this purpose. This deviation of the actual transaction price from the expected equilibrium price is the only exchange cost incurred by customers. These costs are the price for using the intermediary instead of searching for (negotiating and controlling) contracts with other agents, and can therefore be considered as transaction costs.

A dealer model of the bid–ask spread[3]

In order to derive the determinants of the spread let us look at a risk-neutral intermediary, who makes one of the $I(I-1)/2$ submarkets of the I-currency foreign exchange market. At the beginning of each period she sets a spread based on expectations of the order flow from customers, the 'true' long-run equilibrium exchange rate and speculators' behaviour. The dealer then learns the actual orders of her customers, which usually will not equilibrate. After having learnt this open position, the dealer

---

[3] This section borrows to some extent from Black (1991). The model does not follow theories of the bid–ask spreads based on information asymmetries (Bagehot, 1971; Copeland and Galai, 1983; Glosten and Milgrom, 1985; Kyle, 1985), but it includes inventory costs (Stoll, 1978; Amihud and Mendelson, 1982; Ho and Stoll, 1981) and order-processing costs (Roll, 1984). Chapter 5 shows that information-cost effects are transitory and therefore less relevant for the emergence of vehicle currencies. The present model is also close to the early literature on bid–ask spreads and the costs of 'immediacy' (Demsetz, 1968; Tinic, 1972). Other inventory-theory spread models specifically for the forex market are in Allen (1977) and in Suvanto (1993, chapters 2 and 3). Booth (1984) develops a spread model based on information trading, but not necessarily systematic information asymmetries between both dealers and private speculators in the forex market. Lyons (1995) discusses the model of Madhavan and Smidt (1991), which integrates information and inventory-cost aspects – but not order-processing costs – in the light of the forex market.

closes it at the end of the period by transacting with speculators. In this section we still ignore the possibility of vehicle transactions or, in other words, we assume that the market is in a 'barter' equilibrium. This assumption will be relaxed in section 3.3.

For the sake of illustration, let us consider a particular submarket, say the submarket in which French francs (j=FRF) are traded against German marks (i=DEM) and vice versa. If the intermediary is a French bank (e.g. in Paris), then the dealer makes her profit calculations and quotes DEM selling and buying rates in francs. In European quotation (domestic currency units per foreign currency unit) the selling rate for marks is e_{ji}^a and the buying rate is e_{ji}^b, which are set symmetrically around the value of the 'true' equilibrium exchange rate, $\bar{e}_{ji}$, which is constant during the current trading period and known to the bank.[4] Experience tells the dealer that the expected values of actual DEM purchase and sale orders per unit of time (against francs and expressed in marks) are $\bar{x}_{ij} = \bar{x}_{ji}$, but the actual value of the random variables $\tilde{x}_{ij}, \tilde{x}_{ji}$ and $\tilde{e}_{ji}$ – the former two being independently distributed, the latter one being the current exchange rate in the wholesale segment at which she can refinance – she observes only after she has shown the spread, assumed to be binding for this period. One can then write the intermediary's profit in the ij market

$$\tilde{\pi}_{ij} = \tilde{x}_{ij}e_{ji}^a - \tilde{x}_{ji}e_{ji}^b - (\tilde{x}_{ij} - \tilde{x}_{ji})\tilde{e}_{ji} - c_{ij}, \tag{3.1}$$

where $(\tilde{x}_{ij} - \tilde{x}_{ji})$ is the open position (stochastic excess demand for DEM) and c_{ij} is a fixed cost of running this market (connection to Reuters system, etc.) per unit of time. By assuming positive fixed costs ($c_{ij} > 0$) here, there can only be a single dealer per bilateral market ij. A more general concept of dealer price competition is developed in the appendix (pp. 66ff.).[5]

In order to derive the dealer spread, we need to know how the current exchange rate in the wholesale segment, $\tilde{e}_{ji}$, is determined. As she perceives the effective order flow $\tilde{x}_{ij}, \tilde{x}_{ji}$ as being uncertain, the bank expects to be frequently left with open DEM positions. But as our dealer

---

[4] In fact, $\bar{e}_{ji}$ might be interpreted as the rate at which there are no more portfolio adjustments in international trade and investment and, therefore, where asset stocks are constant. In our partial equilibrium model this rate is supposed to be exogenously given as a constant for each trading period. From one period to the other it might follow a random walk (Meese and Rogoff, 1983) or some other stochastic process. As information asymmetries and inventory management through retail prices are absent, there is no reason for the spread to be set asymmetrically around $\bar{e}_{ji}$ (see also the appendix, p. 68).

[5] A contribution on inter-dealer Bertrand competition is Dennert (1993). Suvanto (1993, chapter 3) analyses the case of monopolistic competition among forex dealers at different locations.

restricts herself to her function in exchange intermediation she closes these positions in the same period. Thus she provides whatever amount of liquidity lacking in the retail market by refinancing in the wholesale segment. Since the position-taking traders whom she meets there are supposed to know $\bar{e}_{ji}$ as well, she can do this by 'offering' a different exchange rate. Hence the equilibrium condition can be written in units of currency i (here, the Deutsche mark).

$$\tilde{x}_{ij} - \tilde{x}_{ji} = \alpha_{ji}(\tilde{e}_{ji} - \bar{e}_{ji}). \tag{3.2}$$

The left-hand side can be interpreted as the demand for foreign exchange by the bank and the right-hand side as the supply of foreign exchange by the speculators in the wholesale segment.

Assume that the order flow reveals an excess demand for the German mark (currency i) in the retail segment, then the effort of the intermediary to close her position will induce her to demand marks in the wholesale segment (left-hand side of (3.2) positive). In order to get a corresponding supply of marks by the speculators the German currency has to appreciate to a higher rate with respect to the franc ($\tilde{e}_{ji}$) than $\bar{e}_{ji}$. This is illustrated in figure 3.1. The speculators offer marks because there is a good chance to buy them back at a lower rate in a later period. The sensitivity of them, α_{ji}, is given and known to the intermediary. In other words, she knows the joint probability distribution of $\tilde{x}_{ij} - \tilde{x}_{ji}$ and $\tilde{e}_{ji}$.[6]

From (3.1) and (3.2) and the application of the expectations operator one obtains

$$\bar{\pi}_{ij} = \bar{x}_{ji}(e^a_{ji} - e^b_{ji}) - \text{cov}(\tilde{x}_{ij} - \tilde{x}_{ji}, \tilde{e}_{ji}) - c_{ij} = p_{ij}, \tag{3.3}$$

which is the expected dealer profit. I assume that the ij dealer is a profit centre trying to maximize $\bar{\pi}_{ij}$. For example, the threat of entry by another dealer might drive p_{ij} towards zero (or to some positive value in the presence of entry costs). Defining the (fractional) bid–ask spread

$$s_{ji} \equiv \frac{e^a_{ji} - e^b_{ji}}{\bar{e}_{ji}}, \tag{3.4}$$

and putting (3.2) in (3.3) we can derive the basic relationship governing it

[6] The linear form of the 'supply function' may be obtained from two-period expected-utility-maximization of liquidity-unconstrained risk-averse investors facing an uncertain future wholesale price. Then their sensitivity α_{ij} is the inverse of their (constant) coefficient of absolute risk aversion. Notice that I simplify the algebra of the model by ignoring the influence of possible covariabilities between the ji and other exchange rates on the speculators' behaviour in (3.2), i.e. I assume that order flows in one bilateral market ($\tilde{x}_{ij}$) are independent of those in others ($\tilde{x}_{lm}, l \neq i$ or $m \neq j$). However, none of the main results derived below relies on this assumption.

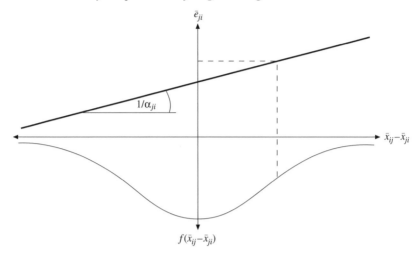

Figure 3.1 Determination of the short-run wholesale exchange rate

$$s_{ji} = \frac{\sigma_{ji}^0 + \gamma_{ji}}{\bar{x}_{ji}}, \tag{3.5}$$

where σ_{ji}^0 is a measure of the volatility of the current FRF–DEM (wholesale) exchange rate, defined in marks

$$\sigma_{ji}^0 \equiv \frac{V(\tilde{x}_{ij} - \tilde{x}_{ji})}{\alpha_{ji}\bar{e}_{ji}} = \frac{\alpha_{ji}V(\tilde{e}_{ji})}{\bar{e}_{ji}}, \tag{3.6}$$

and where

$$\gamma_{ji} \equiv \frac{c_{ij} + p_{ij}}{\bar{e}_{ji}}. \tag{3.7}$$

Because of her dependence on speculators for instantaneous refinancing, she loses on average when transacting with them in the wholesale market. The higher σ_{ji}^0, the heavier these losses. σ_{ji}^0 itself depends positively on the volatility of the net order flow, which determines the variance of $\tilde{e}_{ji}$, on the one hand (see (3.2)), and negatively on the sensitivity of the speculators α_{ji} on the other (see (3.6)). If the order flow is very volatile then high refinancing volumes per period have a high probability, meaning much scope for (expected) refinancing losses. If the speculators' sensitivity is rather low (α_{ji} low), then for a given open position the intermediary has to 'offer' an even more unfavourable exchange rate, meaning once more increased scope for refinancing losses. The intermediary must therefore compensate for a higher volatility of the exchange rate (incorporating order flow volatility and speculators' sensitivity) with a larger spread.

Here, exchange rate volatility can be related to the level of trading volume. If expected changes of the level of trading volume are accompanied by similar changes of the volatility of the order flow, then through (3.6) they will bear (have) some costs (benefit) in the form of increased (decreased) exchange rate volatility. Imagine, for example, that $\tilde{x}_{ij}$ and $\tilde{x}_{ji}$ are sums of independent random variables describing each individual customer's demands and supplies. If volume changes take the form of market entry or exit of customers, then an increase in volume will also increase the volatility of the order flow to the dealer, and vice versa. As discussed later, such an effect can play a role in volume changes through switchings of the exchange pattern from direct to indirect transactions and vice versa. However, if only the expected order size of some customer changes, then the order flow variance for the dealer may also be unaffected.

As can be seen from (3.5), the *direct* (or order-processing) effect of volume changes on the spread is negative. But there *can* be a positive *indirect* (or inventory cost) effect through volatility. Hence, as this model is formulated, the marginal effect of volume on the spread is ambiguous. It can be negative or positive depending on the type of volume changes and the distributions of the order flows, determining whether the direct volume–fixed-cost effect or the indirect volume–volatility effect dominates.

The relation between spreads, volatilities and volumes advanced by (3.5) can be evaluated against the background of the existing empirical literature on bid–ask spreads in the forex market. As discussed *in extenso* in the main empirical chapter of this book (chapter 5) expected volatility increases spreads, while expected volume decreases spreads. Unexpected volumes (or volatilities) also increase spreads, but this effect is of a transitory nature and can therefore be neglected in the present chapter. Concerning the volume–volatility relation, the correlation observed in the forex and other financial markets is less than perfect (Karpoff, 1987; Frankel and Froot, 1990; Jorion, 1996). For example, for the short panel of monthly volumes and volatilities in chapter 5 (measuring the predictable parts) the correlation coefficient is $\rho = 0.03$, while for the daily dollar/yen time series in the same chapter $\rho = 0.5$. It turns out that the indirect volume–volatility effect usually does not fully compensate the direct volume–fixed-cost effect. Summing up, then, the evidence supports the predictions made by the spread model arguing in favour of a negative long-run volume effect.

3.3   Structures of currency exchange

In section 3.2 I introduced a simple model of a forex dealer's bid–ask spread, which enables me determine the transaction costs in the spot forex market and which also performs reasonably well when exposed to the facts. But I ignored one crucial aspect of how trading volumes are determined. While, on the one hand, the (expected) volumes influence the magnitude of the spreads, as (3.5) shows, on the other hand, spreads themselves determine the volumes in different markets. This feedback of spreads into volumes is of a discrete nature, as changes in spreads can make it attractive to switch from direct exchange to indirect exchange or vice versa for some currency pairs, thereby withdrawing trading activity from some markets while adding activity to others (network effects) and affecting volatilities as well.

I introduce this aspect by defining variables $\tilde{z}_{ij}$, describing the optimal currency exchanges for customers (or total final volumes), which can, but need not, be identical to their 'original' currency exchange desires $\tilde{x}_{ij}$. The exchange model takes on the character of a simple extensive-form game, where the dealers in active markets choose their spreads in the first stage, based on their expectations of how the customers will choose their exchange patterns. In the next stage, the customers will actually decide on this pattern, based on the spreads, which are binding for the dealers over the whole period. Finally, in the third stage, the latter refinance with speculators, as described on p. 45. This game may be repeated in each period and the dealers can adjust their spreads only between, not during, periods. Due to the random-order flow to the intermediaries, the currency exchange model is stochastic. We can simplify the whole analysis considerably by writing it in expectations form, i.e. reasoning in averages.

Exchange model

When the dealers consider that the customers can choose between direct exchange and indirect exchange through a vehicle, arbitrarily chosen to be currency I,[7] then their behaviour can be summarized in 7 $I \times I$ matrices with only 0 diagonal elements: Z, Y, X, S, Γ, K and Σ. $X = (\bar{x}_{ij})$ describes the average *originally* desired currency exchanges by the customer entering the retail market, e.g. $\bar{x}_{23}$ is the expected value of the sum of desired purchases of currency 2 against currency 3 in terms of

---

[7] Let us assume for the moment that there is already a (potential) vehicle currency I. The important question which currencies are eligible or natural candidates to become a vehicle is discussed on pp. 54ff. below.

some numéraire at long-term equilibrium exchange rates. In Krugman's (1980) terminology, X may be called the (expected) *structure of payments*, since the desired exchanges will originate in trade or capital transactions between residents of different countries. $\Gamma = (\gamma_{ij})$ is the matrix describing the fixed costs of *making* active bilateral currency markets as defined in (3.7).

$K = (\kappa_{ij}) \geq 0$ describes the potential costs of activating a formerly closed bilateral market. These *set-up costs* are defined to be zero for the incumbent dealer(s) and can be positive for a dealer entering a market which has been inactive in the previous period. (Incumbent dealers are 'inherited' from the past, so their set-up costs are sunk.) A practical example of such set-up costs is the research efforts necessary to find out the potential equilibrium size, volatility and spread of a currently closed market.

While X, Γ and K are exogenous, S, Y, Z and Σ are endogenously determined as follows.

$$S = (s_{ij}) \text{ with } s_{ij}|_{i,j \neq I} = \begin{cases} (\sigma_{ij} + \gamma_{ij})/\bar{z}_{ij} & \text{if } s_{ij} \geq s_{iI} + s_{Ij} \\ s_{iI} + s_{Ij} + \varepsilon & \text{if } s_{ij} < s_{iI} + s_{Ij} \end{cases},$$

$$s_{iI}|_{i \neq I} \frac{\sigma_{iI} + \gamma_{iI}}{\bar{z}_{iI}}, s_{Ij}|_{j \neq I} = \frac{\sigma_{Ij} + \gamma_{Ij}}{\bar{z}_{Ij}} \tag{3.8}$$

is the *structure of transaction costs* (fractional spreads) as motivated from section 3.2. s_{23} for example is the ratio of the difference between ask and bid prices of the exchange rate between currency 2 and currency 3, divided by the middle rate (as defined in (3.4)). One difference between (3.8) and (3.5) in section 3.2 is that markets can be closed now, or have a prohibitively high 'spread'. This can be represented by a 'spread' which is slightly (ε) above that for the indirect transaction through currency I (rather than 'infinite'). s_{iI} and s_{Ij} are the transaction costs in the vehicle markets.

The next issue is how the $\bar{z}_{ij}$s in (3.8) are determined. The dealers know that the customers observe spreads and decide whether they want to realize their original exchange desires ($\bar{x}_{ij}$) directly or indirectly

$$s_{ij} \underset{>}{\overset{<}{=}} s_{iI} + s_{Ij}. \tag{3.9}$$

If the transaction costs of direct exchange for some market ij (left-hand side of (3.9)) are lower than that of going through the vehicle I (right-hand side of (9)) he assumes that customers will 'vote' for the former option. A dealer might also enter a market ij which has been closed in the previous period, if she has found out that it can be re-activated at a profit (after potential set-up costs κ_{ij}). If the direct transaction costs are higher then she expects them to prefer both transactions through the medium of exchange. These decisions determine the (expected) *structure of vehicle use Y* and the (expected) *structure of exchange* $Z = (\bar{z}_{ij})$ – the latter once more Krugman's (1980) term – with

$$Z \equiv X - Y, \tag{3.10}$$

where

$$Y = (\bar{y}_{ij}) =$$

$$\begin{pmatrix}
0 & \delta_{12}\bar{x}_{12} & \delta_{13}\bar{x}_{13} & \cdots & \delta_{1I-1}\bar{x}_{1I-1} & -\sum_{j=2}^{I-1}\delta_{1j}\bar{x}_{1j} \\
\delta_{21}\bar{x}_{21} & 0 & \delta_{23}\bar{x}_{23} & \cdots & \delta_{2I-1}\bar{x}_{2I-1} & -\sum_{j=1,j\neq2}^{I-1}\delta_{2j}\bar{x}_{2j} \\
\vdots & & \ddots & & & \vdots \\
\vdots & & & \ddots & & \vdots \\
\delta_{I-11}\bar{x}_{I-11} & \delta_{I-12}\bar{x}_{I-12} & \cdots & \delta_{I-1I-2}\bar{x}_{I-1I-2} & 0 & -\sum_{j=1}^{I-2}\delta_{I-1j}\bar{x}_{I-1j} \\
-\sum_{i=2}^{I-1}\delta_{i1}\bar{x}_{i1} & -\sum_{i=1,i\neq2}^{I-1}\delta_{i2}\bar{x}_{i2} & \cdots & -\sum_{i=1,i\neq I-2}^{I-1}\delta_{iI-2}\bar{x}_{iI-2} & -\sum_{i=1}^{I-2}\delta_{iI-1}\bar{x}_{iI-1} & 0
\end{pmatrix} \tag{3.11}$$

and $\delta_{ij} \in [0,1]\forall i,j$ are measures of the degree of vehicle use for all bilateral (non-vehicle) markets.

Take the demand for currency 1 against currency 2 as an example. If all such transactions could be expected to be exercised directly, then $\delta_{12} = 0$ such that $\bar{y}_{12} = 0$ and $\bar{z}_{12} = \bar{x}_{12}$. But for any expected indirect transaction ($\delta_{12} > 0$ or equivalently $\bar{y}_{12} > 0$) some volume is withdrawn from the 1-demand side of the 1,2 market and two transactions added in the vehicle markets, one in the *I*2 segment and another in the 1*I* segment. Instead of exchanging currency 2 for currency 1, the customer exchanges 2 for *I* and then *I* for 1. For the supply of currency 1 against currency 2, it is the reverse. The (expected) switch from a direct to an indirect transaction swells the (expected) volume of 'the vehicle market' twofold. Applying the same reasoning to all the remaining non-vehicle markets explains the sums in the *I*th row and the *I*th column of *Y*, which represent the added (expected) volumes in the vehicle markets resulting from indirect exchange.

In order to understand (3.8) it remains to explain $\Sigma = (\sigma_{ij})$, the matrix of exchange rate volatilities on all bilateral markets. As was indicated in section 3.2, $V = (\bar{z}_{ij} - \bar{z}_{ji})$ depends on the structure of exchange. In the case of a non-vehicle market

$$V(\bar{z}_{ij} - \bar{z}_{ji}) = (1 - \delta_{ij})^2 V(\tilde{x}_{ij} - \tilde{x}_{ji}), \tag{3.12}$$

and therefore

$$\sigma_{ij} = \left(1 - \delta_{ij}\right)^2 \sigma_{ij}^0. \tag{3.13}$$

If such a market is exchanged directly ($\delta_{ij} = 0$) then $\sigma_{ij} = \sigma_{ij}^0$ as in (3.5). Otherwise, in complete indirect exchange ($\delta_{ij} = 1$) volatility totally vanishes. In the case of a vehicle market, as a result of the independence of order flows, volatility is the variance of the original order flow, *plus* a sum of the variances of the order flows of all those non-vehicle markets which have switched to indirect exchange through this vehicle market.

$$V(\tilde{z}_{iI} - \tilde{z}_{Ii}) = V(\tilde{x}_{iI} - \tilde{x}_{Ii}) + \sum_{j=1, j\neq i}^{I-1} \delta_{ij}^2 V(\tilde{x}_{ij} - \tilde{x}_{ji}) \; \forall i \neq I \tag{3.14}$$

such that

$$\sigma_{iI} = \left(\frac{1}{\alpha_{iI}\bar{e}_{iI}}\right) \sum_{j=1, j\neq i}^{I} \delta_{ij}^2 V(\tilde{x}_{ij} - \tilde{x}_{ji}) \; \forall i \neq I \tag{3.15}$$

and

$$\sigma_{Ij} = \left(\frac{1}{\alpha_{Ij}\bar{e}_{Ij}}\right) \sum_{i=1, i\neq j}^{I} \delta_{ij}^2 V(\tilde{x}_{ij} - \tilde{x}_{ji}) \; \forall j \neq I. \tag{3.16}$$

Now (3.8), (3.10), (3.11), (3.13), (3.15) and (3.16) permit specifying (3.9) as (3.9′)

$$\bar{x}_{ij}^{-1}\left[(1 - \delta_{ij})\sigma_{ij}^0 + \frac{\gamma_{ij}}{1 - \delta_{ij}}\right] \underset{>}{\overset{<}{=}}$$

$$\left(\bar{x}_{iI} + \sum_{j=1, j\neq i}^{I-1} \delta_{ij}\bar{x}_{ij}\right)^{-1}\left[\frac{V(\tilde{x}_{iI} - \tilde{x}_{Ii}) + \sum_{j=1, j\neq i}^{I-1} \delta_{ij}^2 V(\tilde{x}_{ij} - \tilde{x}_{ji})}{\alpha_{iI}\bar{e}_{iI}} + \gamma_{iI}\right] \tag{3.9′}$$

$$+ \left(\bar{x}_{Ij} + \sum_{i=1, i\neq j}^{I-1} \delta_{ij}\bar{x}_{ij}\right)^{-1}\left[\frac{V(\tilde{x}_{Ij} - \tilde{x}_{jI}) + \sum_{i=1, i\neq j}^{I-1} \delta_{ij}^2 V(\tilde{x}_{ij} - \tilde{x}_{ji})}{\alpha_{Ij}\bar{e}_{Ij}} + \gamma_{Ij}\right].$$

I shall define an equilibrium below as a situation where (average) vehicle use as presumed by the dealers equals the customers' actual (average) vehicle use. Call the optimal vehicle use for the customer (given S) Y^*. Then in equilibrium – i.e. a situation where the customers have chosen the transaction-cost-minimizing exchange decision – $\bar{y}^*_{ij}|_{i,j\neq I}$ is determined by the following correspondence

$$\bar{y}^*_{ij}|_{i,j\neq I} = \delta^*_{ij}\bar{x}_{ij}, \quad \bar{y}^*_{iI}|_{i\neq I} = \bar{x}_{iI} + \sum_{j=1,j\neq i}^{I-1} \delta^*_{ij}\bar{x}_{ij}, \quad \bar{y}^*_{Ij}|_{j\neq I} = \bar{x}_{Ij} + \sum_{i=i,i\neq j}^{I-1} \delta^*_{ij}\bar{x}_{ij}, \quad (3.17)$$

where

$$\delta^*_{ij}|_{i,j\neq I} \begin{cases} = 0 & \text{if} \quad s_{ij} < s_{iI} + s_{Ij} \\ \epsilon[0,1] & \text{if} \quad s_{ij} = s_{iI} + s_{Ij} \\ = 1 & \text{if} \quad s_{ij} > s_{iI} + s_{Ij} \end{cases} \qquad (3.18)$$

For any given pair of currencies, if there is no uncertainty about the spread, in equilibrium the customers will choose 0-vehicle use (direct exchange: $\delta^*_{ij} = 0$) if transaction costs are lower than for the corresponding two transactions for indirect exchange. In the opposite case, they will stick to complete indirect exchange ($\delta^*_{ij} = 1$). In the strict equality case, vehicle use is undetermined in the interval defined by these two bounds, because the customers remain indifferent as to direct and indirect exchange.

The static model encompasses (3.8), (3.10), (3.11), (3.13), (3.15), (3.16), (3.17) and (3.18), which is a non-linear system of $5I(I-1) + (I-1)(I-2)$ equations and an equal number of endogenous variables. An equilibrium is a combination of spreads S, as chosen by the intermediaries based on expected vehicle use Y, and Y^* – the optimal vehicle use – as chosen by customers based on S, such that a dealer cannot make a profit by entering some new market; customers minimize transaction costs and actual average vehicle use (Y^*) equals the dealer's expectations (Y). Original volumes and volatilities (X and Σ^0), fixed costs (Γ) and set-up costs (K), long-run equilibrium exchange rates ($E = (\bar{e}_{ij})$) and sensitivities of speculators ($A = (\alpha_{ij})$) are exogenous.

Definition 1
Given A, E, Γ, K, X, Σ^0, a *forex market equilibrium (FXE)* is a set $\{S,Y,Y^*,Z,\Sigma\}$ such that there is no longer any incentive for dealers to enter a bilateral market, customers minimize transaction costs and $Y \in Y^*$.

This notion of a forex market equilibrium can be formalized more rigorously in terms of Bertrand–Nash price competition between dealers and markets. However, the more precise formulation is notationally so cumbersome that it has been put in the appendix of this chapter. The appendix also illustrates that the main results found below will carry over to the more exact theoretical treatment.

Foreign exchange 'barter' and the emergence of a vehicle currency

In this subsection I want to analyse in which circumstances a vehicle can actually emerge and, if these circumstances are met, which currency will become the vehicle. I first look at a case where generally extreme volatility can make any monetary phenomenon impossible. This can happen if there are no important differences between all currencies – i.e. the forex market is relatively homogeneous or 'symmetric'.

Definition 2

A forex market where all bilateral markets have the same (*a priori*) distribution of order flows, i.e. $\bar{x}_{ij} = x$ and $V(\tilde{x}_{ij} - \tilde{x}_{ji}) = V(\tilde{x}_{i'j'} - \tilde{x}_{j'i'})$ $\forall i \neq j, i \neq j', j \neq j'$, exchange rate volatilities $\sigma_{ij}^0 = \sigma \ \forall i \neq j$, and the same fixed costs $\gamma_{ij} = \gamma \ \forall i \neq j$, is called *symmetric*.

Proposition 1

In a symmetric forex market with at least three currencies ($I \geq 3$), 'barter' (all bilateral markets exchanged directly) is always an FXE if

$$\sigma \geq \gamma \left(1 - \frac{2}{I - 2}\right), \tag{3.19}$$

and it is the only FXE if $K = 0$.

Condition (3.19) states that, in a symmetric forex market, the higher volatility, the lower the total number of currencies and the lower fixed costs, the easier direct exchange becomes. In an extreme case, any vehicle use is made impossible if there are no set-up costs. This is an example of how 'excessive' volatility can destroy money. The reason behind this phenomenon is that, because of the same linearity in volatility and volume changes in the symmetric case, the ratio of volatility to volume in vehicle markets is constant, so that increased vehicle use does not reduce the twofold volatility costs of indirect exchange. In contrast, fixed cost reduction is quite strong, so that the double fixed costs of indirect exchange are quickly driven down by more vehicle use. The case of 'barter' is graphically illustrated in figure 2.1 (p. 16).

Proof

It suffices to show that (3.19) is a sufficient condition for direct exchange to be always cheaper than indirect exchange in a symmetric forex market. I do this in two steps: in step 1 I argue that in the symmetric case the endogenous vehicle volumes and volatilities are linear functions of the number of bilateral markets (completely) exchanged through the respective vehicle markets. In step 2, I exploit this property in (3.9′) to derive (3.19).

By the definition of a symmetric forex market and of a vehicle market, the minimum volume of the latter is x, its original volume without vehicle use. Maximal $I-2$ non-vehicle markets can switch to indirect exchange through this market, where I is the total number of currencies, such that its maximal volume is $x(I-1)$. Thus, for any vehicle market iI $z_{iI} = x(I - I')$ with $I' \in \{1, \ldots, I - 1\}$ and $I' - 1$, the number of non-vehicle markets which have *not* switched to indirect exchange through the iI market. Similarly, because of the additive form of vehicle volatilities found in (15) and (16) (for the δ_{ij}s being either 0 or 1) and the symmetry in definition 1 $\sigma_{iI} = \sigma(I - I')$ (I' as before).

In step 2 I assume that for an arbitrary bilateral market ij the dealers suppose that it is exchanged directly ($\bar{y}_{ij} = 0 = \delta_{ij}$) and I then verify that this is actually an equilibrium if (3.19) holds. I begin by rewriting (3.9') using the expressions from step 1 and take the inequality sign compatible with direct exchange

$$\frac{\sigma + \gamma}{x} \leq \frac{(I - I')\sigma + \gamma}{(I - I')x} + \frac{(I - I'')\sigma + \gamma}{(I - I'')x}, \qquad (3.20)$$

$I' - 1$ and $I'' - 1$ are measures of how many non-vehicle markets have *not* switched to indirect exchange through the iI and Ij markets, respectively. As s_{iI} and s_{Ij} are monotonously increasing in I' and I'' I can set $I' = 2 = I''$. Multiplying by x and rearranging terms gives (3.19). Thus, if (3.19) holds, any bilateral market can continue to function in direct exchange, even when all the other $(I - 1)(I - 2)/2 - 1$ non-vehicle markets are already illiquid. Finally, because of the general symmetry the same reasoning applies whatever I, the (potential) vehicle currency, may be.

If there is no inertia through set-up costs, the system cannot be locked-in in an equilibrium where the current sum of vehicle spreads is larger than the spread which would prevail in the direct market, if the latter would be active. ∎

Of course, if 'excess' volatility is not general, but only limited to certain markets – i.e. there is some asymmetry in the fundamentals – then the less volatile currency will simply emerge as a vehicle currency. Asymmetric volumes work the other way round: the larger the volumes to be traded in one currency (compared to the others), the more likely that this currency will fulfil the vehicle role.

Proposition 2

Suppose fixed costs of market-making are the same in all markets $\gamma_{ij} = \gamma \; \forall i \neq j$. For any currency, arbitrarily chosen to be I, there is a combination of (low) volatilities σ_{iI}^0, $\sigma_{Ij}^0 (i \neq j)$ and (high) expected volumes $\bar{x}_{iI}, \bar{x}_{Ij}$, such that, given all the other exogenous variables, if the initial FXE was forex 'barter', I will automatically emerge as a vehicle currency.

Proof
The proof follows directly from the exchange condition (3.9′) and dealers' market entry and exit decisions. If $\bar{x}_{iI}, \bar{x}_{Ij}$ are sufficiently high without $\sigma^0_{iI}, \sigma^0_{Ij}$ being too large, one, several or all other bilateral markets would have higher transaction costs than the respective vehicle markets and dealers trying to continue making these markets would incur losses and finally have to close them. ∎

Proposition 2 states rigorously what could already be expected from the theory (section 3.2 above) and evidence (chapter 5 below) on transaction costs in forex markets. Currencies with high trading volumes and nevertheless low exchange rate volatilities are natural candidates to perform the vehicle-currency function in forex markets. Apart from the two extremes forex 'barter' (or complete demonetization, proposition 1) and full monetization (i.e. a situation where all non-vehicle currencies are exchanged indirectly through I) there can, depending on the exogenously given original order flows and exchange rate volatilities, also occur equilibria with intermediate vehicle use.

Network externalities, inertia and multiple equilibria

Could there also be multiple equilibria for the same set of trading volumes, volatilities and fixed costs? These could be expected if we consider the character of a medium of exchange as a *network good*.[8] A network good (like for example, telephone connections) becomes the more valuable for its users as use by others increases. This is due to a positive network externality running from a new user to all (or a subset) of the 'incumbent' users (Rohlfs, 1974), which leads to circularity and self-fulfilling forces in the use of network goods.

However, in the case of a vehicle currency the externality need not always be positive. This can be verified by switching one market ij from direct exchange ($\delta_{ij} = 0$) to vehicle exchange ($\delta_{ij} = 1$) in (3.9′). Depending on the relative size of $\bar{x}_{ij}$ as compared to σ^0_{ij} the right-hand side (the transaction costs of vehicle use) could increase or decrease through this switch. In other words, if the indirect volume–volatility effect of a currency unit expected to switch from direct to indirect exchange were

---

[8] For example Pollin and Ullmo (1992, pp. 88f.) describe the different aspects of money as a network good.

positive and stronger than the (always negative) volume–fixed-cost effect, then the externality would be negative and there would be diseconomies of scale in vehicle use and, therefore, the foreign exchange vehicle would rather work as a network 'bad'. In the reverse – say, the 'normal' case – it performs the role of a network good.

Moreover, even in the 'normal' case the scope for multiple equilibria depends also on the degree of inter-dealer or inter-market competition. With completely free entry of dealers on inactive markets and with strong (Bertrand-type) price competition between markets, there is a strong tendency towards a single exchange structure, which minimizes customers' transaction costs. However, the larger the set-up costs $K > 0$ the more difficult it becomes for potentially entering dealers to re-open closed interbank markets. In other words, the higher the set-up costs the more important the *inertia* in the system, and the more *history* matters for the actual equilibrium exchange structures.[9]

Proposition 3

For any bilateral market ij and any single vehicle currency I, there is a (high) level of set-up costs κ_{ij} such that complete indirect exchange for ij is always sustainable, whatever the exchange pattern in all the other markets.

Proof

One can see from the general exchange condition (3.9′) that for finite exogenous variables (and $\bar{x}_{iI}, \bar{x}_{Ij} > 0 \,\forall i, j \neq I$), whatever their values, if δ_{ij} approaches 1 the left-hand side becomes always larger than the right-hand side. When ij has become illiquid and set-up costs are high enough, a dealer wishing to attract the original ij order flow would have to quote a spread which would not allow him to break even in this market. ■

Proposition 3 shows how the system can get locked-in to an exchange structure 'inherited' from the past, which might not change even when the fundamentals become favourable for direct exchange of the ij market. Through this inertia multiple structures can be sustainable as forex equilibria. Moreover, the stronger economies of scale in vehicle use (positive network externality) the more the forex market will have some tendency to be fully monetized through a single medium of exchange.

---

[9] There are certainly other, but not necessarily more realistic ways to bring in some imperfection of the competition between dealers. However, in conjunction with network externalities the effect would be the same – the introduction of some inertia in the currency exchange structure.

Corollary
If set-up costs are large enough, full monetization through a single
vehicle currency is always a forex market equilibrium.

Finally, once such a vehicle is established it does not easily lose its
status when strong network externalities or some set-up costs are at
work. For example, if economies of scale unfold, a vehicle produces the
necessary condition for its existence – low transaction costs – itself. The
system can very well remain in an equilibrium with a vehicle, inherited
from the past, which is now more volatile or *a priori* less heavily traded
than another currency. This result is particularly interesting regarding
the historical experience that dominant international currencies, such as
the pound sterling, maintained a prominent position in the international
monetary system long after the economic dominance of the issuing
country had vanished (chapter 2, section 2.3; see also the following
subsection).

Notice, though, that in the triangular relation between a direct market
and two vehicle markets the lock-in effect of an inactive direct market
does not apply to an active direct market, because the competition
between dealers in active markets is much sharper than that through the
threat of entry, in particular in the present case of (Bertrand-type) price
competition. This limits the number of potential equilibria for given
values of the exogenous variables.

Proposition 4
For any bilateral market ij and any single vehicle currency I, there are
combinations of Γ, X and Σ^0 such that direct exchange for ij is never
sustainable.

Proof
Consider the general exchange condition (3.9′). For $\delta_{ij} = 0$ and finite
values of all *a priori* volumes, volatilities and fixed costs, one can always
find a low level of $\bar{x}_{ij}$, given the other variables, for which the left-hand
side is *always* greater than the right-hand side. The same experiment can
be done with a high level of σ^0_{ij}. ∎

Transitions from one dominant vehicle currency to another

Assume that there is a single vehicle currency intermediating the whole
or a large part of the forex market and that the volume–spread relationship is negative (the 'normal' case of scale economies). Suppose further
that the country issuing this currency is facing a partial or regional
erosion of its dominant role in international trade and investment – i.e.

$\bar{x}_{iI}, \bar{x}_{Ij}$ decline for a few currencies i, j. (Alternatively, one could also think of a destabilization of the vehicle currency through strongly augmented volatility or of a coordinated change in dealer expectations.[10]) If this erosion reaches some *critical level* (or critical mass) with respect to two countries, it might become possible for a dealer (in spite of set-up costs) to re-activate the respective direct forex market for the exchange of these two countries' currencies, so that there is a switch in the exchange structure with a discrete reduction in total vehicle use.[11]

Depending on how strong this initial switch is, it can trigger switches to direct exchange in other bilateral markets as well. This can occur because the first switch can reduce the liquidity of the vehicle currency with respect to up to two other currency pairs in indirect exchange. Again, if critical masses are reached these two will switch as well, and so on. Hence, in certain cases there can be a domino effect of exchange structure changes. In an extreme scenario – say, a very large and global shock on the fundamentals or very strong scale economies in market-making – the original vehicle currency may disappear in a 'catastrophic' fall.

However, if the fundamentals change rather in a gradual fashion (shocks are not big enough) or if the inertia in the system is very important, the decline of the dominant currency may also occur in a long and step-wise manner, with the forex market remaining for some time in equilibria with intermediate use of the original vehicle.[12] History seems to suggest that dominant international currencies tend to lose their status in this step-wise fashion rather than in one big catastrophic regime shift in a short period of time (see chapter 2, section 2.3). The long and step-wise decline of sterling over several decades is the classical example. The more recent observation of some decline in the dollar's role as a vehicle currency hints at slow and partial changes as well (chapters 2 and 4).

If later, or even at the same time, another country experiences an increase in its importance in world trade and finance or even rises to world leadership, an opposite type of movement will occur for that country's currency. For those parts of the forex market which are in a 'barter'-type situation, the emergence of the new vehicle will be very quick, since – as indicated by propositions 3 and 4 – there is less inertia in

---

[10] Regarding the latter, see Krugman (1991).

[11] This critical-mass aspect is a typical phenomenon with the use of network goods, clearly stated in Rohlfs (1974).

[12] Krugman's (1984) figure 8.4 suggests that such intermediate equilibria will be 'unstable'. Hence, it is important to note that in the present theory, depending on the actually prevailing values for the exogenous variables, these intermediate equilibria, if they exist, can but need not be unstable (Hartmann, 1994). Further discussion of stability issues will be provided in the following subsection and n. 16.

direct exchange than in indirect exchange, and critical masses can be reached more quickly. However, for those bilateral markets which are still exchanged through the former dominant vehicle currency, network externalities and switching costs will delay the advance of the challenger.

Multiple vehicle currencies and the stability of the international monetary system

Until the previous paragraph I have assumed that there is no more than one (potential) vehicle currency. Looking back through history, it seems logical for us to find a dominant international medium of exchange (see chapter 2). Before the First World War sterling was the dominant international currency and following the Second World War the dollar finally took over. Nonetheless, in spite of dominance there were almost always other international currencies of differing importance around.[13] Recent developments and prospects in the world economy, such as regional free trade areas and currency unions, for example, have brought us closer to a multipolar international monetary system. Especially if the internationalization of the Japanese yen further advances or the European single currency, the euro, emerges as a major challenger to the US dollar (chapter 4) a bipolar or tripolar currency system might be predicted (Alogoskoufis and Portes, 1992). The present theory can provide a basis for such claims.[14]

Proposition 5

There is a level of set-up costs $K \geq 0$ such that in a forex market with more than three currencies, there exists at least one equilibrium with more than one vehicle currency.

[13] The possibility of endogenously emerging *multiple* media of exchange has been mentioned in the monetary literature, but there was little systematic elaboration. (See, for example, Brunner and Meltzer, 1971, p. 800; Jones, 1976, p. 767, n. 13; Kiyotaki and Wright, 1989, pp. 938, 941, 944; Oh, 1989, pp. 115ff.) Matsuyama *et.al.* (1993) prove that in a two-region search framework for goods exchange there exist equilibria where a medium of exchange from abroad circulates parallel to the local one. However, currency exchanges occur only in the special case where the external medium of exchange is a perfect substitute for the locally produced good. The strategic market games literature has developed models where any individual can issue her own credit certificates, which are generally acceptable as means of payment in goods exchanges (Shubik, 1990; Sorin, 1994). In another paper Starr and Stinchcombe (1993) point out that multiple media of exchange can be transaction-cost-minimizing, when the marginal costs of trading are negligible and the fixed costs of running trading posts differ from post to post. Niehans (1969, pp. 721ff.) finds that several media of exchange can be exchange-cost-minimizing when variable transaction costs for the exchange of two goods differ between agents.

[14] The following reasoning, based on the theoretical model already developed, has gained inspiration from the intuitive analysis of Paul Krugman (1984).

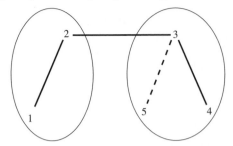

Figure 3.2 Small forex market with two vehicle currencies

Proof
First, let me assume for the moment that the forex market has only four currencies. Suppose further that currencies 2 and 3 are two (potential) vehicles with 1 belonging to the currency area of vehicle 2, and 4 belonging to the currency area of vehicle 3. This structure is illustrated in figure 3.2, where a straight line between two currencies stands for an active bilateral market. (Ignore the dashed line with currency 5 for the moment.) It is easy to see that this situation is sustainable as an equilibrium. From proposition 2 we infer that the indirect exchange of the 1,3 and the 2,4 markets is always self-sustaining for some κ_{13} and κ_{24}. In fact, the same logic applies to the 1,4 market which is exchanged indirectly through *two* media of exchange.[15] Now, add currency 5 in 3's area, as indicated by the dashed line. Once more, proposition 2 shows that the new structure is sustainable as well, since 5 is supposed to be exchanged indirectly with all other currencies except with the vehicle 3. Consequently, in the same manner as currency 5 we can add as many other currencies as we want, either to the 2-area or to the 3-area, provided that it is sufficiently costly to open up the respective markets, while keeping an equilibrium situation. This concludes the proof. ∎

One can offer two further examples of situations with more than one vehicle. The first is Krugman's (1984, p. 267ff.) 'bipolar structure of exchange' and the second is a 'tripolar (currency) world' as might be inferred from Alogoskoufis and Portes (1992). Krugman's 'bipolar world' is illustrated in figure 3.3, which corresponds, in principle, to figure 8.2 in his article. The only difference from the five-currency

[15] The appearance of exchange chains longer than two transactions is in opposition to the search-cost approach of Jones (1976), applied to the foreign exchange market by Chrystal (1984). But it is compatible with the ameliorated version of the Jones model by Oh (1989).

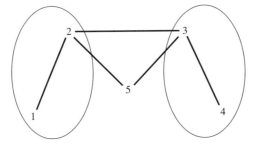

Figure 3.3 Krugman's (1984) 'bipolar structure of exchange'

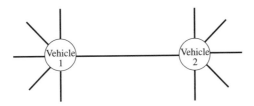

Figure 3.4 Strictly bipolar forex market

('strictly' bipolar) structure in figure 3.2 is that, although there remain the two currency areas, currency 5 does not belong to either of them and is exchanged directly with both of the vehicles 2 and 3. However, in order to exchange 5 and 4 (5 and 1), 3 (2) is used as vehicle. Remembering proposition 4 we see that this situation can, but need not, be an equilibrium in the present model. It could be the case, even assuming the exchange pattern of figure 3.3 at the outset, that volumes and volatilities are such that the transaction costs of directly exchanging 5 and 2 are higher than the transaction costs of going through vehicle 3. An example of such a situation could be, for example, that the 3,5 market was (*a priori*) much more active than the 2,5 market, and that 5 showed no great difference in terms of volatility with respect to 2 and 3. Then, if the differences in volumes were big enough, customers would desert the 2,5 market and we would be back in the situation represented by figure 3.2, which *is* an equilibrium (under the assumptions in proposition 5).

We have seen in the proof of proposition 5 that in the model a *strictly* bipolar system (as illustrated in figure 3.4) is always a forex market equilibrium, if inertia is strong enough. Then, the question suggests itself: is there the possibility of a tripolar structure of foreign exchange (i.e. a world with three vehicle currencies) which is sketched in figure 3.5. Concerning the sustainability of such a situation the reasoning used with

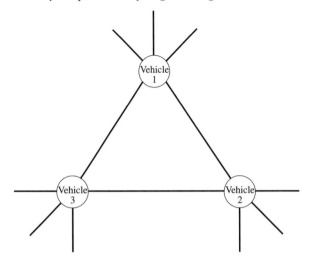

Figure 3.5 Strictly tripolar forex market

respect to currency 5 in figures 3.2 and 3.3 applies. As long as the transaction costs of exchange between the three vehicles are such that the spread of one bilateral market is not greater than the sum of the two spreads on the other two bilateral markets (see proposition 4), the exchange pattern described is viable, if the relations of non-vehicle currencies are, once more, ensured by the inertia in closed interbank markets.

The conclusion is that a tripolar world with three currency areas, each having one dominant currency which serves as the forex vehicle within the area and provides the only connection to the exterior world, is possible, at least in theory. Interestingly enough, the triangular core of the system can be sustainable even if the three currency areas are of rather uneven size. The reason is that low exchange rate volatility of a vehicle can compensate for its lower volume.

There is no point in continuing the exercise with additional vehicles. First of all, even on a global level, there are very few currencies which actually seem to have the potential to play a role as media of exchange in the forex market. Secondly, economic theory identifies more factors which limit the number of vehicle currencies. One is the costliness of the separation of the standard of value function from a medium of exchange. As Suvanto (1993, chapter 5) has shown with a combinatorial exercise, a unique standard of value in the forex market dramatically reduces the costs for detecting arbitrage opportunities. Another factor involves the economies of scale in using media of exchange, which can make many vehicles quite unlikely for a given degree of inertia.

In the past multiple international currencies have often been associated with instability in the international monetary system (Eichengreen, 1987). The inter-war period, during which both the US dollar as well as the pound sterling were very important, for example, is often seen as a period of instability and monetary disorder (Kindleberger, 1973a). Independent of whether this particular period should be characterized as an unstable equilibrium with two dominant currencies or rather a very slow transition from an equilibrium with one dominant international currency to another with another dominant international currency, it is worthwhile analysing what the present theory has to say about the link between structural instabilities and the multiplicity of international currencies.

For this purpose, it is expedient to define 'instability' as a situation in which small changes in the fundamental trade and investment flows or financial market expectations lead to large changes in the exchange structure, and therefore large changes in trading volumes and exchange rate volatilities. In the present theory such a situation can emerge whenever one or several markets are close to a critical mass, as described in earlier subsections.[16] Notice first that this can occur quite independently of the number of exchange media prevailing in the forex market. Moreover, a strictly bipolar equilibrium, such as the one depicted in figure 3.4, can be very stable, if inertia is rather strong. However, weakly bipolar structures, such as the one depicted in figure 3.5, or barter-type situations, may be less stable, since networks of many directly linked currencies exhibit less inertia and critical masses are, therefore, reached more 'easily'.

While strictly bipolar or tripolar systems may be no less stable than exchange structures with many direct currency markets, a situation of full monetization through a single vehicle currency will in many circumstances be very stable, particularly if economies of scale and inertia are strong. This is due to the strong 'ratchet' effect of indirect exchange in that case. It is important, then, to bear in mind that multiple vehicle currencies can (but need not) be associated with instability in the forex market.

---

[16] The extreme case of an unstable exchange structure is a situation where one or several bilateral markets are exchanged partly directly and partly indirectly through a vehicle, i.e. $0 < \delta_{ij} < 1$. This can occur if for those markets $s_{ij} = s_{il} + s_{lj}$ holds. Clearly, this is a 'knife-edge' situation, where the slightest shock would shift the exchange structure. See Hartmann (1994, figure 3) for a graphical illustration of 'knife-edge' and stable equilibria.

As a last remark I should, perhaps, emphasize that the cases sketched in figures 3.4 and 3.5 are rather extreme benchmarks, illustrating most clearly the possible multiplicity of vehicle currencies, but not claiming to be totally realistic. In the forex market of the 1990s one does not find a clear-cut decomposition in currency areas, which are connected only through their vehicle to the exterior world. The main reason is probably that in these cases some originally desired currency exchanges would have to be undertaken in three, instead of one or two, transactions. Rather we observe a complex 'Krugman-type' network of markets with several of the bigger currencies playing a role like that of currency 5 in figure 3.3 above and where exchange chains are never longer than two transactions (see chapter 4, section 4.2). Nevertheless, as we have seen above and as is further discussed in the appendix, this feature need not prevent the system from reaching an equilibrium with more than one vehicle. But this equilibrium may be less stable than the theoretical benchmark equilibria.

3.4   Conclusions

In this chapter I have argued that the use of vehicle currencies, or media of exchange in the forex market, is mainly driven by transaction costs but also by the costs of activating closed interbank markets. As practically the whole turnover of the market goes through the hands of dealers, transaction costs can be measured by the spread between their selling and their buying price for certain currencies. Expanding on a simple dealer model by Black (1991) we see that the most basic factors determining spreads are exchange rate volatility, (expected) market volume and order-processing costs of market-making.

Differences in volumes and volatilities in the numerous bilateral currency markets determine an exchange structure with a complex network of open interbank markets. Very small or very volatile markets will switch to indirect exchange through a vehicle currency and remain closed. A fundamental aspect of these media of exchange in general is a network externality working through the thickness (or thinness) of the market(s). But in spite of possible economies of scale in use, it is not guaranteed that the market mechanism will lead to a single vehicle. In fact, with the help of the theoretical model one can identify forex market equilibria with none ('barter'), one, two, or even three vehicles. Once a vehicle currency is established, very large changes in the fundamentals (or dealer expectations) may be necessary for another currency to take its place, since changes in the exchange structure (dealers re-activating formerly closed markets) can be costly themselves and these set-up costs in conjunction with economies of scale result in inertia. Therefore, the 'dethronement' of a vehicle currency can occur in a slow and step-wise fashion or after a dramatic collapse, depending on the size and nature of shocks hitting the international monetary system. Situations with multiple vehicle currencies need not be characterized by a high degree of instability, however.

The model presented can explain a number of facts observed in the history of international currencies, as outlined in chapter 2. First, it can explain the typically hierarchical structure of the international monetary system, where a single currency usually dominates one or several other key currencies on the global level. Secondly, it underlines the fact that the currency of a country which is very important in international trade and investment will usually emerge as the dominant international currency, provided that its exchange rate is not overly volatile. This important role of volatility (risk) has been much neglected in most of the international currency literature. The model also shows why changes in the importance of international currencies occur so slowly, in particular it can explain why formerly dominant currencies may remain major key currencies long after the fundamental trade and investment flows of the country issuing them have ceased to 'justify' their position.

In addition to the explanation of these historical facts the theory of vehicle currencies advanced here can also make three general contributions to the theory of exchange media. First, it can show in which circumstances general price instability can lead to the disappearance of money, the return to barter. Secondly, it can provide a rationale for multiple media of exchange. And finally, it can underline the fact that network externalities through exchange media can sometimes be negative (exchange cost increasing) instead of positive (exchange cost reducing).

As discussed in more detail in chapter 5, the empirical predictions about the relationships between forex spreads, expected trading volumes and exchange rate volatilities which can be derived from the model turn out to be confirmed by the data. Finally, we can apply the logic of the present model to explain the emergence of the Deutsche mark as a competing vehicle currency to the US dollar for trading among European currencies and also to make predictions about the potential of the euro, the future single European currency, to become a vehicle currency after its introduction (scheduled for 1999) as is done in chapter 4.

By definition, a theoretical model can never cover *all* the details of reality. Hence, the present model also neglects a number of additional factors possibly contributing to a currency's potential to become a vehicle in the spot forex market. One is the availability of a wide range of financial instruments and other services in this currency (Swoboda, 1969). Since my model is limited to the spot currency markets it cannot take this aspect into account. Another factor is forex dealers' and investors' confidence in prospects for a stability oriented monetary policy of the vehicle country (Tavlas, 1991). While the model gives a prominent role to exchange rate stability, it does not provide an explicit link between that and monetary policy issues. Both these issues will be addressed in the wider context of chapter 4.

However, the model *can* explain the effect of time zones and the resulting intra-day seasonality in trading activity and exchange rate volatilities (Dacorogna *et al.*, 1993) on the currency exchange structure. If one were able to consider intra-day patterns of forex turnovers, it might turn out that the exchange structure of the market varied in the course of the day: for example, mark vehicle transactions may only occur during European trading hours when Tokyo is already closed and New York has not yet opened.

Appendix: multiple vehicles with inter-dealer price and entry competition

The purpose of this appendix is to give a more rigorous account of the concept of forex dealer and market competition underlying the discussion in the main body of chapter 3 and to provide some simple examples illustrating the potential existence of multiple media of exchange, in a hierarchical or non-hierarchical relation, in the forex market. More precisely, I assume Bertrand–Nash competition among incumbent dealers and entry competition between incumbents and outside dealers within any bilateral market as well as between different markets.

I proceed again in step 1 by writing the spread model for a single bilateral market, briefly discussing the consequences of different cost functions. Depending on the shape of the cost function there is one dealer per market facing entry competition or several incumbent dealers mainly competing with each other. In step 2 more markets are considered simultaneously such that each dealer takes into account not only the other dealers' reaction functions but also the exchange-cost-minimizing reaction functions of the customers creating inter-market competition between dealers. In step 3, I shall distinguish 'hierarchical' bipolar exchange structures from 'non-hierarchical', strictly bipolar, systems. As discussed in chapter 2, section 2.3, hierarchical relationships between the international key currencies have thus far been the rule in the history of international money.

A.1 Inter-dealer competition in a single market

Linear order processing cost functions

Consider a market like the one described in section 3.2. Let me assume that there are two incumbent dealers competing in the market to provide exchange services for customers. The dealers' profit functions can be written as

$$\tilde{\pi}_{ij}^h = \tilde{x}_{ij}^h e_{ji}^{a,h} - \tilde{x}_{ji}^h e_{ji}^{b,h} - (\tilde{x}_{ij}^h - \tilde{x}_{ji}^h)\tilde{e}_{ji} - c_{ij}, \qquad (3A.1)$$

$\tilde{x}_{ij}^h \geq 0$ is dealer h's ($h \in \{1, 2\}$) customer demand for currency i against j and $c_{ij} \geq 0$ the fixed costs of making market ij. Since both dealers' order flows add up to total order flow ($\tilde{x}_{ij}$), the equilibrium condition is analogous to (3.2)

$$\tilde{x}_{ij}^1 + \tilde{x}_{ij}^2 - \tilde{x}_{ji}^1 - \tilde{x}_{ji}^2 = \alpha_{ji}(\tilde{e}_{ji} - \bar{e}_{ji}). \qquad (3A.2)$$

Assumptions A.1:

(i) A currency is a homogeneous 'good'. Hence, each dealer's order flow is

$$\tilde{x}_{ij}^1 = \eta \tilde{x}_{ij}, \ \tilde{x}_{ij}^2 = (1 - \eta)\tilde{x}_{ij},$$
$$\tilde{x}_{ji}^1 = \mu \tilde{x}_{ji}, \ \tilde{x}_{ji}^2 = (1 - \mu(\tilde{x}_{ji})),$$

where

$$\eta \begin{cases} = 1 & \text{if } e_{ji}^{a,1} < e_{ji}^{a,2} \\ \sim U(1/2, 1/12) & \text{if } e_{ji}^{a,1} = e_{ji}^{a,2} \\ = 0 & \text{if } e_{ji}^{a,1} > e_{ji}^{a,2} \end{cases}$$

and

$$\mu \begin{cases} = 1 & \text{if } e_{ji}^{b,1} > e_{ji}^{b,2} \\ \sim U(1/2, 1/12) & \text{if } e_{ji}^{b,1} = e_{ji}^{b,2} \\ = 0 & \text{if } e_{ji}^{b,1} < e_{ji}^{b,2} \end{cases}$$

When dealer prices are equal, then the demand and supply shares η, $1 - \eta$, and μ, $1 - \mu$ are uniformly distributed between 0 and 1 [$\sim U(1/2, 1/12)$] and independent of the original currency exchange desires $\tilde{x}_{ij}$.

(ii) Other potential dealers are waiting outside and may enter market ij, if they can make a (strictly) positive expected profit by doing so. An incumbent dealer with a (strictly) negative expected profit will drop out of the market.

(iii) Dealers are risk-neutral and therefore maximize expected profits with bid and ask prices as their strategic variables.

Definition A.1:

A *Bertrand–Nash equilibrium (BNE I)* in this market is an array of prices $e_{ji}^{a1}, e_{ji}^{b2}, e_{ji}^{a2}) \geq 0$ such that $\bar{\pi}_{ij}^1, \bar{\pi}_{ij}^2 \geq 0$ are maximized, given the prices of the other dealer, and customers' exchange needs fulfilled.

Result A.1:

In a Bertrand–Nash (BNE I) equilibrium

(i) the expected profit(s) of the incumbent dealer(s) is (are) driven to zero,

(ii) bid–ask spreads are strictly positive and symmetric around the 'true' equilibrium price $\bar{e}_{ji}$,

(iii) they are given by

$$e_{ji}^a - e_{ji}^b = \frac{2\alpha_{ji}^{-1} V(\tilde{x}_{ij}) + c_{ij}}{\bar{x}_{ij}} = \frac{\alpha_{ji} V(\tilde{e}_{ij}) + c_{ij}}{\bar{x}_{ij}}. \tag{3A.3}$$

If $c_{ij} > 0$, then only a single dealer can survive. If $c_{ij} = 0$, then both dealers may remain in this market.

Arguments:

(i) Since dealers are identical, if an incumbent dealer makes a positive profit, then the other incumbent dealer or an entering dealer can show a slightly lower ask price or a slightly higher bid price, which will bring him all the order flow and still a positive profit. Therefore potential undercutting will drive profits to zero.

(ii) Since the expected costs of market-making are always positive a dealer who sets ask prices smaller or equal to bid prices will always lose money and drop out of the market. The distribution of sell orders is the same as the distribution of buy orders. Thus a dealer setting an asymmetric spread makes a negative profit or will be undercut by another dealer on the market side with the larger spread.

(iii) Suppose that both dealers are in the market. Then they must have identical bid and ask prices and the order flow is shared according to the realizations of η and μ. Expected profits are then

$$\pi_{ij}^{1,2} = \frac{\bar{x}_{ij}}{2} s_{ij} - \frac{1}{\alpha_{ji}} V(\tilde{x}_{ij}) - c_{ij},$$

for dealer 1 and 2. Zero profits imply the spreads

$$e_{ji}^{a,1} - e_{ji}^{b,1} = \frac{2\alpha_{ij}^{-1} V(\tilde{x}_{ij}) + 2c_{ij}}{\bar{x}_{ij}} = e_{ji}^{a,2} - e_{ji}^{b,2},$$

while for a single incumbent dealer the spread is (3A.3), which is strictly smaller as long as $c_{ij} > 0$. Consequently each dealer has the incentive to undercut such that there cannot be a BNE I with more than one dealer, when there is a dominating fixed-cost effect. (In this case the (hypothetical) spread is monotonously increasing with the number of dealers supposed to be in the market, where the factor in front of c_{ij} is equal to their total number.) If $c_{ij} = 0$, then the last spread equation is exactly identical to (3A.3) and thus independent of the number of dealers in the market. No undercutting is possible and two (or more) dealers are sustainable in a BNE I.∎

From (3A.3) one easily derives (3.4)–(3.7) in section 3.2 of the main text.

Are there more cost structures of market-making so that there can be more than one dealer in a Bertrand equilibrium? Consider the case with positive but constant marginal order processing costs $C_{ij}(\eta\tilde{x}_{ij} + \mu\tilde{x}_{ji})$, $C_{ij}([1 - \eta]\tilde{x}_{ij} + [1 - \mu]\tilde{x}_{ji})$ and no fixed costs. Then expected profits are

$$\tilde{\pi}_{ij}^{1,2} = \frac{\bar{x}_{ij}}{2} s_{ij} \frac{1}{\alpha_{ji}} V(\tilde{x}_{ij}) - C_{ij}\bar{x}_{ij} \tag{3A.4}$$

and – with $\tilde{\pi}_{ij}^{1} = 0 = \tilde{\pi}_{ij}^{2}$ – spreads become

$$e_{ji}^{a,1} - e_{ji}^{b,1} = \frac{2V(\tilde{x}_{ij})}{\alpha_{ji}\bar{x}_{ij}} + 2C_{ij} = e_{ji}^{a,2} - e_{ji}^{b,2}. \tag{3A.5}$$

It can be checked that in this particular case (3A.5) also holds for a single dealer as well as for any higher number of dealers. Hence for any given number of incumbent dealers there is a BNE I with spreads as in (3A.5). The same result holds when $C_{ij} = 0 = c_{ij}$.

Non-linear order-processing-cost functions

With non-linear order-processing-cost functions, say of the quadratic form $c_{ij} + C_{ij}(\tilde{x}_{ij}^{h'} + \tilde{x}_{ji}^{h'})^2$ for some dealer h', the analysis is no longer so easy. Then, for certain parameter combinations, the zero-profit spread function can be lower for some number of dealers $H^* > 1$ than for any other positive integer H.[1] I do not take this case any further, but it is worthwhile noting that changes in exogenous variables (or parameters)

---

[1] However, for other parameter combinations it may happen that $H^* = 1$ or $H^* \to \infty$.

may have more complex effects on prices (or spreads), because they may also affect H^*, the equilibrium number of dealers.

Set-up costs, market entry and profits

Set-up costs, denoted κ_{ij}, are defined to be zero for the incumbent dealer(s) and strictly positive for dealers newly entering a market ij. (Incumbent dealers are 'inherited' from the past such that their set-up costs are sunk, new dealers have to pay them in the current period.) For a single market, if there is only one incumbent dealer (fixed costs dominate), then this dealer's expected profits equal κ_{ij}. If his profits were to exceed κ_{ij}, another dealer could enter, undercut and still make some profit.[2] With several incumbent dealers (constant marginal costs) – with or without set-up costs – profits would be driven to zero.

A.2   Exchange structures with inter-dealer and inter-market competition

I now return to the question of the exchange pattern and the case for multiple vehicle currencies. Now customers again decide on the basis of dealer spreads how they exchange their original demands and supplies of currencies. Direct exchange for a particular pair of currencies ij might – in certain situations – be more costly than (unique or multiple) indirect exchange(s). Bilateral markets without an active dealer cannot be used (or have prohibitive transactions costs). Dealers can make any market ij by presenting spreads which maximize their profits given the spreads of the other dealers and the exchange pattern chosen by the customers.

Assumption A.2:
Each forex dealing company ('bank') can serve more than one market, but its cost function is separable with respect to markets and it cannot cross-subsidize between markets.

This assumption ensures that when one firm makes more than one market, then each market maker is a *profit centre* with independent

---

[2] This notion is akin to the concept of contestable markets (Baumol *et al.*, 1982). Notice that entry strategies *are not Nash* strategies, where every agent takes the strategy of the rival as given and constant. If this were assumed for entry strategies, then single incumbents would always have an incentive to deviate with their price strategies and Bertrand–Nash equilibria non-existent. Entry threat must be 'permanent' – it must be there even if no entry occurs. However, when there are at least two other active bilateral markets (requiring at least three currencies), as discussed further below, then profits in the ij market might be reduced below κ_{ij} when indirect exchange possibilities were sufficiently cheap for customers (inter-market dealer competition).

revenue and cost responsibility (Tygier, 1983). It mainly serves to avoid overloading the following extended definition of a Bertrand–Nash equilibrium. Nevertheless dealers of the same company in different markets could also be allowed to coordinate their price policies in order to 'conquer' bilateral markets from other companies without changing the main arguments below. Under assumption A.2 we can think of a representative dealer *per market ij* and thus suppress additional indices for dealers in the notation.

Definition A.2:
A *foreign exchange market equilibrium (BNE II)* is a collection of spreads $s^* = (s_{12}^*, s_{13}^*, \ldots, s_{ij}^*, \ldots, s_{I-1I}^*)$ and an array of (expected) trades $\bar{z}^* = (\bar{z}_{12}^*, \ldots, \bar{z}_{ij}^*, \ldots, \bar{z}_{I-1I}^*)$ $\forall i \neq j$ such that
(i) $\bar{\pi}_{ij}(\bar{z}_{ij}^*[s^*], s_{ij}^*) \geq \bar{\pi}_{ij}(\bar{z}_{ij}^*[s_{-ij}^*, s_{ij}], s_{ij}), \bar{\pi}_{ij}(\bar{z}_{ij}^*[s^*], s_{ij}^*) \geq 0 \forall i \neq j$ with $\bar{z}_{ij}^* > 0$, $s_{ij}, s_{ij}^* \geq 0$;
(ii) $\bar{z}^*[s^*]$ minimizes customers' transaction costs for given s^* and satisfies their exchange needs $\bar{x} = (\bar{x}_{12}, \ldots, \bar{x}_{ij}, \ldots, \bar{x}_{I-1I})$.

The main purpose of chapter 3 was to show that there can be multiple media of exchange in the forex market. In the model as it stands now – with fierce inter-dealer price and entry competition and set-up costs of market entry – a multitude of different exchange patterns can emerge, depending on the assumptions on the initial market pattern, the dealers' cost structures and the exogenous variables. In this appendix, I content myself with the discussion of some illustrative examples, highlighting cases with two vehicle currencies, as currently observed in the world forex market.

Examples with strong economies of scale in vehicle use

Consider a forex market with $I = 5$ currencies and $\bar{x}_{ij} = 1 \forall i \neq j$. Assume the (expected) profit function $\bar{\pi}_{ij} = s_{ij}\bar{z}_{ij} - 1$. (Under certain assumptions such a case may be constructed from (3A.3). It is not meant to be extremely realistic, but relatively useful for illustration purposes.) Notice first that without set-up costs full monetization with a single vehicle currency is the only BNE II. Strong economies of scale in use lead to a 'monopoly money'.[3] This exchange pattern is illustrated in figure 3A.1 with currency 5 arbitrarily chosen to be the vehicle. (As can be seen from figures 2.2 and 4.1 in chapters 2 and 4 respectively, it is analogous to the situation actually observed from the 1960s until the late 1980s, when the US dollar had the position of currency 5.) The numbers at each arc

[3] See also the corollary to proposition 3 in the main text.

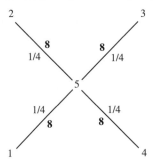

Figure 3A.1 Example 1 – full monetization with a single vehicle currency ('monopoly money')

describe the volume $\bar{z}_{ij} + \bar{z}_{ji}$ (bold type) and the spread in the market. It can be checked that no dealer can attract enough volume to realize a positive profit by making other markets.

Now assume that the set-up costs for a new dealer in a market are $\kappa_{ij} = 1$. These set-up (or switching) costs introduce some *inertia* in the structure of exchange (Krugman, 1984). The exchange pattern in figure 3A.1 still remains a possible equilibrium, although in the case of a single 'inherited' dealer per market facing entry competition spreads would go up by $1/2\bar{z}_{ij}$ and profits become strictly positive due to the 'barrier to entry' provided by set-up costs. Consider now the exchange structure sketched in figure 3A.2 (example 2), which corresponds to the strictly bipolar case in figure 3.4 in the main text. There are two vehicles, currency 5 and currency 4. 1 and 2 go always through 5, and 3 goes always through 4. Exchange of 1 against 3 and 2 against 3 require double vehicle use, three transactions in all. Notice that vehicle 4 and 5 have a similar status, their relationship is 'non-hierarchical'. The complete structure of exchange is summarized in matrix Z_2.

$$Z_2 = \begin{pmatrix} 0 & 0 & 0 & 0 & 4 \\ 0 & 0 & 0 & 0 & 4 \\ 0 & 0 & 0 & 4 & 0 \\ 0 & 0 & 4 & 0 & 6 \\ 4 & 4 & 0 & 6 & 0 \end{pmatrix}$$

The spreads are computed for the case of a single dealer per bilateral market, hence the optimal spreads give positive profits. For the 3,4 and 4,5 markets there is a continuum of spreads compatible with this type of double-vehicle equilibrium. In the figure I have chosen the spreads which

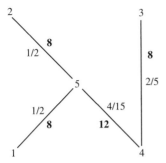

Figure 3A.2 Example 2 – strictly bipolar ('non-hierarchical') exchange structure

give equal profits of 3/5 to both dealers. The obvious possibility of deviation would be that some dealer tries to activate market 3,5. However, as long as $s_{34} + s_{45} \leq 2/3$ the set-up costs prevent this. There are forex market equilibria with two vehicle currencies.

Comparing single- and double-vehicle equilibria in examples 1 and 2 shows that the number of open markets (4) is the same, while (expected) overall volume is higher in the bipolar case (36 units). These two facts remain valid, when the number of currencies is above 5. Interestingly enough, total transaction costs paid by customers are higher in the polar (8 units) than in the bipolar (7.2 units) case.[4]

The next example is constructed in a way to reproduce a structure of exchange which has important aspects in common with the structure currently observed in the forex market (see chapter 4). In order to make the point I have to introduce some asymmetry. I do this by assuming that $\bar{x}_{14} = \bar{x}_{41} = 2 = \bar{x}_{34} = \bar{x}_{43}$. Moreover, to diminish the number of equilibria I assume in this example that there is more than one dealer per bilateral market, resulting in zero profits in general. All the other exogenous variables are the same as in the previous example. Look at figure 3A.3 and matrix Z_3 to see the exchange flows hypothesized.

$$Z_3 = \begin{pmatrix} 0 & 0 & 0 & 3 & 2 \\ 0 & 0 & 0 & 0 & 4 \\ 0 & 0 & 0 & 3 & 2 \\ 3 & 0 & 3 & 0 & 2 \\ 2 & 4 & 2 & 2 & 0 \end{pmatrix}$$

[4] Notice that it would be the same (four units) when dealer profits are eliminated by intra-market price competition.

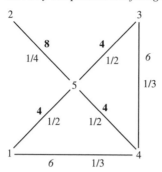

Figure 3A.3 Example 3 – weakly bipolar ('hierarchical')
exchange structure

Again there are two vehicles, 4 and 5. Currency 2 is always exchanged
through 5, but 1 and 3 go through 4 when they are to be exchanged
against each other and through 5 when they are to be exchanged against
2. No currency goes *always* through 4. Although both 4 and 5 are vehicle
currencies, they are of somewhat different quality. In a way the existence
of type-2 currencies makes the position of 5 appear 'stronger' than that
of 4. The exchange structure is 'hierarchical': vehicle currency 5 has
active markets with all the other currencies, while vehicle currency 4 has
no active interbank market with 2. It is somewhat cumbersome but
straightforward to check that the spreads and (expected) trades in figure
3A.3 are, in fact, a forex market equilibrium (BNE II).

  This equilibrium entails more active markets (six) than with a single
(or two) vehicle(s) (four). Therefore total transaction costs borne by
customers are also higher. However (expected) overall transaction
volume is *lower* (28 units) than with a single vehicle (40 units) or a
bipolar system as in figure 3A.2 (42 units).

  At the risk of over-selling the practical relevance of this example one
might give some names to the numbers at the nodes of this network.
Currency 5 plays a role similar to that of the US dollar, while currency 4
resembles the Deutsche mark (see chapter 4). Currency 1 and 3 may be
two other EU currencies – say, the French franc and the Danish kroner.
Currency 2's role is analogous to that of the Canadian dollar, for
example. Clearly, in this example – as in practice today – the dollar is a
global vehicle currency, while the mark is a regional vehicle currency.
One might tend to object first that, in reality, there are many more
currencies, but it is already intuitively clear that one can add more
currencies of the 1–3 type or the 2 type without putting the sustainability
of the roles of 4 and 5 in a BNE II in question. Second, it may be pointed

out that the assumptions on the structure of payments does not correspond to those in reality. However, what really matters is the ratio of volatility to volume. In this sense assuming higher volume for EMS markets in this example ($\bar{x}_{34} > \bar{x}_{35}$) could also be interpreted as a way of saying that EMS markets have a more advantageous volume–volatility relation compared to dollar markets.

4   Currency competition between the euro, the dollar and the yen

> When it comes to a new international money to replace the dollar, if it be replaced within the near-term future, I find it impossible to fasten on a firm prediction ... The safest prediction is that there will be another transitional period, like that between the world wars, after which a new continental or national leadership will emerge.
>
> *(Charles Kindleberger, 1993)*

4.1   Introduction[1]

European Economic and Monetary Union (EMU) will be the most important event in the international monetary and financial system since the unravelling of the post-war international monetary order in 1973 (Bergsten, 1997). No later than July 2002 all currencies of countries participating in full monetary union will have to be completely replaced by the single European currency, the euro. This is the bottom line of the changeover scenario, as adopted by the 1997 Madrid Summit (European Council, 1995). The currency unification, which is planned to start on 1 January 1999 with the irrevocable fixing of exchange rates among the qualifying European Union (EU) members, will cause a shock to the international monetary system. Recent history has seen the breakup of important currencies, such as those related to the disintegration of the Soviet Union and the Austro-Hungarian Empire after the First World War. However, the introduction of a common currency by a number of previously separate important trading and investment nations has not happened at any rate on this scale.[2] The main purpose of chapter 4 is to

---

[1] This chapter draws on some of the material assembled in Hartmann (1996b, 1997a, 1997c). Part of it was presented at the Centre for European Policy Studies (CEPS) working party meeting on 'The Passage to the Euro' (Brussels, May 1997). Examples from 'The Future of the Euro as an International Currency: A Transactions Perspective' are reproduced with the kind permission of CEPS.

[2] There have been important monetary unions between independent states earlier in history – for example, the Latin Monetary Union (1865–1914/27) and the Scandinavian Monetary Union (1873–1914/31). In none of these cases, though, were national monies replaced by a common currency (Cohen, 1993).

evaluate the consequences of EMU for the future international use of the major currencies.

Some numbers – assembled in table 4.1 – help illustrate the importance of the countries involved in EMU for the global economy. All fifteen EU nations together make an economic unit at least as large as the US economy, and in many respects larger than any other country in the world. Current EU GDP exceeds US GDP by 16 per cent (column (2)), the EU population exceeds that of the USA by 40 per cent (column (4)), EU exports (outside the Union) exceed US exports by 22 per cent (column (5)), EU aggregate money supply exceeds US money supply by 11 per cent (when US money market funds are taken into account (column (6)[3]), outstanding claims in total EU capital markets (bank assets, bonds and equities) are about 19 per cent larger than those in the USA (last column). By all these measures Japan is clearly a smaller economy than the other two.

However, this picture requires a number of important qualifications: First, current exchange rate deviations from purchasing power parity (PPP) seem to favour the EU when one currency (here, the dollar) is used as the common denominator. After correction for this fact, EU and US GDP have about the same size (table 4.1, column (3)). While it is not certain at the time of writing that EMU will start with all fifteen EU countries, it is not totally impossible that – at some future date – Canada and Mexico could build a monetary union with the USA. Also, the capital markets figures in column (7) give an imprecise picture, because when securities markets are distinguished from banking markets, the former are larger in the USA while the latter are larger in Europe (Prati and Schinasi, 1997), and because EU markets are not as yet as integrated as most of the domestic US markets. The safest statement to make is, perhaps, that after EMU the domestic 'monetary habitats' of the dollar and the euro will be of comparable size. But how about their international reach?

In chapter 2, section 2.3 we have tracked the international use of currencies until the mid-1990s. In spite of some decline during the 1970s and the 1980s, the US dollar's position had consolidated again by that time and it has remained the most important and clearly dominant international currency in almost all respects on the global level until the

---

[3] It has to be emphasized here that financial innovations in the USA and differences in payment systems have the effect that M1, the measure employed in table 4.1, is biased downwards compared to Germany or Japan. However, I found that the relatively low number for the USA survives for broader money aggregates (e.g. M2). Adding funds invested in money market funds to M1 would increase US money supply by 557 bn USD (or 30.4 per cent of world M1), still lower than aggregate EU M1. Moreover, the ratio of Japanese to US M1 was of the same order at the end of 1990 and 1991 as well, so that the USA credit crunch in 1992 alone cannot be held responsible for the relative low US figure.

Table 4.1 *The EU, the USA and Japan in the world economy, 1991–6*

(1)	Gross domestic product (2) 1995 (at market rates)		Gross domestic product (3) 1996 (at 1991 PPP)		Population[d] (4) 1995		Merchandise exports[e] (5) 1995 (at market rates)		Money stock[f] (6) 1991 (at market rates)		Capital markets[i] (7) 1995 (at market rates)	
	bn USD	%	bn USD[b]	%[c]	m.	%	bn USD	%	bn USD	%	bn USD	%
EU-15 (intra-EU trade)	8,382	30	7,430	20	372	7	2,047 (1336)	40 [19] (26)	1,800[g]	38	27,270	n.a.
United States	6,952	25	7,575	21	263	5	585	12 [16]	1,059[h]	22	22,865	n.a.
Japan	5,109	18	2,571	8	125	3	443	9 [12]	1,091	23	16,375	n.a.
Germany	2,413	9	n.a.	n.a.	82	1	524	10 [–]	398	8	6,509	n.a.
World total	27,846	100	n.a.	100	5,645	100	5,080 [3,744]	100 [100]	4,760	100	n.a.	100

Note:

n.a. not available; bn = billion, m. = million.

Sources:

[a] World Bank (1997, CD ROM) with author's calculations.

[b] Funke and Kennedy (1997, table 1); 1996 OECD projections.

[c] IMF (1997b); very slight inconsistencies with the previous column, due to the difference between GDP projections and GDP realizations.

[d] World Bank (1997, CD ROM) with author's calculations.

[e] IMF (1996b) with author's calculations; post-EMU figures in square brackets.

[f] UN Statistical Yearbook (1995, CD ROM) with author's calculations.

[g] Excludes Sweden, for which no information is available.

[h] Incorporating US money market funds from United States Federal Reserve Board (1996), the figure increases to 1,616 bn USD (30.4 per cent of total world M1).

[i] Prati and Schinasi (1997, table 1); sum of total bank assets, aggregate stock market capitalizations and total bonds outstanding.

present day. The second most important currency is the German mark, which has developed a strong regional role within Europe at the expense of the dollar. The Japanese yen's place is at no. 3, with a weaker regional role in Asia.[4] In the face of the size jump of the European domestic 'monetary habitat' – with the fifteen EU countries together being about four times the size of Germany by different measures in table 4.1 – will the euro be able to become a serious rival to the dollar?

In chapter 3 I developed a theory of vehicle currencies which can help us understand to which type of exchange structures international currency competition can lead. In particular, it was shown that two types of structures may be sustainable in equilibrium. First, the 'hierarchical' structures, which have been observed during most of history, in which among several international media of exchange a single one clearly dominates and, secondly, 'non-hierarchical' structures (strictly bipolar or tripolar) where two or three international media of exchange share the leadership. A related question addressed in the present chapter therefore is which type of structure is likely to emerge in the international monetary system after EMU.

I first take a step back and review the emergence of the Deutsche mark as a foreign exchange (forex) vehicle currency for European monies, illustrate the current structure of currency exchanges and then discuss what is different about a discontinuous change, such as the introduction of a new currency such as the euro. In section 4.3 I focus on the impact of EMU on the currency composition of foreign exchange trading volumes. Distinguishing immediate ('arithmetic') effects from dynamic follow-up ('economic') effects an attempt is made to evaluate whether the dollar can maintain its vehicle role, whether the euro is likely to overtake the mark and expand its vehicle role and whether the yen might emerge as a third vehicle currency. The remainder of the chapter then looks – via an analogous two-step approach – at the international money functions beyond the forex market. An extensive section 4.4 addresses the issue of the currency denomination of world trade after EMU and studies in which direction the evolution of intra- and inter-regional trade flows will drive global trade invoicing shares. Section 4.5 discusses central banks' reserve holdings. The important role of national and international securities markets for the competition between international currencies is scrutinized in section 4.6 and some overall conclusions about international currency competition after EMU are drawn in section 4.7.

---

[4] The yen's position is disputable for foreign trade invoicing (see section 4.4 and table 4.4 on p. 101 or Chapter 2, table 2.2, p. 36) but stronger in international investment (chapter 2, section 2.3).

Before starting the analysis of the future currency competition between the euro, the dollar and the yen, I should perhaps point out that I shall not give much emphasis on scenarios about what could happen during the months immediately before and after 1 January 1999. This is, first, because speculative capital flows in and out of the European currencies/euro can be very sensitive to all types of news about joining countries and the political decisions regarding the composition of the Council of the European Central Bank (ECB). Secondly, during the transitional period until 2002 – stage IIIA – national denominations of the euro will still be legal tender in the respective countries. While most wholesale transactions – money markets, large-value payments systems, new issues of government debt, trading on the main stock exchanges, etc. – will be all in euro, right from the start of stage III, many retail transactions are likely to still be executed in national denominations (Schlesinger *et al.*, 1996). Before 2002 the 'domestic monetary habitat' of the euro will not be well established. For both these reasons I consider it virtually impossible to make any reasonable predictions about the *external* role of the euro during these transitional phases. Most of the predictions undertaken further below can apply safely only to stage IIIB, June 2002 and beyond.[5]

4.2   The emergence of the Deutsche mark as a forex vehicle currency and the 'simple arithmetics' of EMU

Let us start with the forex market again. As has been pointed out already in chapters 2 and 3, the exchange structure of the forex market can be understood as a network between currencies. One representation is in terms of graphs, as in figure 4.1 (reproduced from chapter 2, figure 2.2). The currencies are the nodes (*USD*, *DEM*, etc.), *liquid* (or active) bilateral markets are the arcs connecting the nodes with each other. Some bilateral markets may be illiquid (no arc), such as that for Japanese yen (JPY) against Canadian dollar (CAD) in figure 4.1.[6] Exchanging these two currencies implies two transactions through two liquid markets, *JPY/USD* and *USD/CAD*. The theory of vehicle currencies developed in chapter 3 explained such exchange patterns, considering the transaction costs of going through a direct bilateral market as compared to the sum of the transaction costs of using several bilateral markets (indirect exchange).

---

[5] McCauley (1997, section 1) looks at some issues regarding the transitional period.
[6] The national surveys underlying the BIS reports show some residual turnovers for markets that are considered to be illiquid. However, these turnovers are so small that they can be neglected for our purposes.

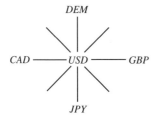

Figure 4.1 Structure of exchange in the interbank forex market from the 1960s to the mid-1980s

The particular exchange pattern depicted in figure 4.1 describes the basic structure of the forex market in the 1960s (Aliber, 1969; Swoboda, 1969), the 1970s (Kenen, 1983) and, at least, the early 1980s (Black, 1991). The dollar is the single vehicle currency. Most other 'cross-currency' transactions are exercised indirectly involving two USD transactions. Non-USD transactions are a small residual. As already pointed out in chapter 2, section 2.3, Kenen (1983) reckons that in 1980 between 90 and 99 per cent of all interbank foreign exchange turnover had the dollar on one side of the transaction. However, Black (1991) observed that the USD share was decreasing in the course of the 1980s.

By the early 1990s the general pattern showed a clear change, since the Deutsche mark (DEM) had emerged as a second vehicle currency. This change has been documented by at least two European central banks. The Banque de France (Pineau, 1993) writes in its monthly bulletin:

La progression de la part relative des transactions en DEM/FRF … confirme les progrès réalisés en matière d'intégration économique et financière européenne. Par ailleurs, elle consacre *le rôle du mark comme monnaie véhiculaire pour les opérations faisant jouer les devises du SME*. Le fait que *la devise allemande ait largement supplanté le dollar dans cette fonction* est reflété par la fraction très substantielle des opérations réalisées au comptant (85% du total).[7]

Similarly, one reads in Danmarks Nationalbank's Monetary Review (Andersen, 1992):

_____

[7] The growth in the relative share of DEM/FRF transactions … confirms the progress made towards European economic and financial integration. Moreover, it reflects *the role of the mark as vehicle currency for transactions in EMS currencies*. The fact that the German currency has largely substituted the dollar in this function is reflected in its substantial share in spot transactions (85% of the total); my own emphasis. The number mentioned by the Banque de France applies to the Paris market, but the French central bank did not provide the full currency breakdown of spot transactions on request. Only the currency breakdown of total turnover over all forex instruments is published (Pineau, 1993). SME=Système Monétaire Européen (European Monetary System (EMS), comprising countries participating in the European exchange rate mechanism).

The great significance of the D-mark reflects that *by far the majority of transactions in Danish kroner against other European currencies are made via the D-mark.* DKK/NLG trading is thus most often broken down as DKK/DEM and DEM/NLG.[8]

The Bank for International Settlements (BIS, 1993) reports that the importance of the mark on a world level, as compared to US dollar or global volume growth, has increased disproportionately in the three years between its 1989 and 1992 forex turnover surveys, especially in the spot market. By April 1992, 71 per cent of global *inter-dealer spot* turnover had the dollar on one side of the transaction, while the share of mark inter-dealer spot turnover reached 57 per cent. Deducting 31 per cent of direct USD/DEM transactions, which are counted twice in the sum of the two previous items, it turns out that 97 per cent of global inter-dealer spot forex trading has either the USD or the DEM on at least one side of the transaction. (Virtually the same number can be found with turnovers in April 1995, where the total dollar share was 69 per cent, the total mark share 57 per cent and direct USD/DEM transactions 29 per cent: BIS, 1996.)

In table 4.2 I assembled interbank spot turnovers from the *national* surveys underlying the BIS aggregates.[9] Included in the table are all those countries whose central banks provided deep enough currency breakdowns to distinguish total inter-dealer spot volume in USD, as traded by banks located in the respective country, from total inter-dealer spot volume in DEM and from direct USD/DEM transactions. Comparing columns (2) and (3) for different regions, one sees that in most European countries DEM turnover exceeds USD turnover,[10] whereas in other regions covered, such as South Africa, North America, the Middle East, Asia and Oceania, it is the other way round.

Last but not least, there has been the following change in the set-up of Reuters forex information screens: while the classical Reuters 'FXFX page' showed only USD quotes, there has been a second page which showed 'cross-currency' (basically DEM) quotes. However, these DEM

---

[8] Emphasis my own.

[9] I am indebted to Richard Portes for his tremendous help in convincing the central banks to provide these data and to the central banks themselves for their extraordinary cooperation.

[10] The same seems to be true for some Central European countries (McCauley, 1997, table A4.2, p.60; notice though that the data in McCauley's table do not distinguish between spot and derivatives turnovers which, as will be argued below, is not advisable). The two exceptions in Europe, where dollar turnover is slightly larger than mark turnover, are the UK and Switzerland, which are larger and more international trading centres. However, even in these centres the mark is the vehicle currency for *intra-European trading*, but the share of transactions in *non-European currencies*, which go through the dollar, is larger.

Table 4.2 *Regional roles of dollar and mark in spot forex trading, 1992 (per cent of total interbank spot turnover)*

Region/ Country (1)	Total USD volume[a] (2)	Total DEM volume[a] (3)	Direct USD/ DEM volume (4)	Residual volume[b] (5)	Total in all currencies[c] (6)
Europe					
Belgium	51.4	77.9	35.1	5.8	100
Denmark	35.8	86.6	26.6	4.2	100
Finland[d]	33.2	95.5	30.5	1.8	100
Germany	76.5	96.3	74.1	1.3	100
Italy	>44.7	>45.8	7.4	<16.9	100
Netherlands	44.5	69.8	22.8	8.5	100
Norway	57.5	77.6	38.4	3.3	100
Portugal	37.9	88.5	30.8	4.4	100
Spain	39.6	68.9	16.0	7.5	100
Sweden	46.2	83.3	33.6	4.1	100
Switzerland	59.4	54.6	22.1	8.1	100
UK	67.0	59.1	28.3	2.2	100
Africa					
South Africa	97.9	32.8	31.9	1.2	100
North America					
Canada[e]	89.6	>23.0	22.7	<10.1	100
United States	80.6	56.9	38.7	1.2	100
Middle East					
Bahrain[e]	93.7	>30.1	28.2	<4.4	100
Asia					
Hong Kong[e]	83.0	>43.2	n.a.	n.a.	100
Japan[e]	89.7	>27.5	21.0	<3.8	100
Singapore[e]	80.6	>35.2	35.2	<19.4	100
Oceania					
Australia	87.7	n.a.	n.a.	<12.3	100
New Zealand	94.4	41.0	36.6	1.2	100

Notes: April 1992 national turnover surveys provided by central banks. n.a. not available.

[a] Includes direct USD/DEM turnover. A large part of this turnover has usually the respective local currency on one side. > means that gaps in reporting have been identified for the respective currency, which may result in an overestimation of residual volume in column (4).

[b] Residual calculated as 100−(column (1)/+column (2)/−column (3)). Includes remaining cross-currency turnovers and gaps in reporting – for example, non-European countries often do not report all DEM turnovers.

[c] Normalized to 100 per cent.

[d] April 1995 data.

[e] Includes customer (retail) turnover.

quotes exhibited bid–ask spreads of about double the size of USD spreads, because they were computed 'synthetically' from the corresponding two USD spreads. In the early 1990s Reuters added a new page ('WXWY') where banks could, and actually did, feed in 'real' DEM quotes with other European currencies. The fact that the quotes on this new page had spreads similar to USD spreads on FXFX confirms the fact that by that time there were highly active intra-European DEM markets.[11]

All this evidence strongly indicates that by 1992 the DEM had taken over as a vehicle currency in *intra-European* spot forex trading. The current structure of exchange in world forex markets is illustrated in figure 4.2. There are two vehicle currencies, the dollar (*USD*) and the mark (*DEM*). European currencies are represented by the Danish kroner (*DKK*) and the French franc (*FRF*), Asian currencies by the Hong Kong dollar (*HKD*), currencies from the Western Hemisphere and Oceania by the Canadian dollar (*CAD*) and the Australian dollar (*AUD*), respectively. Asian, Western Hemisphere and Oceania currencies are exchanged through the dollar, both among each other and with European currencies. For example, a *CAD/DKK* transaction goes *CAD/USD* and *USD/DKK*. European currencies among each other are exchanged through *DEM* but for the rest of the world the *USD* is still their vehicle; *DKK/FRF* goes *DKK/DEM* and *DEM/FRF*, whereas *DKK/AUD* goes *DKK/USD* and *USD/AUD*. The *JPY* is special in so far as it has a very liquid direct market with the DEM but – apart from this – it is linked to other European or non-European currencies through the USD (like other Asian currencies).[12]

It is thus important to note that there is (to date) no evidence that the yen has gained any noticeable role as a forex vehicle currency in intra-Asian trading, where the dollar is clearly dominant (and the mark plays virtually no role). This is also visible from the last BIS turnover survey's (1997b, table 1–G) and McCauley's (1997, table A4.2, p. 60) accounts of domestic currency turnovers in Australia, Hong Kong, Japan, New Zealand, Singapore, South Korea, Taiwan and Thailand. For all these countries local currency trading against the US dollar covers an overwhelming part of total turnover (varying between 92 and 99 per cent of all turnover). Local currency against yen and mark transactions are

---

[11] I am grateful to Michel Dacorogna, Rakhal Davé and Ueli Müller from Olsen & Associates for having pointed me to these changes in the Reuters environment.
[12] Notice that trading volumes in South and Middle American, Eastern and Central European as well as African foreign exchange markets (except South Africa) are currently not covered by BIS (1993, 1996) turnover surveys. McCauley (1997) reports some additional forex turnover data for several emerging market countries.

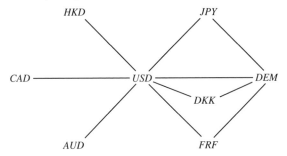

Figure 4.2 Current (weakly bipolar) exchange structure in the spot interbank forex market

negligible fractions of dollar turnovers. Moreover, from the data communicated to me by the Bank of Japan, one can see that in Japan only 1.6 per cent of total spot turnover has yen on one side of the transaction and neither dollar nor mark on the other. (This also shows that the residual for Japan reported in table 4.2 (column (5)) is mainly due to gaps in reporting of DEM turnovers.)

The respective positions of the two existing vehicle currencies, the dollar and the mark, are quite different. While the dollar has relatively liquid markets with practically all other currencies – serving as a global vehicle currency – the mark's role as a vehicle is limited to European currencies. This exchange structure is only *'weakly bipolar'* and therefore 'hierarchical', as derived from the theoretical model in chapter 3 and illustrated, in particular, in figure 3A.3 (p. 74). At the current stage there does not seem to be evidence of any of the twenty-six countries' currencies covered by BIS triannual forex turnover surveys being connected to all the other currencies through the mark alone. Thus a 'strictly bipolar' system, as illustrated in figure 3.4 (p. 61), has *not* (yet) emerged.[13] Given the absence of a vehicle role for the yen, a move to a (weakly or strictly) 'tripolar' currency system (Alogoskoufis and Portes, 1992), although possible in theory (section 4.5 below and figure 3.5) is presently not visible in the *forex market* either.

The exact timing of the emergence of the mark is somewhat hard to determine. The April 1989 BIS turnover survey (BIS, 1990) and those of the nineteen national central banks involved do *not* indicate vehicle use of the mark, but it has to be mentioned that the Bundesbank did not participate in this survey, implying some under-estimation of DEM

---

[13] Remember from chapter 3 that in the *'strictly'* bipolar' system some transactions would have to be made in *three* steps: one currency against vehicle 1, vehicle 1 against vehicle 2 and vehicle 2 against another currency.

trading volumes at that time. As has been discussed in great detail in chapter 3 and as will be empirically tested in chapter 5 (quite successfully, as it turns out), the two major determinants of the potential of a currency to become a forex vehicle are high (expected) trading volume and low exchange rate variability. Two other factors, which have not been explicitly integrated in the model of chapter 3, are large and sophisticated domestic financial markets (Swoboda, 1969) and a stability oriented domestic monetary policy (Tavlas, 1991). While the Bundesbank has for a long time benefited from a high degree of anti-inflationary credibility, higher trading volume, lower exchange rate volatility and developing financial markets seem to have played important roles for the timing of the emergence of the mark.

The creation of the EMS in 1978 meant low exchange rate variability of the mark – the currency of the most important trading and investment nation in the European Community – and therefore lower transaction costs in trading with respect to many other European currencies during the 1980s.[14] The liberalization of capital markets in the second half of the 1980s (Tavlas, 1991), which also signalled a more accommodating stance of the Bundesbank *vis-à-vis* potentially exchange rate-increasing capital inflows, meant an evolution to greater depth and width of German financial markets. At the same time, more and more European central banks used the German currency for their interventions in the EMS (chapter 2, section 2.3, pp. 35ff.). These developments may have rendered the mark *eligible* as an intra-European forex vehicle, although inertia in the exchange structure prevented bilateral DEM markets swiftly reaching the critical masses at which they could be activated by dealers.

The important development, which may have lifted the mark to today's status, is related to the phenomenon of *convergence trading* in Europe at the end of the 1980s and beginning of the 1990s (Group of Ten, 1993, pp. 10–12, 46ff.). In this period many international investors took short positions in DEM in order to benefit from interest rate differentials with other European currencies, believing that there was low realignment risk. This increased the trading activity between the mark and other European currencies culminating in the reversal of these positions and several shocks in the form of the EMS crises of the early 1990s.[15] Although hard evidence is not available to test these hypotheses

[14] The positive correlation between exchange rate volatilities and bid–ask spreads, due to inventory cost effects, is a very strong finding in forex micro-structure analysis (see chapters 3 and 5). Consult Giavazzi and Giovannini (1989) for the story of limiting exchange rate volatility within Europe.

[15] See Goldstein *et al.* (1993); Group of Ten (1993); Portes (1993) for the story of these currency crises and for the role of convergence trading.

in a rigorous way, convergence trading and its consequences may have produced the *lock-out*, reflected by forex dealers activating intra-European DEM markets, allowing the exchange structure to shift to an equilibrium with the mark as a second, but regional, vehicle currency.

An interesting feature of this regime shift in the exchange structure in world currency markets is the fact that it has been largely limited to the spot market. In the forex swap market, for example, virtually all inter-dealer turnover (97 per cent of the total) still has the USD on one side of the transaction (BIS, 1996). In the smallest forex market segment, the *outright forward* market, the situation is again different. Here the USD share is also larger than in the spot market (80 per cent) but the DEM share is smaller (36 per cent). Only 89 per cent of inter-dealer turnover involves USD or DEM on one side, the remaining 11 per cent being spread out more evenly over smaller currencies than in the case of spot trading. The less important role of the mark in forex derivatives trading may, in part, be due to late financial liberalization and less developed financial markets in Germany. It also reflects the absence of a second 'vehicle currency' in these markets. The more even currency distribution of non-USD forwards indicates their direct use for hedging purposes. *Forex swaps* mainly serve dealers to shift the *timing* of currency risk exposures from spot or forward transactions by simultaneously buying and selling two forward contracts with different maturities. Since this type of transaction replaces currency risk by credit risk (BIS, 1996, p. 18), the volatility advantages of the Deutsche mark within Europe do *not* lead to lower transaction costs and an exchange structure analogous to the spot market.

The situation of the euro will, of course, be different from that of the mark in the late 1980s. On the one hand, there will be a discontinuous change – a jump in the size of the 'domestic monetary and financial habitat' compared to any previous European currency. As has been shown in the Introduction to this chapter, this initial shock or size jump can increase the domestic economy by a factor of four, compared to Germany, the largest European economy, if all fifteen EU countries do actually qualify and join EMU. On the other hand, in the presence of majority voting in the ECB's policy-making council, it will not automatically inherit the anti-inflationary monetary policy credibility from the Bundesbank, which will rather have to be built up over time. Moreover, EMU-area financial markets will at the start of full monetary union not be as integrated as the domestic markets in the USA or Japan. And finally, because of the 'simple arithmetics' of uniting a number of national currencies into a common one, the *external* shock to the international monetary and financial system may be much smaller than the *internal* shock might suggest (see section 4.6 on both these points).

In order to illustrate this latter point in the context of forex trading, it is useful to decompose global forex turnover into three components, the first one pure intra-EMU trading, the second one turnover between EMU currencies and currencies of the rest of the world (ROW) and the third one intra-ROW trading. Total world forex trade is the sum of intra-EMU, EMU–ROW and intra-ROW turnover. The first component is simply erased by EMU. From day 1 of stage III there will no longer be any forex market for currencies of 'in'-countries, which will have been absorbed by the euro. The second component switches from EMU–ROW currencies to euro–ROW currencies, without any change in aggregate size. However, every bilateral euro–ROW currency market will necessarily be larger than even the largest pre-EMU currency market with the respective ROW currency. The last component, intra-ROW trading, will remain completely unchanged. Hence, EMU implies in the first place a reduction of global forex turnover of the order of intra-EMU trading, and euro turnover is likely to start at a level corresponding to the sum of EMU currency trading with monies not participating in the union. Hence, because of the substantial 'arithmetic' reshuffling of forex turnovers through the currency union, the simple sum of current EU currency trading volumes may be a misleading guide to future euro trading in the forex market.

Notice that this 'simple arithmetics' of EMU applies in various forms to the measurement of international currency use with respect to most of the other functions of international money (table 2.1) as well. The cases of investment currency and reserve currency use are similar, though not analogous, to that described *in extenso* above, because international transactions do not disappear but convert into 'domestic' transactions. For example, a Spanish resident holding a DEM deposit, say, in Germany or the Banco d'España holding German government paper in its reserve portfolio will experience the conversion of their claims in 'domestic' assets, denominated in the euro. So the total amount of 'international' investments and official reserves reduce by the amount of intra-EMU holdings. Similarly, foreign trade-vehicle use reduces by the amounts of EMU-currency invoicing within the EMU area. Notice, that from a political point of view intra-European investment or trade between 'in'-countries is still *foreign* investment or trade. However, from the point of view of international currency competition intra-European holdings or transactions cannot be counted for the euro any more, because as for the case of a New York citizen holding a dollar bond issued by a Californian municipality or trade between Tokyo and Osaka the currency of denomination is the 'domestic' one, which faces virtually no competition *within* the currency area, be it the USA, Japan or the

EMU-'in' countries in Europe. As we shall show now for one international currency function after the other, starting with foreign exchange trading, this initial 'arithmetic' effect is of considerable importance and may well dominate any subsequent adjustments to a new economic equilibrium for some time after the union has started.

4.3   EMU and forex markets

This section evaluates the impact of EMU on turnovers in the forex market. The pivotal role of forex markets for international currency use (see chapter 1 and chapter 3), reflecting the world exchange structure as opposed to the original payments structure in international transactions, should be remembered. I first estimate 'starting levels' of turnovers in euro, dollar and yen on the basis of the 'simple arithmetics' of EMU sketched in the previous section. I then discuss potential dynamic follow-up effects in order to evaluate how the final equilibrium exchange structure (see chapter 3) could look. However, this will also depend on the effects of EMU on the fundamental trade and investment flows. I shall look at those in subsequent sections before a final evaluation is made. The aim is to assess, first, whether the euro may be able to gain a role as a forex vehicle currency and, second, whether it is likely to achieve a larger vehicle role than the Deutsche mark before EMU, potentially even threatening the US dollar's dominant position as the global vehicle currency. I shall also look at the role of the yen in post-EMU forex markets and under what circumstances it might achieve some vehicle role in the future.

The direct impact of EMU

Scenarios on volumes after full EMU can be derived from the three-yearly BIS (1993, 1996) turnover surveys plus additional information provided by central banks in the underlying local surveys, which measure the trading activity in and between the twenty-six most important forex centres in the world. In what follows I shall focus on spot trading, both inter-dealer and dealer–customer.[16] I assume that the switch to the euro is made at current exchange rates with the euro at par with its predecessor, the ecu (European Council, 1992, 1995). As explained earlier the main procedure is to eliminate within-EMU-area turnover and add up EMU currency and ROW currency turnovers for the euro.

I shall compute post-EMU forex turnovers for four different scenarios

---

[16] Since these estimates have been made the BIS has calculated similar figures for *total* volumes, aggregating spot and derivatives turnovers (BIS, 1997a; McCauley, 1997).

about the 'ins' and the 'outs', which are listed in column (1) of table 4.3. 'No EMU' stands for the status quo in April 1995 (no 'ins'). 'Core EMU' assumes that only Austria, Belgium, France, Germany, Luxembourg and the Netherlands join the monetary union. The remaining two scenarios assume that all European Union (EU) countries are 'in', in one case excluding the UK and in the other case including the UK.[17]

Table 4.3 contains levels of daily spot trading volumes in USD, DEM and JPY as well as their shares in total spot volume. In columns (4) and (5) I estimate the level of intra-EMU trading volume eliminated through the currency unification and the hypothetical spot trading volume in euro after the switch. The overall reduction of world spot forex trading is most important (88 bn USD per day or 18 per cent of the total) when the whole EU participates in EMU. It is the lowest (61 bn USD or 12 per cent), when only core countries qualify. Although the *levels* of USD and JPY volumes remain unaffected, the reductions in global volumes imply increases in their share of total spot volume from 71 per cent to 81–87 per cent for the USD and from 22 per cent to 25–27 per cent for the JPY.

Before EMU 54 per cent of overall spot trading had the DEM on one side of the transaction and the ecu accounted for only 2 per cent of trading. After EMU euro trading covers a larger *percentage share* of the whole market than DEM trading before. With all EU countries in EMU euro trading would be highest with 61 per cent, while with a core EMU euro trading (55 per cent) would have only a slightly larger share than the DEM before EMU. Based on these estimations, the *absolute levels* of euro trading would not be very different from those of the DEM before EMU. Under full EMU it would be slightly higher, in the other cases it would be lower. In other words, the elimination of intra-EMU trading offsets most of the EMU-external volume 'gained' for the euro through the currency unification.

The fact that intra-EMU trading lost largely offsets the increase in EMU-external trading switching to the euro has to do with the importance of the DEM as the forex vehicle for European currencies. For example, a bank having French francs (FRF) and needing Belgian francs (BEF) usually exchanges its FRF against DEM and the DEM against BEF. Therefore, joining BEF, DEM, and FRF into one currency implies

---

[17] At the time of writing, the decision on which countries would join EMU was still several months ahead. However, as it turns out at several points in the analysis below, the fact whether single countries will join or not has – with the exception of the UK – only a minor impact on the scenarios calculated. For example, adding Finland as a new 'core' country, would not have any noticable impact on forex results, because the Finnish forex market is small (about the size of South Africa's market). More scenarios for different groups of EMU-'in' countries are discussed in Hartmann (1997a). None of the main conclusions reached below is affected by limiting the attention to four scenarios.

Table 4.3 *Level and currency composition of spot forex trading volume before and after EMU, 1995 data*

EMU scenarios ('ins'/'outs') (1)	USD volume (2) bn USD	%	DEM volume (3) bn USD	%	Eliminating EU volume (4) bn USD	%	Euro volume (5) bn USD	%	JPY volume (6) bn USD	%	Global volume (7) bn USD	%
No EMU (4/95)	351.4	71.1	268.3	54.3	0.0	0.0	(8.2)[a]	(1.7)[a]	109.0	22.1	494.2	100.0
Core EMU[b]	351.4	81.0	0.0	0.0	60.6	12.3	236.9	54.6	109.0	25.1	433.6	100.0
Full EU (not UK)	351.4	82.8	0.0	0.0	69.8	14.1	241.4	56.9	109.0	25.7	424.4	100.0
Full EU (with UK)	351.4	86.6	0.0	0.0	88.4	17.9	249.9	61.1	109.0	26.9	405.7	100.0

Notes:
[a] Ecu volumes.
[b] Austria, Belgium, France, Germany, Luxemburg, the Netherlands.
Author's calculations from BIS (1996) and national surveys provided by central banks. Numbers based on daily averages over April 1995. The horizontal sum of currency volumes is larger than 100 per cent of global turnover, because for example direct USD/euro volume is counted twice, once in USD volume and once in euro volume. If all other currencies were included, then the total would amount to 200 per cent of global turnover. Global volume, in column (7), has been normalized to 100 per cent.
Source: Hartmann (1996b).

a double reduction in intra-European trading. In contrast, practically all USD vehicle transactions remain since they happen in the trading of non-EU currencies. USD turnovers in table 4.3 contain much vehicle volume, while euro turnovers contain very little vehicle volume as 'inherited' from the DEM. Altogether, it appears that the position of the euro in absolute terms compared to the mark will be weaker in spot foreign exchange trading than in international goods trade. (This comes from the limited role of the mark as a trade vehicle currency in the narrow sense, even within Europe, see section 4.4). However, in relative terms the euro would be clearly more important than the mark right from the start, if the UK joined the common currency.

The fact that a particular non-core country is 'in' or 'out' has only a minor impact on the starting level of the euro in spot forex trading (rows (3) and (4) in table 4.3). This result is similar to the case of international trade (see below), but more pronounced. Again the only exception to this rule is the participation, or not, of the UK which changes the euro starting level by four percentage points. I have done exactly the same simulations with data from the April 1992 BIS survey. As reported in Hartmann (1996b), there do not appear any important differences between the results for the 1992 data and those for the 1995 data reported here, because the shares of the main currencies in global forex trading have hardly changed in the three years between these two surveys.

Follow-up effects of EMU

Of course the scenarios in table 4.2 all make use of the drastic simplification that the international structure of payments remains unchanged through EMU. Moreover, it is assumed that there are no qualitative changes in the structure of exchange outside of the EMU area, except the unification of several bilateral markets. In terms of figure 4.2, DEM would have been replaced by the euro (EUR) and, for a large union where all EU countries participated, DKK and FRF would have been absorbed as well. That is to say that, although the volumes in EMU–ROW currency pairs all switch to the euro, no prediction is made whether this will lead to any secondary switches in the exchange structure, such as the establishment of, say, a liquid CAD/EUR market or the euro replacing the dollar as the vehicle in some bilateral ROW markets. Those numbers have to be interpreted as the 'starting levels' of the dollar, the yen and the euro directly after EMU. However, they might not be forex market equilibrium levels, as defined in chapter 3. For example, since the bilateral euro markets are larger than the former

DEM markets, the figures for the euro will rather represent lower bounds for the more long-term perspectives of the new European currency.

Predictions about these potential secondary switches are extremely difficult to make, because it is not known with precision when a critical mass will be reached, so that the exchange structure changes. Remember from the theory in chapter 3 that critical masses are determined by the fundamental payments levels, the incumbent exchange structure (current forex volumes), exchange rate volatilities (including market expectations about these variables), fixed costs of market-making and, if applicable, the costs of re-activating formerly closed markets (set-up costs), which simultaneously determine the structure of effective or hypothetical transaction costs for all bilateral markets. While there is now some fairly precise information about the current forex volumes, the problem is to link them with less precise information on the underlying payments volumes.[18]

The responsiveness of exchange rate volatilities further complicates matters, because they cannot be assumed to remain constant when market sizes change as a consequence of exchange structure switching. Finally, set-up costs of formerly closed or non-existent markets can be particularly important for a new currency, such as the euro; however, one has very little idea what size they may have. (In contrast, fixed costs of market-making may be considered as small compared to, say, inventory costs of market-making such as those introduced by exchange rate volatility and may, thus, be neglected.) Accepting, then, that it is virtually impossible to derive actual equilibria analytically with any reasonable degree of precision, one should try and make some more qualitative scenarios.

One potential scenario is illustrated in figure 4.3. In this case it is assumed that secondary switches lead to liquid markets between the euro (*EUR*) and the main currencies in Asia and Oceania, such as the Australian dollar (*AUD*) and the Singapore dollar (*SGD*). Notice, however, that for the currencies in the upper half of the figure the USD still performs all vehicle transactions, while the EUR would do this only for the currencies in the bottom half, where I put for illustration purposes the Swiss franc (*CHF*) and the Norwegian kroner (*NOK*). One should also add Central and Eastern European as well as Mediterranean or former CFA-zone countries to this latter group. Although for reasons of

---

[18] An attempt to make this link with the help of new data on gross international investment flows and the notion of inter-dealer 'hot potato' trading (Lyons, 1996) has been undertaken by Portes *et al.* (1997). Since the main point of this paper is to highlight the role of investment decisions for currency internationalization in general, I shall deal with it in greater detail in section 4.6 below.

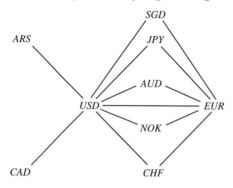

Figure 4.3 Hypothetical new (bipolar) equilibrium exchange structure in the spot interbank forex market after EMU

space and clarity not explicitly indicated in figure 4.2, the DEM (or for the African currencies the French franc) performs the vehicle function for this latter group of currencies already, and the EUR would just take it over. In this scenario, though, the EUR would not develop any direct markets with all the Western Hemisphere currencies, issued by countries geographically close to the USA (*CAD, ARS* (Argentine peso)).

Another scenario, with a further extended role of the euro, would be represented by a system where the common European currency had liquid markets with *all* other currencies in the world (i.e. in terms of figure 4.3, *CAD* and *ARS* would join *JPY*, *SGD* and *AUD* in the upper half of the figure. Furthermore, in an even further extended euro scenario, the new European currency would take over some vehicle role for the currencies in the top of figure 4.3, say, for the exchange of *JPY* or *SGD* against *NOK* or *CHF*). However, this may be as far as the euro can get in the most optimistic scenario from a European perspective and after a considerable period of time following the completion of stage IIIA in June 2002.

The two major factors influencing the relative likelihood of all these scenarios (apart from virtually unmeasurable set-up costs) will be bilateral trading volumes and exchange rate volatilities. For example, in cases of non-EMU currencies which are covered by the BIS surveys and where currently a liquid DEM market exists, the higher bilateral turnover through the changeover to the euro is apparent. For example, total Swiss franc (CHF)/DEM spot trading was 11.5 bn USD per day in 1992, total CHF/euro trading would have been 13.8 bn USD with full EMU, a jump of 20 per cent. Norwegian kroner (NOK)/DEM trading was 0.3 bn USD and NOK/euro would have been 0.4 bn USD, an increase of the order of one-third. Similar orders of magnitude will apply to the hypothetical volumes in markets which are currently exchanged through the dollar, reducing 'hypothetical' transaction costs and, hence, enhancing the scope for the opening of more direct euro markets than existed for the mark.

The other important factor is the attractiveness of the euro in terms of exchange rate volatility. As shown in the theoretical chapter 3 and strongly underpinned empirically in chapter 5, high volatility is an obstacle for a currency to become a forex vehicle, because it increases transaction costs. Normally, short-term euro volatility will increase compared to the DEM through the volume–volatility correlation caused by financial market micro-structure effects (Tauchen and Pitts, 1983; Karpoff, 1987; Jorion, 1996). For example, for the short panel and for the time series of volumes and volatilities in chapter 5 the correlation coefficients are 0.03 and 0.5, respectively. However, in the light of the spread estimations in these chapters it is unlikely that the indirect effect from volumes through volatilities on spreads can offset the direct volume-effect reducing spreads (see also chapter 3, section 3.2).

However, euro volatility will depend on more than simply turnover – for example, it will depend on the exchange rate regime with respect to other currencies. Hence, the more countries explicitly peg their currencies against the euro or implicitly target their home currency's exchange rate against the euro the more likely, *ceteris paribus*, that it will perform vehicle functions for those currencies. (Remember the EMS effect described in section 4.2.) Optimal pegs depend on geographical trade links and foreign-currency denominations of (public or private) debts. Bénassy-Quéré (1997) traces the explicit and implicit exchange rate-targeting strategies of thirty-five countries (sixteen Western European, four Central and Eastern European countries (CEEC) as well as fifteen Asian) over the period 1989–95 with a measure of monthly relative exchange rate volatilities of those currencies with respect to the dollar, the mark and the yen. The data shows, for example, the dollar's volatility advantages over the yen in Asia over the sample period, which did not deteriorate until 1995. It also shows that although CEECs gave some weight to the mark as an anchor, the German currency did not as yet have clear volatility advantages over the dollar in this region.

This picture is confirmed and extended by McCauley's moving-regression analysis of different countries' *daily* exchange rates with the dollar and the mark (or yen) between 1994 and 1997 (1997, graphs 2 and 7). While the Polish *zloty*, the Czech *koruna* and the Hungarian *forint* share about half of the mark's movements, the Russian rouble as well as eight different Asian currencies closely aligned themselves with the dollar at this time. The same applies to the Canadian and the Australian dollar.

Furthermore, from McCauley's evidence the Moroccan *dirham* shares about three-quarters of mark movements, while the South African rand lost links to the mark and moved closely with the US dollar. Comovements between the Turkish lira as well as the New Israeli shekel and the mark are also relatively small. Saudi riyal fluctuations are virtually identical to dollar fluctuations (see Hartmann, 1997b, table 1). However, the arrival of EMU may well bring exchange rate targeting in the regions around the EU closer to the euro, not only in the CEECs but also in the Southern Mediterranean countries.

Similarly, the more stability oriented the monetary policy of the ECB, and the more this translates into less volatile euro exchange rates, the larger the scope for the euro as a vehicle currency. A number of studies, notably Cohen (1997) and Benassy-Quéré *et al.* (1997), have argued that a floating euro exchange rate is likely to be more volatile than, say, the Deutsche mark rate or some weighted European average with respect to non-European currencies. However, others have objected that this need not be so, neither in theory (Martin, 1997) nor in practice (Masson and Turtelboom, 1997). In any case, these studies mainly refer to macroeconomic volatility (i.e. the adjustment path of the exchange rate in response to macroeconomic shocks at a monthly or even longer frequency), which may, but need not, coincide with short-term (daily or intra-day) volatility as most relevant for forex transaction costs. Although the volume–volatility correlation in forex and other financial markets suggests that euro short-term volatilities could be higher than, say, DEM short-term volatilities (because bilateral euro markets will be larger than former bilateral DEM markets), it is difficult to predict in advance whether certain euro volatilities (with respect to non-USD currencies) will be 'worse' than those of the dollar (with respect to the same currencies) in a floating rates environment. It goes without saying that the introduction of capital controls, impairing the convertibility of the euro, would reduce its prospects of becoming a forex vehicle currency close to zero.

A question not directly related to EMU, but also important, deals with changes in the role of the yen in the forex markets. In particular, will the Japanese currency emerge as a vehicle for the other Asian currencies? This will depend in part on continuing regional economic integration increasing fundamental intra-Asian payments flows and, thus, ('hypothetical') intra-Asian currency turnovers. The yen might also get a boost from reduced volatility, if in the aftermath of the 1997 Asian currency crises many countries of that region abandon dollar pegging and targeting and switch to a strong role for the yen in their exchange rate stabilization policies. However, first, basket pegging (to a weighted average of the dollar, the yen and the euro) with less volatility advantages for the Japanese currency might be considered more likely than pure yen pegging (Williamson, 1996) and, second, the competitive edge to open direct yen markets in Asia will probably need to come from Japanese banks in the first place. Independent of how long after the current Asian crises new, more yen oriented, exchange rate arrangements can be found, as long as the Japanese banking system has not overcome its formidable domestic problems, a major obstacle for the emergence of the yen as a forex vehicle currency will remain. This may even be reinforced if the liberalization of financial-services trade and the opening of domestic Asian financial markets, as agreed in the 1997 World Trade Organization (WTO) deal on GATS (General Agreement on Trade in Services), is fully implemented, giving US and European banks better access to the Asian markets.[19] Evaluating these four arguments, one might conclude that for the years after EMU, the currency exchange structure *within* Asia is more likely to remain as it currently is (dollar-dominated) than to experience a dramatic shift.

It turns out that the euro will start at a relatively low level of spot forex trading volume since much of the DEM's vehicle transactions will be eliminated through EMU and, therefore, the new single European currency will 'inherit' only a very small vehicle role. Nevertheless, it is likely to develop some more direct markets with non-European currencies, increasing its turnover in the years after the changeover. The potential of the euro to become a forex vehicle for other ROW currencies, and therefore to some extent challenge the USD's global role, appears to be limited, however. This potential is of course highest for trading between Western European non-EMU currencies. Central and Eastern European as well as some African currencies may also be exchanged through the euro, given that they develop free private markets for foreign exchange. Knowing the current strength of the dollar in the Americas and Asia the chances of the euro as a forex vehicle in these two regions are extremely low; at best, it may develop some more direct markets with currencies in these regions. From the persective of forex markets alone the euro's role as a vehicle, as defined in chapters 2 and 3, is likely to start on a relatively low level and to remain regional for the foreseeable future.

4.4   EMU and foreign trade invoicing

In this section I want to review briefly the current knowledge about the choice of foreign trade vehicle currencies (see chapter 2, table 2.1, p. 14)

---

[19] A discussion of the issues revolving around financial services trade liberalization is contained in Kono *et al.* (1997).

in order to draw some inferences about the use of the euro, the dollar and the yen in international trade invoicing after the introduction of the single European currency.

Stylized facts of trade invoicing behaviour

A number of regularities have been observed in the choice of currencies for the invoicing of international trade (Grassman, 1973; Page, 1977, 1981; Scharrer, 1981; Black, 1990; Tavlas, 1991; van de Koolwijk, 1994):

1. For trade in manufactured goods between industrial countries the major part of contracts are denominated in the exporter's currency and most of the remaining contracts are denominated in the importer's currency, while third-currency invoicing is relatively rare ('Grassman's Law').[20]
2. For trade between industrial and developing countries the industrial country's currency or a third currency (usually the US dollar) is used in most cases.
3. Inflationary currencies are used less in their country's foreign trade than less inflationary currencies.
4. Trade in primary products is usually invoiced in dollars (and hardly at all in sterling).
5. The US dollar is the only currency for which the share of foreign trade invoiced in that currency *substantially* exceeds the share of the respective country in world trade. German mark invoicing is important within Europe, but invoicing in mark only slightly exceeds Germany's trade share.

This list suggests that the invoice currency decision is mainly related to the type of good and country considered, perhaps also to the counterparties' sizes (bargaining power) and sophistication, to monetary stability and incumbency. In chapter 2, section 2.2, we surveyed theoretical models by Bilson (1983); Viaene and de Vries (1992); and Matsuyama *et al.* (1993), as well as other explanations by McKinnon (1979) for these stylized facts.

One factor influencing foreign traders' invoicing decisions is monetary network externalities (or 'thick-market' externalities). The basic idea is to some extent analogous to the mechanism already described extensively in chapter 2 and in chapter 3 for forex vehicle currencies. Additional users of a medium of exchange increase the utility of its incumbent users,

---

[20] Grassman's Law highlights the home-currency preference in international trade. However, there are some important exceptions to it (for example, Finland, Italy or Japan).

because the latters' transaction costs diminish. Again, these network externalities imply some circularity in the use of exchange media and, *ceteris paribus*, a certain tendency towards concentration. They can also be responsible for an important degree of inertia in the use of exchange media: once a medium is established and expectations have become consistent with equilibrium, it becomes all the more difficult for another medium to take its place.

In the case of international trade denomination exporters and importers will agree on a currency for invoicing and settlement, which can be bought, sold or hedged at low transaction costs in the forex market or which has a relatively high degree of acceptability for other transactions. Forex transaction costs (including potential hedging costs) and acceptability for other transactions explain the widespread home-currency preference in international trade ('Grassman's Law').[21] If there is *no* home-currency preference – because, for example, the local currency is very small or unstable – an already important international currency with a deep and broad foreign exchange market and a high degree of international acceptability will be preferred to other 'third' currencies.

Further factors in invoicing decisions in international trade, which have not been considered in the analytical literature, suggest that potential international currencies should not be affected by capital controls and have deep and broad financial markets (beyond that for foreign exchange). Capital controls obviously increase transaction costs for international traders and financial markets are important for the efficient management of foreign exchange exposures acquired through international trade activity. Finally, tax rates and ownership structures may sometimes play a role (Goeltz, 1980), in particular for the trade activities of multinationals (including their internal transfer pricing practices).

The direct impact of EMU

In a first step to determine the future role of the single European currency in trade invoicing one can compute potential euro use on the basis of historical data on invoicing practices and international trade flows. A useful data set of invoicing practices in seven industrial countries and OPEC has been collected by the European Commission and published by a study group of the ECU Institute (1995). Although estimations of

---

[21] The latter aspect is also emphasized in the monetary random-matching model of Matsuyama *et al.* (1993), in which a domestic and a foreign agent are assumed to meet with lower likelihood than two domestic agents (see also chapter 2, section 2.2).

invoicing practices outside these seven countries rely on some drastic simplifications, this source together with statistics specifying regional breakdowns of international trade flows (UN, 1995) can be used to make some predictions about approximate invoicing currency use after EMU.[22] The results and how they were reached are summarized in table 4.4.[23]

The left-hand side of table 4.4 (column (1)) shows the importance of the major currencies in export invoicing in 1992, as reported by the ECU Institute (1995).[24] The dollar (USD) remains the clearly dominant currency in international trade, whose share in global invoicing in 1992 still exceeded the US' share in international trade (12.3 per cent) by a factor of almost four. The second most important currency in international trade is the Deutsche mark (DEM). Although slightly up compared to 1980 (see chapter 2, table 2.2, p. 136), its share in trade denomination in 1992 was only four percentage points higher than Germany's share in world exports in the same year (11.8 per cent). This reflects the fact that, in contrast to the US dollar the German mark plays hardly any role as a trade vehicle currency in the *narrow* sense (i.e. for countries other than Germany), not even within Europe (see van de Koolwijk, 1994). Finally, the Japanese yen (JPY) is surprisingly weak in international trade invoicing (4.8 per cent in 1992), which is only about half of Japanese exports (9.3 per cent) and even less than the roles of the French franc (6.3 per cent) or the British pound (5.7 per cent).

On the right-hand side of table 4.4 (columns (2) and (3)) I present estimates of the part of 'international' currency uses which would have been erased if EMU had happened in 1992 and those which would have remained. Intra-EMU trade 'disappears' as *international* trade and becomes *regional* trade denominated in the 'domestic' currency, the euro. This implies a 'reduction' of total world trade by 26 per cent (if all EU countries were 'in', last row). EMU-to-rest-of-the-world (ROW) trade remains unchanged, except that all trade that was denominated in an EMU currency before now switches to the euro. Rows EU-4 and EU-5 report the trade vehicle currency uses (erased or remaining) for all EMU currencies together for which invoicing data are available; in the first case

[22] The details about how invoicing practices in regions for which explicit information was unavailable were estimated are given in the background paper by van de Koolwijk (1994).

[23] The trade figures reported in this chapter relate to total merchandise trade, because, first, figures on services trade are relatively unreliable and very incomplete and, second, the available information on currency invoicing in international trade relates to merchandise trade alone.

[24] I am not aware of any more recent and similarly comprehensive source of world trade invoicing practices.

Table 4.4   *Estimated trade invoicing in major currencies before and after EMU, 1992 data*

	World (1)		Intra-EMU[a] (2)		Extra-EMU[a] (3)		
	bn USD	%	bn USD	%	bn USD	%[b]	%[c]
USD	1,740.5	47.6	141.1	3.9	1,599.4	43.7	59.4
JPY	175.5	4.8	4.3	0.1	171.2	4.7	6.3
DEM	559.4	15.3	296.6	8.1	262.8	7.2	9.8
FRF	230.4	6.3	116.8	3.2	113.6	3.1	4.2
GBP	208.4	5.7	103.0	2.8	105.4	2.9	3.9
ITL	124.3	3.4	61.9	1.7	62.4	1.7	2.4
NLG	102.4	2.8	48.3	1.3	54.1	1.5	2.0
EU-4[d]	1,016.5	27.8	523.6	14.3	492.9	13.5	18.3
EU-5[e]	1,224.9	33.5	626.6	17.1	598.3	16.4	22.2
EU-15[f]	–	–	–	–	679.1	16.6	25.2
Exports	3,656.1	100.0	963.0	100.0	2,693.1	100.0	100.0

Notes:
[a] Estimated from national export figures and invoicing practices.
[b] Percentage of pre-EMU world exports.
[c] Percentage of post-EMU ('extra-EMU') world exports.
[d] France, Germany, Italy, the Netherlands.
[e] As in note *d plus* UK.
[f] Euro invoicing resulting from EU currencies not included in rows above estimated from those countries' exports to non-EU countries assuming 50 per cent home-currency invoicing: 80.8 bn USD (2.2 per cent of pre-EMU exports, 3 per cent of post-EMU exports).
Sources: Hartmann (1996b) and some additional estimates.
1992 invoice data for five EU countries, the USA and Japan from ECU Institute (1995), trade statistics from *United Nations Statistical Yearbook 1993* (UN, 1995). EU-15 pre-EMU invoicing as well as columns (2) and (3) author's own estimates and calculations.

including the UK and in the second case excluding it.[25] Thus, on the right of these rows one finds estimates of the future use of the euro in international trade in absolute terms, in per cent of pre-EMU world trade and in per cent of post-EMU world trade.

It appears that, with UK participation in EMU, a sum amounting to at least 17 per cent of pre-EMU world exports would be 'lost' for euro invoicing, because it is now regional trade. This is about half of the total amount of EU-currency invoicing and more than the total share of Deutsche mark invoicing before EMU. (Without the UK this number

[25] As in the case of foreign exchange, I do not address the problem of which countries will be 'in' EMU and which will be 'out' in greater detail. This is mainly because a greater variety of scenarios would not change anything fundamental for the conclusions drawn below.

reduces to 14 per cent.) Hence, one can infer that total euro invoicing will be 16.4 per cent (13.5 per cent) of pre-EMU world trade or 22.2 per cent (18.3 per cent) of post-EMU world trade.

These estimates may be imprecise for two reasons. On the one hand, they could under-state the likely starting level of the euro in international trade, since the Commission data cover only the five *major* EU currencies. On the other hand, the available data do not contain information on differences between intra-EU trade invoicing and EU-to-ROW trade invoicing. Therefore the assumption has to be made that the currency distribution of trade invoicing is the same in both cases. This assumption may lead to an over-estimation of future euro use, although the Deutsche Bundesbank (1991) found it to be roughly valid for the German case.[26]

Addressing the former problem first, a back-of-the-envelope estimation based on the assumption of 50 per cent home-currency invoicing of exports from the remaining ten EU countries results in an additional 80.8 bn USD of euro invoicing (row EU-15–row EU-5 in table 4.4).[27] The main reasons why the inclusion of these countries has only a minor impact on future euro invoicing (about 2 per cent of world trade) are that, first, their weight in international trade is comparatively small and, second, the larger part of their trade becomes 'domestic' trade after EMU. Including them in the estimations implies that roughly a quarter of world trade would be invoiced in euro, right from the start of EMU. It is also apparent from this result that – apart from the EMU core countries and the UK – the fact that a particular country is 'in' or 'out' does not have an important impact on the potential of the euro to become an important international trade vehicle currency. (Remember the analogous finding for forex trading in section 4.3.)

In order to check against the possible overestimation of euro use in table 4.4 I compare four scenarios of euro invoicing in EU exports (assuming that all countries participate), which are reported in descending order of euro use in table 4.5. The most optimistic scenario (from a European perspective, column (1)) assumes that 92 per cent of EU exports after EMU will be denominated in euro, which is the share of dollar invoicing in US exports (ECU Institute, 1995). The most pessimistic scenario (from a European perspective) hypothesizes a share of 55

---

[26] The difference between mark invoicing of German exports to non-European countries and to European countries is very small (Deutsche Bundesbank, 1991, pp. 41ff.). The reason is that mark invoicing of Germany's trade with the USA is lower than the average, whereas mark invoicing with most other non-EU countries (in particular with developing countries) is much higher than the average. Nevertheless, this home-currency invoicing pattern might still be different for other EU countries.

[27] The average of home-currency invoicing for the five EU currencies explicitly reported in table 4.4 is 49.8 per cent of their exports.

Table 4.5   *Scenarios of euro invoicing after EMU*

Scenarios of invoicing shares	Euro invoicing in EU exports		Euro invoicing in world exports[a]	
	% of EU exports (1)	bn USD (2)	bn USD (3)	% of world exports (4)
Like USA	92	566	741	28
Like EU-15[b]	82	505	679	25
Like Germany	77	474	648	24
Like France	55	339	513	19

Notes:

[a] Euro invoicing in EU exports *plus* euro invoicing in the ROW, the latter estimated to be 174.3 bn USD (not in the tables). Shares in percentage of post-EMU world trade.

[b] Euro invoicing in EU exports for EU-15 (505 bn USD) estimated from world euro invoicing for EU-15 in table 4.4 (679 bn USD) *minus* the estimate of euro invoicing in the rest of the world in note (*a*) above (174 bn USD). The resulting number (505 bn USD) is 82 per cent of total EU exports (616 bn USD; calculated from the difference of total EU-15 exports and intra-EU exports in table 4.1).

Source: Hartmann (1996b).

per cent euro invoicing, corresponding to the current fraction of franc invoicing in French trade. The other two cases correspond to the export-invoicing shares as implied in table 4.4 (82 per cent) and to the current mark-invoicing share in German exports (77 per cent). *Grosso modo*, the results from table 4.4 can be confirmed. Under the new scenarios total euro invoicing will be between 19 and 28 per cent of (post-EMU) world trade. The most likely *starting* scenario, that the invoicing of EU foreign trade will roughly resemble current invoicing of German trade, results in a share of 24 per cent of world trade denominated in euro.

Concerning the impact of EMU on non-European currencies, *absolute* dollar invoicing will diminish, while the change for the Japanese yen is negligible (table 4.4). This is due to the fact that the dollar still plays some role as a trade vehicle currency (in the narrow sense) within Europe (for example, for some oil trade; see McCauley, 1997) and the yen does not play any such role at all.[28] Nonetheless, the dollar will be able to maintain its dominant role in international trade directly after completion of EMU, with a fraction of 44 per cent of pre-EMU trade and 59 per cent of post-EMU trade being denominated in the US currency

---

[28] However, the reduction of total dollar invoicing by about 4 per cent of world trade reported in table 4.4 might be a little bit too high, due to the assumption that the currency distribution of European trade invoicing is the same for EU-internal and for EU-external trade.

(table 4.4). This is more than twice as much as the likely initial level for the euro.

The reductionary effect of the 'simple arithmetics' of EMU on future euro trade invoicing seems to be less pronounced than the case in forex trading. For example, the estimated euro share for full EMU in section 4.3 would be seven percentage points larger than the mark's pre-EMU share. In foreign trade invoicing, the total advantage of the euro, compared to the mark, would be 9–10 percentage points. The main reason for this phenomenon is the fact that the mark seems to be hardly used as a foreign trade vehicle currency in the *narrow* sense, even not within Europe.[29]

Follow-up effects of EMU

The numbers for euro invoicing found in column (3) of table 4.4 and in rows 3 and 4 of table 4.5 have to be interpreted as estimates of the *starting level* of the new European currency. Two different aspects can indicate more about the evolution of international euro use *after* the original switch. One aspect concerns structural changes in international trade flows, the other relates to future monetary policies and funda-mental changes in invoicing practices due to network effects. Starting with network effects, given the comparable sizes of the US and EU-15 economies and Europe's larger share in international trade than, say Germany's, it is quite likely that invoicing in domestic currency of EU exports will reach the level of the USA and, therefore, euro invoicing will rise to 28 per cent of world trade (table 4.5, row 2).

At the beginning of this section, evidence was cited showing the importance of the type of good traded and the origin of counterparties for the use of invoicing currencies. For example, trade in manufactured goods among industrial countries is mainly denominated in the exporter's currency. Hence by extrapolation of trends in manufactured goods trade among these countries it may be possible to say more about the evolution of the future rivalry between the euro, the dollar and the yen. Table 4.6 summarizes the relevant developments in the 1980s and early 1990s. It shows that manufactured trade among industrial countries (adjusted for intra-EU trade) rose by a cumulative 142 per cent between 1980 and 1993. While Japan's trade grew disproportionately (208 per cent), the US lagged behind, though by less than the EU. Looking at the average annual growth rates, it appears that (lately) the USA has expanded manufactured trade quicker than the EU or Japan. What impact do the

---

[29] Van de Koolwijk (1994, pp. 55–9) shows this for France and Italy, for example.

different regional growth rates have on the respective shares in total intra-industrial-country manufactured goods trade? Since 1980 the EU's share seems to be slightly down, from 32 to 29 per cent, while Japan's share rose from 16 per cent to 21 per cent. No important changes in the regional decomposition of trade among these countries occurred in more recent times (between 1988 and 1993). Taken together these numbers do not indicate important trends favouring any of the three main currencies.[30]

In table 4.7 I use the same measures as in table 4.6 in order to analyse the development of trade flows from industrial countries to developing countries. Based on stylized fact 2, cited at the beginning of this section, an increase in an industrial country's market share of exports to developing countries implies an increase in that country's domestic currency's use in international trade. Table 4.7 shows, again, that Japan's exports expanded most, while the EU's trade growth to developing countries was relatively low, both in the long and in the short run. Concerning market share the EU has lost about eight percentage points since 1980, while Japan has gained more than six percentage points. However, since 1988, again, no important trends can be observed favouring any of the three large currencies over the others. (Notice that table 4.7 did not include CEECs in the 'developing country' category, which will be considered separately in table 4.11, p. 110.)

From the previous tables it has appeared that trade shares usually change very slowly and, thus, so does the currency distribution of world trade invoicing. In particular, there do not seem to be important trends in the recent past on the *global* level. This is not very surprising, given the fact that for some time intra-regional trade in the three large blocs (Western Hemisphere, Europe and Asia) had tended to grow quicker than inter-regional trade. Table 4.8 shows the intra-regional trade developments of the four main regions of developing and transition countries compared to that of total world trade. The largest and fastest-growing trade region of these is Asia, accounting in 1993 for about 12 per cent of world trade. Given the strong position of the US dollar as a trade vehicle currency in the narrow sense in this region, it acts as a strong supporter of the US currency's role in total world trade.

The other three regions are very small and unlikely to cause dramatic changes in global trade invoicing. However, Latin American trade has grown slowly but steadily in the last few years, also providing some support for the dollar. CEE trade has broken down as a consequence of the fall of communism at the turn of the decade. The decline in intra-

---

[30] The share of manufactured goods trade in total merchandise trade was increasing over the period considered in table 4.6.

Table 4.6 *Development of manufactured goods trade among industrial countries (excluding intra-EU trade), 1980–93*

	Export growth rates							Share of total exports						
	1980–93ᵃ	1988–9	1989–90	1990–1	1991–2	1992–3	Averageᵇ	1980	1988	1989	1990	1991	1992	1993
EU(12)ᶜ	112.1	4.0	15.2	−5.9	4.3	−3.4	2.8	32.0	30.3	29.8	30.4	28.9	28.9	28.5
USA	134.5	14.5	18.8	3.9	1.8	0.3	7.9	23.0	19.0	20.5	21.6	22.7	22.1	22.6
Japan	207.8	3.3	1.1	4.2	4.7	1.3	2.9	16.2	22.0	21.4	19.2	20.2	20.3	21.0
All ICᵈ	141.9	6.7	16.7	0.3	5.1	−1.9	5.4	100.0	100.0	100.0	100.0	100.0	100.0	100.0

Notes: ᵃ Cumulative growth rate.
ᵇ Average of yearly rates between 1988 and 1993.
ᶜ Data excluding new EU members (Austria, Finland, Sweden).
ᵈ All industrial countries, excluding intra-EU(12) trade.
Sources: United Nations Statistical Yearbook 1992, 1994 (UN, 1994, 1996; country groupings from UN Annex I), author's calculations.

Table 4.7 *Development of industrial countries' trade with developing countries, 1980–93*

	Export growth rates							Share of total exports						
	1980–93ᵃ	1988–9	1989–90	1990–1	1991–2	1992–3	Averageᵇ	1980	1988	1989	1990	1991	1992	1993
EU(12)ᶜ	62.1	8.0	19.0	3.3	11.1	4.6	9.2	42.0	35.6	35.6	37.5	35.1	34.9	34.1
USA	113.6	13.4	6.3	15.3	13.5	6.1	10.9	26.2	27.0	28.3	26.7	27.9	28.3	28.1
Japan	162.9	5.1	9.7	18.2	13.2	12.0	11.6	20.4	25.2	24.4	23.7	25.5	25.7	27.0
All ICᵈ	100.3	8.2	12.9	10.2	12.0	7.0	10.1	100.0	100.0	100.0	100.0	100.0	100.0	100.0

Notes: See table 4.6.
Sources: See table 4.6.

Table 4.8 *Development of developing and transition countries' intra-regional trade as compared to that of world trade, 1980–93*

	Export growth rates							Share of total exports						
	1980–93[a]	1988–9	1989–90	1990–1	1991–2	1992–3	Average[b]	1980	1988	1989	1990	1991	1992	1993
Asia[c]	322.4	12.3	12.1	18.5	14.1	11.0	13.6	5.3	8.5	8.9	8.9	10.5	11.1	12.3
Latin America[d]	53.6	26.0	9.2	14.6	23.8	17.9	18.3	1.1	0.5	0.6	0.6	0.7	0.8	0.9
Eastern Europe[e]	−71.1	−17.7	−18.1	−62.0	−24.7	1.4	−24.2	3.8	4.1	3.1	2.3	0.9	0.6	0.6
Africa	135.8	15.3	25.1	−1.3	5.7	0.8	9.1	0.1	0.1	0.1	0.2	0.2	0.1	0.2
World	82.0	7.3	12.9	0.5	7.9	−0.4	5.6	100.0	100.0	100.0	100.0	100.0	100.0	100.0

Notes: [a],[b] see table 4.6.
[c] Excludes Japan (industrial country).
[d] South and Central America.
[e] Central and Eastern Europe, including successor countries of former USSR.

Sources: See table 4.6.

regional trade had, however, stopped by the end of the sample period. Notice that this region once accounted for about 4 per cent of world trade. If it recovers this share in the future it may give a boost to the euro, because the EU tends to expand its trade with this region faster than the USA (see table 4.11). Intra-African trade, although growing faster than total world trade, is much too small to make any noticeable impact on the global level.

Depending on how industrial countries' trade links with these regions evolve their respective currencies may through network externality effects gain more influence in the denomination of their intra-regional trade. Therefore, I turn now to inter-regional trade. Of particular importance is of course the 'battle for Asia'. In table 4.9, I show the development of EU, US and Japanese exports with this region (excluding the Middle East and, hence, the major oil-exporting countries). In contrast to what one might have expected from the current discussions about the lack of competitiveness of countries from the 'old continent', EU exports to Asia grew much quicker than those originating in the USA, and the EU's trade share has risen slowly but steadily from about 21 per cent in 1980 to about 25 per cent in 1993 (mainly at the expense of the USA).[31] Given the still continuing weakness of the Japanese yen as a foreign trade vehicle currency, a continuation of these trends would imply a growing role for the euro together with a reduction of the dollar's dominance in Asia. On the other hand, Japan's trade links with its neighbours are rising at a similar – or more recently even quicker – pace, which may well raise the profile of its currency in this region.

In trade with Latin America (table 4.10) the USA is clearly dominant and the dollar is the major vehicle currency. EU shares are not expanding and Japan's share has done so only very slightly. Although the US share has not further increased in the recent past, there is little doubt that the euro or the yen have little scope to gain market share in this region.

However, this is different for the CEECs (table 4.11), where pro-nounced trends are visible. EU exports to this region grew quicker than those of the USA. Japanese exports strongly contracted. Therefore the EU accounts for an ever larger share of industrial-country exports to these countries, implying a growing role for the euro in inter-regional trade and much scope for it to develop a vehicle-currency role in the narrow sense in these countries' intra-regional trade.[32] If this trade

---

[31] However, it is not impossible that this trend in merchandise trade could be partly offset by a reverse trend in services trade.

[32] It is true that trade figures for the ex-communist bloc during the 1980s may suffer from valuation problems. However, it is unlikely that distortions in the price systems explain the pronounced regional divergence of trade flows reported in table 4.11.

Table 4.9 *Development of industrial countries' trade with Asia (excluding Middle East), 1980–93*

	Export growth rates							Share of total exports						
	1980–93[a]	1988–9	1989–90	1990–1	1991–2	1992–3	Average[b]	1980	1988	1989	1990	1991	1992	1993
EU(12)[c]	288.7	12.8	18.7	1.7	9.3	13.3	11.2	20.6	23.6	23.9	25.7	24.2	24.6	25.3
USA	160.0	16.1	6.3	6.2	4.8	7.2	8.1	34.7	30.5	31.9	30.6	30.1	29.3	28.5
Japan	231.0	7.0	8.3	17.9	11.2	15.6	12.0	26.5	27.8	26.8	26.2	28.7	29.6	31.0
All IC[d]	216.9	11.0	10.7	7.9	7.6	10.9	9.6	100.0	100.0	100.0	100.0	100.0	100.0	100.0

Notes: See table 4.6.
Sources: See table 4.6.

Table 4.10 *Development of industrial countries' trade with South and Central American developing countries, 1980–93*

	Export growth rates							Share of total exports						
	1980–93[a]	1988–9	1989–90	1990–1	1991–2	1992–3	Average[b]	1980	1988	1989	1990	1991	1992	1993
EU(12)[c]	58.1	7.3	17.9	10.2	16.1	6.8	11.7	29.1	26.0	25.8	27.0	25.9	25.3	26.0
USA	98.0	12.3	10.1	17.3	19.2	3.0	12.4	49.9	54.1	56.2	54.9	56.0	56.3	55.7
Japan	86.4	2.1	9.7	26.1	23.0	5.7	13.3	11.2	11.1	10.5	10.2	11.2	11.6	11.8
All IC[d]	77.5	8.2	12.7	15.0	18.5	4.2	11.7	100.0	100.0	100.0	100.0	100.0	100.0	100.0

Notes: See table 4.6.
Sources: See table 4.6.

Table 4.11 *Development of industrial countries' trade with Central and Eastern Europe (including countries of the former USSR), 1980–93*

	Export growth rates							Share of total exports						
	1980–93[a]	1988–9	1989–90	1990–1	1991–2	1992–3	Average[b]	1980	1988	1989	1990	1991	1992	1993
EU(12)[c]	98.7	16.4	7.4	29.7	14.7	6.2	14.9	56.6	55.5	57.1	60.2	68.6	71.2	71.5
USA	44.8	45.0	−19.9	10.6	12.4	6.2	10.9	9.1	8.4	10.8	8.5	8.2	8.4	8.4
Japan	−38.5	−3.9	−11.9	−13.5	−35.6	19.5	−9.1	8.5	9.0	7.7	6.6	5.0	2.9	3.3
All IC[d]	57.4	13.2	1.8	13.8	10.5	5.8	9.0	100.0	100.0	100.0	100.0	100.0	100.0	100.0

Notes: See table 4.6.
Sources: See table 4.6.

returned to levels observed before the overthrow of communism, the euro could extend its share in world trade invoicing by several percentage points.

For reasons of space and the limited size of trade flows in this region I do not report industrial countries' trade with Africa. It should just be noted that Europe's export share to the whole of Africa has tended to decline in recent years, giving some small advantages for the USA and Japan.

The theoretical discussion at the beginning of this section underlined another factor in trade invoicing practices, domestic inflation rates and variabilities (stylized fact 3). Whether the euro becomes more attractive than the dollar or the yen on this level very much depends on the future monetary policy conducted by the ECB. Assuming that US and Japanese monetary policies remain unchanged, an ECB establishing an inflation record like that of the German Bundesbank in the past may foster euro invoicing in international trade, although given low inflation in the recent past in practically all industrial countries the potential impact may be rather small. If the ECB conducted a monetary policy which is some weighted average of historical policies in the EU, however, then the euro could become less attractive than the dollar in terms of price stability.

One factor in the future performance of the ECB is the fundamental approach to monetary policy taken. Masson and Turtelboom (1997) have simulated potential post-EMU volatilities in several macroeconomic variables, using the IMF's multi-country model MULTIMOD, depending on whether the ECB pursues monetary or inflation targeting. Whereas, in these simulations, inflation targeting resulted in a lower variability of short-term interest rates and the dollar/euro exchange rate than monetary (M3) targeting, inflation variability was lower only for contemporaneous (same-year) inflation targeting, not for forward-looking (next-year) inflation targeting. From that perspective contemporaneous inflation targeting would be the option most beneficial for euro internationalization through trade invoicing. Another factor is the independence and price stability orientation of the ECB, as determined by its Statute (European Council, 1992). This element clearly hints at low inflation and, therefore, a high attractiveness of the euro for international traders. The political decision about the composition of the ECB's governing council and the popular acceptance of ECB policies in EMU countries, two more factors, cannot be judged at the time of writing, more than six months before the decision on EMU member countries has been taken.

Although the Bank of Japan has during the 1990s produced a lower inflation rate than the USA or Germany, Japanese inflation tends to be more volatile than that of its two competitors, which makes the yen less attractive as a trade-invoicing currency.[33]

Invoicing regularity 4 (p. 98) stipulated that trade in primary products is to a large extent priced in US dollars. An argument which has been brought forward is that if EU-15 as a whole was a larger importer of certain homogeneous goods than its competitors, then the euro could replace the dollar for these goods. The most important commodity is, of course, oil. According to World Trade Organization data (WTO, 1996, tables IV.13–IV.17) world fuels exports amounted to 349 bn USD in 1995 or 6.9 per cent of total merchandise trade. Deducting 57.8 bn USD of fuels trade between Western European countries (and 15.6 bn USD between Northern American countries) amounts to a post-EMU share of roughly 8.0 per cent. Western Europe has the largest share of fuels imports from the rest of the world (outside Europe), amounting to 26.6 per cent of the total. Japan and North America (imports from outside the region) follow, with shares of 19.6 and 19.3 per cent, respectively (the US share alone would be 21.6 per cent). From these data, expectations that the euro has a chance to replace the dollar as the main invoicing currency for fuels can be confirmed.

However, there are other considerations than simply comparing global demand shares. First, potential distortions through deviations of market exchange rates from equilibrium levels have to be kept in mind (remember from the discussion of table 4.1 that current exchange rates seem to 'favour' European trade shares). Secondly, there are regional differences. Europe receives about the same quantities of fuels from Africa as North America receives from Latin America, and gets most of the rest from the CEECs. The main importer from the Middle East is Japan (leading the EU and the USA), which imports most of the rest it needs from Asia – intra-Asian fuels trade alone accounts for roughly 16 per cent of the world total. Given that Middle Eastern, Latin American and Asian countries have clearly had a preference for the dollar up to now, the euro may have a difficult start. Thirdly, McCauley (1997) points out that for many countries commodity prices in dollars are currently less volatile than they would be in Deutsche mark. Fourthly, at present the main derivatives markets for these products are in the UK and in the USA, and they function mainly in dollars, which will further enhance the network advantages of the US currency, in particular if the UK stays out of EMU. These arguments point to potential inertia in commodities

---

[33] In constrast to Tavlas (1992, table 2), who uses quarterly consumer price inflation (CPI) rates, I find with monthly CPI rates that this phenomenon has not disappeared during the 1980s and is still present by the mid-1990s.

invoicing which may favour incumbency – the dollar – over global demand share – the euro – for quite a while.

An event which could make a difference would be UK EMU membership. This would shift the London commodity markets (International Petroleum Exchange, London Bullion Market, London Metal Exchange, etc., which in some cases even lead US markets), to the euro, improving the situation for the European currency. Given the regional differences in commodities demand described above, one potential scenario could be a split of commodities pricing in a dollar zone, with derivatives markets located in, say, Chicago, and a euro zone, with derivatives markets located in London. With 8 per cent of post-EMU world trade being fuels trade and about 4 per cent other primary goods trade there would be some potential for the euro to close part of the gap to the dollar described in table 4.4 above.[34]

Summing up, one can predict that the euro should start with a share of approximately one-quarter of world trade after the European currency changeover, which is clearly more than the Deutsche mark today. This will also be much more than yen invoicing but considerably less than US dollar invoicing, probably accounting for about 6 and 59 per cent of world trade respectively. Because of the increased size of the 'domestic' economy and international trade relations, the euro is likely to expand its role in the years after EMU through network effects. However, the information on changes in trade flows collected and inertia in invoicing practices do not hint at dramatic changes in the global currency composition of international trade after full monetary union. The 'arithmetic' effect of the initial switch is likely to be much more important than dynamic follow-up effects over the short and medium term. What one might expect is a rather gradual increase of euro invoicing, which occurs mainly in the regions close to the EU, such as in trade with non-EMU European countries, the CEE countries as well as the Southern and Eastern part of the Mediterranean. Trade in homogeneous commodities has the potential to lift the euro share in the future, but many uncertainties about UK participation in EMU and the powers of inertia remain. The US currency is, thus, likely to remain dominant on the global level and, in particular, in the Western Hemisphere and in

---

[34] Kenen (1995, p. 112) has written that

> The size of its [the euro's] domain outside Europe will depend partly on the evolution of pricing practices in the major commodity markets. If some of them switch to ECU [euro], many commodity-exporting countries may begin to invoice their exports in ECU [euro] and will join the ECU [euro] zone. One cannot even rule out a shift to the pricing of oil in ECU [euro], rather than dollars, which would extend the euro zone into the Middle East.

Asia. There are little signs of an important change in the yen's weak position in foreign trade, even in Asia, although – as in the case of foreign exchange trading – new exchange rate arrangements after the dust of the recent Asian crisis has settled may make a difference.

4.5   EMU and official reserve holdings

The next two sections deal with the impact of EMU on international investments in the future three leading world currencies – the dollar, the euro and the yen. I shall start with central banks' investments for their forex reserve holdings and address private investments and the role of European financial market development afterwards.

As reported in chapter 2, European central banks participating in the European Monetary System (EMS) began in the second half of the 1980s to use Deutsche mark in considerable amounts for their exchange rate-stabilizing interventions. This indicates that Deutsche mark holdings may today comprise a substantial part of EU countries' official forex reserves (outside Germany). Since these will convert into 'domestic' assets under EMU, the initial 'arithmetic' effect on the global currency distribution of reserves may be important. In order to estimate this effect one needs information on the amount of EU currencies in the central banks' portfolios joining EMU. The currency breakdowns of individual countries' official reserves is, in most cases, confidential, but one can infer from Masson and Turtelboom (1997, table 5) that EU countries hold at least 31 per cent of their foreign reserves in their own currencies. Assuming that half of non-specified currencies are from Europe as well (and the rest dollars) and that half of non-gold-backed ecu reserves are private ecus, this share rises to 41 per cent.[35]

From this a rough estimate of the instantaneous effect of EMU on global reserve holdings is derived in table 4.12. At the start of monetary union about two-thirds of global official reserves will be in US dollars, 19 per cent in euro and 8 per cent in yen. (This is very close to McCauley's, 1997, table 13, estimate, who finds a slightly higher dollar and a slightly lower euro share.) Again the only EU currency really making a difference for the euro is the British pound. If the UK would stay out of EMU, the euro's starting level will decline by about 3–4 percentage points (see the more general sensitivity analysis reported in square brackets).

---

[35] The proper treatment of holdings in official ECU is important, because they will convert back into dollars and gold reserves, against which they have been issued, in stage III of EMU, and not into national euro denominations (Kenen, 1995, p. 114). In 1990 EU countries (excluding Luxembourg) held about 42 per cent of their reserves in EU currencies.

Table 4.12   *Global reserve currency composition before and after EMU (in per cent of total world reserves), 1995 data*[a]

	Before EMU	After EMU
USD reserves	62	69
Euro reserves	26	19
(DEM)	(14)	(–)
[sensitivity analysis][b]		[15–21]
JPY reserves	6	8
Total reserves	100	100

Notes:
[a] It is assumed that non-specified currencies in IMF reserve data are half USD and half EU currencies; non-gold-backed ecus are switched half in USD and half in EU currencies, unless specified otherwise.
[b] Sensitivity analysis for varying EMU members (core EMU versus full EMU) and varying assumptions on ecu reserves; only the minimum and the maximum are shown.
Sources: Author's estimates and calculations using data in IMF (1997a) and in Masson and Turtelboom (1997).

To which extent will the world's central banks embrace the euro as a reserve asset after the initial changeover? The fact that the aggregation of official EU reserves will lead to a much larger amount of dollar reserves in the hands of the ECB and national EMU central banks (compared to EU trade flows, for example) than usually observed for industrial countries has triggered much discussion in financial markets as to whether heavy official dollar selling should be expected, quickly reducing the US currency's share in total world reserves.[36] And, indeed, Leahy (1996) estimates econometrically that sales of dollar reserves could be of the order of 35 per cent of their current level.

However, this reasoning is now more and more coming to be questioned. First, as long as the new European System of Central Banks (ESCB) is concerned with establishing credibility in the markets and, perhaps, also facing potential transitional forex market volatility, 'in'-countries' and the ECB's reserve managers may feel comfortable with a big cushion of US dollars. Valuable attempts to link the currency composition of reserve holdings with optimal portfolio optimization produce, at best, mixed results (Heller and Knight, 1978; Dooley *et al.*, 1989; Masson and Turtelboom, 1997), whereas debt denomination, exchange arrangements or trade links seem to be more important

[36] McCauley (1997, annex 3) provides a comprehensive account of this discussion.

(Dooley *et al.*, 1989). Not unrelated to that, most countries' official reserve managers seem to be reluctant to seek changes in their reserve holdings proactively (see McCauley, 1997, p. 56, paraphrasing Machlup), so that their currency compositions exhibit substantial inertia.

Expanding on Eichengreen and Frankel (1996), Eichengreen (1997) has advanced a test of this hypothesis. He regresses twenty-five yearly observations of the US', the UK's and Japan's compositions of official reserves on the respective country's output and trade shares as well as on reserve compositions one-year lagged. The lagged dependent variables turn out to be the by far most significant explanatory variables with parameter values ranging between 0.58 and 0.86. Eichengreen (1997, p. 15) interprets this result as a 'powerful testimony to the influence of history' (see also the historical account of reserve holdings in chapter 2).

Instead of dramatic shifts in the currency composition of the world's forex reserves, a rather gradual diversification over time towards the euro can be expected. One of the reasons for the dominant role of the US dollar in official reserves is the deep and broad market for short-term government paper in New York. As shown in table 4.1, the size of EMU financial markets will be considerable, but they will not be fully integrated right from the start of the union (see below). As this integration proceeds over time, as the more bank-based European financial system evolves towards more securities market orientation, and provided that the ESCB establishes monetary policy credibility, non-EMU reserve managers will find the euro more attractive and shift part of their funds into the new European currency, in particular when their countries have decided to give some weight to the euro in their exchange rate policies and when there is a liquid bilateral market with the euro in interbank forex trading (which in itself depends on trade and investment links, see sections 4.3, 4.4 and 4.6). However, given the low starting level for the euro, inertia and dollar incumbency, only *neighbouring* countries – in particular, participants in the ERM II, the new exchange rate mechanism succeeding the EMS for countries not joining the EMU in the first wave – will be strongly inclined to go into the euro, and the new European currency is not likely to come close to the global position of the US currency in the foreseeable future.

In spite of some slow growth in the last twenty years, the yen has traditionally played an even less important role as an official reserve asset than the Deutsche mark. Garber (1996) has explained this by the less deep and less broad domestic yen government Treasury bill market compared to New York, and by the fact that the use of alternative assets is discouraged by various taxes.[37] He points to the more proactive role of the US Federal Reserve in providing financial services for foreign central banks. While financial liberalizations and the April 1998 'Big Bang' in Japan may foster financial market development and enhance the attractiveness of the yen as a reserve asset, it is not clear whether the Bank of Japan will switch to a more 'commercial' attitude towards providing financial services for foreign reserve managers;[38] Japanese domestic markets are in addition smaller than those of the USA or the aggregate of the EU. As long as there is turmoil in Asian financial markets and in the Japanese banking system, the yen is unlikely to gain much more of reserve managers' confidence.

4.6   EMU, international investment and the evolution of European financial markets

Central bank reserve holdings and even international trade are nowadays clearly smaller than international lending and securities investment as well as forex trading (discussed in section 4.3). At the end of 1996 total official forex holdings amounted to 1 bn SDR (roughly 1.5 bn USD; IMF, 1997a), which compares, for example, to 3,225.5 bn USD of outstanding international debt securities alone (BIS, 1997b). Total world trade of 5,080 bn USD in 1995 (table 4.1, column (5)) is less than a third of cross-border bond and equity transactions by the Group of 7 (G-7) largest industrial countries.[39] These facts provoke the thought that investment-currency use could be more important than trade invoicing or official reserve holdings for the internationalization of currencies. Although 'purists' might object that investment in a store of value is not 'money use' in the narrow sense (chapter 2), it can still be a major source of international payments flows and through this channel (as described, for example, in Hartmann, 1994, and chapter 2 above) an important determinant of the exchange structure in the forex market, which can feed back through network transaction cost effects into vehicle-currency use (and also further investment decisions).[40]

---

[37] According to a recent study by the New York Fed (Fleming, 1997, table 2) a small but significant share of US Treasury securities turnover is actually traded in Tokyo. However, most of this 'off-shore' trading happens in maturities of two years and longer (between 2 and 6 per cent of the total – including also the New York and London markets – trading in these securities), while Tokyo US Treasury bill trading is very small.

[38] Such a change in attitude is at least as unlikely for the ESCB.

[39] I estimated from McCauley (1997, table A3.4) and Portes et al. (1997, table 7) that these transactions from the G-7 countries must have been equal or larger than 17,151 bn USD in 1995 (after correction for double counting).

[40] A similar circular mechanism is described in Bénassy and Deusy-Fournier (1994).

The link between domestic financial market depth and currency internationalization

The strongest case following this line of argument to date has been made by Portes *et al.* (1997), who sketch some elements of a potential three-country transaction-cost model linking international trade and investment with the exchange structure in currency markets.[41] In this framework thick-market externalities apply not only to forex markets but also to domestic financial markets. When investors shift funds from foreign countries to a country *A* not only transaction costs in the *A* currency markets decline but also transaction costs in *A*'s domestic (say, government bond) market do (whereas those in the countries facing disinvestment go up), further attracting international investors. However, micro-structure effects from volumes on volatilities, potentially dampening the strength of thick-market externalities (theoretically and empirically 'verified' in chapter 3, Karpoff (1987); Frankel and Froot (1990); Jorion (1996), and numerous other studies), are disregarded. Moreover, since there is apparently no uncertainty over financial market returns, international diversification of intermediaries' portfolios over several currencies on the basis of risk–return considerations does not appear in any of the scenarios presented (see the discussion of investment currency theory in chapter 2, section 2.2). In the framework chosen different 'steady-state' structures of currency use in forex, trade and investment can be sustained by transaction costs depending on the initial conditions, exogenous values for trade and investment flows as well as market expectations on those structures.

Portes *et al.* (1997) have collected a formidable data set comprising spot foreign exchange turnovers, cross-border trade, equity and bond flows *between* the USA, Europe and Japan as well as domestic government bond turnovers *within* the USA, Europe and Japan. In order to discriminate between the different structures of international currency use they link these with bid–ask spreads and the empirical relationship between trading volumes and transaction costs derived in Hartmann (1997b).[42] As a result of this first empirical simulation they conclude that EMU will immediately shift the global equilibrium from what they have

---

[41] The basic notions of this framework are akin to the trade-forex model of Rey (1997), discussed in the theoretical survey of chapter 2.

[42] For each bilateral forex market the degree of vehicle use is derived as the difference between total spot dealer–customer turnover and the turnover which can be accounted for by the fundamental payments flows resulting from cross-border trade and investment. Inter-dealer turnover is assumed to be linked to dealer–customer turnover through a fixed multiplier reflecting inventory management in the form of 'hot-potato' trading (Lyons, 1996, 1997).

defined to be the 'status quo' equilibrium to their 'quasi-status quo' equilibrium, in which the US dollar keeps its 'status quo' position as the absolute forex vehicle for currency exchanges between Europe and Asia but the euro takes over all the financial investment flows between these two regions.

In a second step the authors assume that the domestic component of European transaction costs (say, the spread in government bond markets) declines to (or below) the level of US domestic transaction costs. This is based on the argument (p. 29) that 'within a time horizon of five to ten years, financial market integration will be completed within Europe', which may have the effect described because of the similar aggregate sizes of both areas' domestic financial markets. Under this assumption a new set of simulations leads the authors to conclude that there are multiple equilibria, including both a 'medium euro' scenario and a 'big euro' scenario. The former scenario implies that the dollar still retains its forex vehicle role (though with lower trading volume against the yen) but the euro takes over as the dominant international investment currency, with asset flows between Europe and Asia as well as between Europe and the USA being primarily in euro. The latter, 'big euro', scenario implies that the European currency also takes over as the forex vehicle – i.e. in this case the only international role of the dollar is in investment flows between the USA and Asia. These results are further substantiated with a sensitivity analysis, varying the elasticity of transaction costs to trading volumes.

The analysis leads Portes et al. (1997) to the following two strong conclusions: first (p. 37), 'scenarios in which the euro does share international currency status more or less equally with the dollar are indeed plausible scenarios'. Second (p. 14), 'the future of the euro will be determined on the financial markets not on the goods markets'. In this latter respect they attach quite an important degree of responsibility to European policy-makers' decisions, such as the ECB's stance towards capital inflows or unremunerated reserve requirements and its readiness to act as a lender of last resort in financial crises. They also point to regulators' inclinations to pursue financial deregulation as well as to their own and central bankers' efforts to promote cost-effective euro-payment systems. And they note that, in their view, private initiatives to harmonize market conventions and to consolidate markets are already under-way.

There are a number of issues which could be raised regarding the analysis underlying these conclusions. The first is related to the authors' interpretation of the 'status quo'. As has been pointed out above, and illustrated in figure 4.2 (p. 85), there is a highly liquid direct spot forex market between the mark and the yen (which is actually the fifth largest in the world; BIS, 1996, tables 1–B and 1–C), and the dollar plays only an EU–Asia vehicle role for the other European currencies whose trading with Asian currencies is more limited. The exchange structure between the present three major currencies – the dollar, the mark and the yen – is *direct* exchange, already today.[43] Hence, by assuming 'total indirect exchange' through the dollar between Europe and Asia, any switch in the exchange structure to more euro use appears more dramatic in the framework chosen than it would be in practice.

Similarly, by treating the world as a three-country system and by neglecting any partial investments in different countries for diversification purposes, changes in investment behaviour are more drastic than one would expect in practice, with equally drastic consequences for transaction costs through network externalities. In particular, this framework excludes at the outset the more gradual type of changes in international currency use observed in history and described as one potential scenario in chapter 3. Finally, switches in the currency or domestic-asset exchange structures are costless for the financial intermediaries considered (e.g. zero set-up costs). One might claim, indeed, that given the low starting levels of euro use, smaller regional developments within or at the periphery of the three large areas (America, Europe and Asia) may be more likely in the first place than any large switches in the triangular relationship *between* these three blocs.

Prospects for further European financial market integration and implications for investment currency competition

McCauley (1997, table 13) has advanced an estimate of euro, dollar and yen starting levels in international banking and financial markets, applying the 'simple arithmetics' of EMU to BIS data on international bonds, cross-border bank liabilities to non-banks, foreign-currency liabilities to domestic non-banks and euro-notes outstanding. According to this data, the total share of the euro would be 13 per cent of the total, as compared to a current sum of 34 per cent for all EU currencies together.

---

[43] As has been pointed out in section 4.2 (p. 87), the situation is somewhat different for outright forwards and swaps, for which the mark–yen market is the ninth largest of those specified in the BIS (1996) survey. Notice, however, that the theoretical framework on which the authors' arguments are based considers only spot forex markets. Swap transactions, for example, are different in nature. They serve as a means to manage the *timing* of the actual payments involved with other (mainly spot) transactions, helping dealers to optimize their liquidity and exchange rate risk exposures. In this context, it may be advantageous for dealers to manage mark exposures and yen exposures separately in the deeper dollar–mark and dollar–yen swap markets.

Even compared to the previous estimates on foreign exchange turnovers, international trade and foreign reserves, this is a surprisingly low number, indicating considerable cross-currency finance within Europe.[44] The dollar's share after EMU would be 53 per cent (40 per cent before EMU), and the yen's share 15 per cent (12 per cent before EMU). Again, it has to be cautioned that this provides a purely static picture. But in the presence of some circularity and inertia, is a quick portfolio shift balancing the relative positions of the dollar and the euro, as also claimed (for example, by Bergsten, 1997), plausible?

One argument that could be brought forward in favour of strong follow-up effects is that the historical experience of gradual changes in international currency use and of the extension of regime changes over several decades may be less applicable today than it has been in the past, because nowadays financial markets are much more important than they were, say, at the end of the sterling era and technical progress has enabled them to adjust their international investment behaviour much more quickly than was previously the case. If these modern financial markets alone drive the extent to which national currencies are used with respect to all international money functions, which is the main notion behind the Portes *et al.* (1997) prediction, then the transition to an important role of the euro could, in fact, be quicker.

The view that financial markets would do the job alone and that foreign traders and official reserve managers would just follow behind as an unimportant appendage strikes me as a slight over-statement. In spite of their relatively small size financial institutions tend to monitor trade flows and official reserves very carefully, and changes in these variables can influence financial market expectations to a considerable extent. However, quite apart from this, three key factors will decide whether quick changes in investment currency use after EMU are likely or not. The first factor is the size of the initial shock on the international monetary and financial system, which can produce the lock-out from the current, partly self-fulfilling equilibrium. Introducing a common currency in a number of advanced economies implies a discontinous change in the system, which is different from the gradual rise of a single nation in the world economy and therefore limits the applicability of historical analogies to, say, the emergence of the US dollar or the Deutsche mark. The second factor, as rightly stressed by Portes *et al.* (1997), is the extent and

---

[44] Henning (1997, table 5) estimated a smaller arithmetic effect on the basis of some more ad hoc assumptions on intra-European investments. McCauley (1997, pp. 6–9) observes that non-German investors tended to centralize their EU investments in marks, although other EU currencies offered higher yields.

speed with which European financial markets will integrate under a common currency, such that international investors and debt managers find it equally attractive to put their money in or raise money from the European markets than to do so in the USA (or Japan).

The third factor, which could – in theory – be at least as important as any liquidity/transaction-cost effects, is the post-EMU correlation between US, EMU-area and Japanese financial market returns. Should euro/dollar or euro/yen returns be lower than the current correlations observed for European currencies, then a higher potential for diversification effects could further increase investment demand for the new European currency, if international investors feel over-exposed to dollar risk.

Unfortunately, there is considerable uncertainty about what these future correlations may look like. With the help of the IMF's multi-country model, MULTIMOD, Masson and Turtelboom (1997) simulated potential future dollar, yen and euro short-term government debt returns after EMU from the perspective of an international investor. Although their main interest was in optimal official reserve holdings, and not in private investment, their results suggest that euro/yen correlations could be lower than historical mark/yen correlations, whereas euro/dollar correlations could turn out to be higher than historical mark/dollar correlations. Notice, however, that there may also be some counter-balancing effects involved. Reduced correlations may make it not only more attractive for Americans to hold more euros in their portfolios but can also give incentives for Europeans to take on more dollars, for example. Finally, and somewhat analogous to reserve holdings, due to home bias actual portfolio changes might be more modest than those predicted international capital asset pricing theory.[45]

Regarding the first argument, the initial shock of EMU on the international economy is, in my view, frequently over-estimated, mainly because the working of the 'simple arithmetics' of EMU is often not well understood or not taken seriously. In contrast to the internal size jump of the 'domestic monetary habitat' for the euro, the *external* size jump is more modest because Europe's trade and investment to the rest of the world is much more limited than intra-European trade and investment (see the various evidence for this provided above). Furthermore, not all EU countries are likely to join EMU right from the start, which creates an element of 'sequencing' in the initial shock. The three shocks which

---

[45] See, for example, French and Poterba (1991) or Tesar and Werner (1992). International investment theory is discussed in the theoretical survey in chapter 2.

finally undermined sterling and promoted the dollar were the unravelling of the gold standard and two world wars. Is the EMU really a change of a comparable order of magnitude?

Regarding the second key argument EMU's impact on *internal* financial markets is potentially large, but it is likely to be spread out over quite a significant period of time, given the present heterogeneity and fragmentation of the national segments. This latter point needs some more elaboration.[46] *Money markets* have usually been strongly separated by national borders and, therefore, market micro-structures tend to be extremely country-specific. Those differences relate to the type of intermediaries, such as discount houses in London and repo market-makers in Paris; to the way trading is organized, such as screen-based trading systems versus decentralized telephone markets; to the types of instruments traded and their relative importance, such as repurchase agreements or interbank deposits; to the existence or not of minimum reserve requirements for money market instruments; to payment and settlement systems and legal and tax provisions as well as the regulatory environment; and, last but not least, to domestic market conventions. The way in which national monetary policy is conducted is, of course, a strong factor shaping these arrangements, but it is not the only one.

It is often been said that the single monetary policy for the whole euro area and the connection of national real-time gross settlement systems (RTGS) through TARGET (the Trans-European Automated Real-Time Gross Settlement Express Transfer System) will automatically lead to an integrated EMU-wide money market in euro. And without any doubt the unifying effect will be strong with little scope for the occurrence of important short-term interest rate differentials in normal circumstances from one 'in'-country to another. In other words, there will be 'a single private money market yield curve' (for maturities ranging from overnight to one year), 'and the markets' choice of reference rates between offshore and onshore rates will depend on the ECB's reserve requirements' (McCauley and White, 1997, p. 6).

However, the single yield curve does not imply that an investor will be indifferent between going to Frankfurt, London or Paris for her liquidity management in euro. Some micro-structural differences may continue to exist, leading Prati and Schinasi (1997, p. 18) to conclude that it is

an open question ... whether the different market structures characterizing the interbank markets in each [EMU] member country will survive or whether

---

[46] In the following discussions of European financial markets I shall be drawing on the work by others, in particular on that by McCauley and White (1997) and Prati and Schinasi (1997).

market pressures – acting through price differentials – will lead to a single EMU-wide interbank market'.[47]

This contrasts with the present US money market, which is highly integrated with most of the activity concentrated in New York. In any case, McCauley and White (1997, p. 6 and table 5) interpret data about current derivatives trading in private money market instruments as indicative of smaller future aggregate euro-money market turnover than future aggregate US turnover. (By the same measure, euro-money markets would still be more liquid than Japanese money markets.)

Folkerts-Landau and Garber (1992) argue that a proactive stance of the central bank in the smoothing of daily liquidity fluctuations is an important factor in the stabilization of a market-based financial system, such as that of the USA, which experiences sharp liquidity shortfalls in money markets more frequently than universal bank-based systems. Therefore, a 'narrow' central bank, not having important financial stability functions, will have incentives to discourage the transformation of a bank-based system into a market-based system. The Maastricht Treaty and the publications of the European Monetary Institute about (EMI) the future monetary framework of the ESCB (EMI, 1997) rather tend to point towards a more 'narrow', 'Continental European model' under EMU, with little financial stability functions – unlike, for example, the broader and more active role of the US Federal Reserve. Whether the ECB will make use of reserve requirements for monetary policy purposes, and to what extent they will be remunerated, is also of importance in this regard.

While this type of argument would suggest limitations to financial market growth in Europe, the *practice* of ECB procedures may still turn out to be different. For example, national central banks within the ESCB, having lost some of their former responsibilities, may find themselves in a competitive position *vis-à-vis* their neighbours to attract large shares of EMU-area financial markets to their own constituencies. The instrument could be the regulatory powers, which have been delegated to the *national* supervisory authorities (European Council, 1992), be they integrated in the national central banks or not.[48]

---

[47] In contrast to interbank markets, Prati and Schinasi (1997, p. 18) consider that the decision that the ECB will use repurchase agreements as the main instrument for implementing monetary policy could prove to be a strong, and decisive, incentive for the development of an EMU-wide market for repurchase agreements (repo market).

[48] Goodhart and Schoenmaker (1995) describe the relations between monetary policy and financial regulatory bodies in seventeen industrial countries. A more recent description of these institutional structures in more than seventy-five countries is provided in Goodhart *et al.* (1998).

One financial stability-related function, which has been given to the ECB (and is currently being prepared at the EMI), is the establishment of the TARGET payment system, linking the national RTGS systems. Through the requirement to cover emerging intra-day overdrafts with collateral, RTGS systems have an important safety component, but in return the opportunity costs of collateral make them also relatively costly, compared to net settlement systems. Folkerts-Landau *et al.* (1996) even argue that the increased need for collateral may reduce overall liquidity in financial markets. Hence, depending on the relative attractiveness of private intra-European large-value net payments systems and TARGET pricing (still to be decided at the time of writing), European payment systems might be cheaper or more costly to use and more or less favourable for financial market liquidity than US payment systems, with implications for the attractiveness of investing in the euro.[49]

Another key financial market for the competition between Europe, the USA and Japan is the *government bond market*. One major difference between the EU and its two main competitors is the absence of a large central budget at the federal level. On the one hand, the removal of currency risk between EU currencies will (and already does) reduce yield differentials substantially but, on the other hand, owing to differences in national debt levels and economic as well as demographic divergences, bond markets will increase the emphasis given to the pricing of credit risk (Goodhart and Lemmen, 1997; McCauley and White, 1997; Prati and Schinasi, 1997). It is generally accepted that credit risk differentials will be smaller than previously existing currency risk differentials, even more so if the Growth and Stability Pact (GSP) turns out to be credible, but those credit-risk yield differentials will also be persistent, because a central EU budget is not in sight in the foreseeable future. One implication could be that the EMU government bond market will not be served by a single futures contract (McCauley and White, 1997). Numbers giving the sum of all current EU government debt markets (such as those which entered the financial market aggregates in table 4.1) and comparisons of those with the US market for an evaluation of future relative liquidity must be therefore interpreted with caution.

Further obstacles to full integration of EU government or private bond markets after EMU are differences in market conventions and micro-structures as well as domestic regulatory environments, both in

---

[49] One difference between the US Federal Reserves Fedwire RTGS and European systems is that the latter (including the arrangements envisaged for TARGET) do not allow for intra-day overdrafts that are not fully collateralized. In contrast, the Fed grants this possibility and charges intra-day 'interest rates' for overdrafts. Some observers reckon that this could make Fedwire a less costly RTGS for banks.

primary and secondary markets, akin to those mentioned for money markets.[50] For example, the 1993 European Investment Services Directive (ISD), introducing a 'single passport' for securities firms and the home-country principle to avoid regulatory discrimination by host countries, exempted 'rules of conduct' from the general principle, which may affect, say, dealers in private primary bond markets. The Giovannini Report (European Commission, 1997) seems to have taken the view that the costs of harmonization of market conventions must be borne by the markets themselves. While there is certainly consensus in the markets that harmonization is desirable, considerable resistance emerges as soon as deviations from the national familiar systems become costly. Substantial differences in conventions within Europe still exist with respect to settlement periods, coupon frequencies (annual versus semi-annual), day counts and banking holidays. While the difficulties to agree on procedures for redenominating existing debt instruments into euros is rather a transitory problem (although also a difficult one), some of the other differences may remain even in the long run.

The introduction of the euro also implies forces for the integration and consolidation of European *equity markets*, which were until very recently highly fragmented. Frankel (1996), for example, finds strong effects of exchange rate regimes on international stock return correlations. Prati and Schinasi (1997, p. 35) predict that the 'most likely development is that a European-wide equity market for blue-chip stocks will emerge into a single electronic exchange with a screen-based automated order-driven trading system'. The smaller national bourses will rather specialize in non-blue-chip domestic companies. It appears unlikely at the present time that any EU country would let its domestic stock market disappear altogether, so that domestic company shares will be traded only in foreign countries. Recent strategic alliances between the Frankfurt, Paris and Zurich markets signal the determination of Continental exchanges to reap at least some of the potential benefits of consolidation.

However, if the UK joins EMU at some stage one scenario is the development of fierce competition between the London Stock Exchange (LSE) in conjunction with the London International Financial Futures and Options Exchange (LIFFE) and the Continental alliances. The London market might take on this challenge, instead of joining the Continental alliances, because of the current leading position of the LSE among European bourses. London's domestic market capitalization was

---

[50] It is not possible to address all these points in greater depth in the present book. For a brilliant discussion of the issues surrounding the impact of EMU on government bond markets with extensive references to the previous literature, see McCauley and White (1997).

in 1996 the second largest market in Europe 2.5 times larger than that in Germany, and 95 per cent of total EU turnover in non-domestic stocks was traded in London (Prati and Schinasi, 1997, table 12). If certain stocks are traded in London as well as on Continental exchanges, total liquidity in these stocks need not correspond to the sum of their current trading volumes (unless the LSE connects to the Continent through an automated trading system). Very recently, the likelihood of a different scenario, in which the LSE connects to the Continent through an automated trading system even before the UK joins, has increased considerably through a 'letter of intent' signed by the London and Frankfurt exchanges to establish a joint electronic trading platform for European 'blue-chip' shares. In any case, the aggregate market capitalization of the New York Stock Exchange (NYSE) is even larger than the European aggregate over all national markets. Tokyo stock market capitalization is roughly the same as the European aggregate *without* the UK.

One regulatory obstacle for further European stock market integration may originate in the concept of a 'regulated market', as incorporated in the ISD. This notion allows EU countries to discriminate against foreign over-the-counter (OTC) markets, if they consider that trading volumes should be concentrated on more transparent organized exchanges with formal securities listings (Steil, 1996, chapter 4). Another obstacle relates to differences in European securities clearing and settlement standards, such as different access conditions, securities forms (paper-based or book-entry) or taxation of trades as well as non-harmonized settlement cycles, which increase cross-border transaction costs through diseconomies of scale (Giddy *et al.*, 1996). The introduction of a European central securities depository (CDS or 'Euro-hub') could reduce this problem. The Giovannini Report sounded pessimistic regarding a standard settlement period for the whole of Europe. Finally, mutual recognition of prospectuses for new equity offerings is currently not ensured; in several EU countries it is often not possible for firms from another member country to launch a public offer using a prospectus drawn up in accordance with the 1989 Commission's Prospectus Directive.

As a general matter, it is quite important for post-EMU financial markets whether the UK joins the union at a later stage or not. London is not only the largest stock market in Europe, but also leads other EU countries in foreign exchange, derivatives (BIS, 1996) and international bonds trading. Moreover, some of the world's leading commodity exchanges are also in London, whereas the Continent does not have any market of comparable size. Although the previous share trading example has shown that the participation of the UK need not in all cases lead to a beneficial liquidity/transaction-cost effect, the standing of London as an international financial centre, and the broadness, depth and sophistication of its markets should on balance give a boost to the scope of the euro as an attractive investment currency.

As has already been noted at the beginning of this chapter, the structural difference between the European (more bank-based) and the American (more market-based) financial systems is reflected in the measures of aggregate bank assets and aggregate stocks outstanding in securities markets. The EU has the larger *banking markets* whereas the USA has the larger securities markets. The share of bank assets as a percentage of the total assets held by banks *and* financial institutions, for example, is 73 per cent in France, 77 per cent in Germany and 56 per cent in the UK, which is comparable to Japan (79 per cent). This percentage is, by contrast, only 22 per cent in the USA (McCauley and White, 1997, table 4). The introduction of the euro, with the related size jump in *existing* securities markets, could accelerate the process of disintermediation in Europe, reducing the importance of traditional bank lending to the benefit of further growth of securities markets. If such a development gained momentum and EU financial regulators and central bankers took an accommodating stance towards it, Europe's securities markets could grow beyond the present of US markets' size.

However, it is now widely accepted that, even with considerable competitive pressures through technological change, the growing role of private pension funds and financial deregulation, the restructuring of European banking systems is advancing at a surprisingly slow pace. Prati and Schinasi (1997, p. 52) claim that after the start of EMU 'counterbalancing factors suggest that any shift of financial activity away from the large European universal banks will be gradual'. One could add that even when this gradual restructuring and consolidation of EU banking markets is complete, the European financial system will not necessarily look exactly like the US system. If EU universal banks succeed in continuing their diversification into investment business, they may still maintain a larger lending activity than US non-universal banks, implying less development for EU securities markets.

The main conclusion which emanates from this summary of the likely impact of EMU on Europe's domestic financial markets is that, while there are some important initial size jumps involved, the full development and restructuring of these markets will be a gradual process,[51] and due to

---

[51] A similar conclusion has already been reached by Peter Kenen (1995, p. 118) who writes that:

> the size of the increase in demand for ECU[euro]-denominated assets will depend on the contribution of EMU to the unification and quality of EC [EU] asset markets, and this will take place gradually.

the segmenting effects of national borders continuing to exist within the union they may even not attain the same degree of integration as the domestic markets in the USA or Japan over a longer time horizon. Overall, considerable uncertainties remain.

Having said this, I find it extremely hard to believe that EU financial markets will in a comparatively limited period of time attract as many non-EU investors as would be necessary to shift the international monetary and financial system to a new regime where the euro either shared international dominance on an equal basis with the dollar or even displaced the US currency from that position. A ten-year period may be at the lower end of the period necessary to put the euro in a position to get close to the currency which has dominated the international monetary and financial system for the last forty years. The historical experience of gradual changes in the use and replacement of international currencies, although not directly applicable to the international impact of the euro, is still alive. However, while the new European currency may lag behind the dollar for a substantial period of time, it should immediately jump to no. 2, and start extending its initially small advantage compared to the Deutsche mark, leaving the Japanese yen well behind.

4.7   Conclusions

In the present chapter I have, first, discussed the emergence of the Deutsche mark as forex vehicle currency and, then, the potential impact of EMU on the international use of the major currencies. In line with the theoretical model in chapter 3, the mark's emergence was explained by enhanced international transactions via Germany and exchange risk-reduction effects, both related to continuing European integration and the EMS, as well as by further development of Germany's financial markets.

The creation of a new money for a considerable number of important industrial countries is different from historical experiences with emerging international currencies. First, EMU implies a substantial discontinuity in the size of the 'domestic monetary habitat' and, secondly, financial markets are more important and more dynamic today than they have been when the pound sterling or the dollar rose to world dominance. Taking these differences into account, I come to the conclusion that the euro, the future single European currency, will immediately become the second most important currency in the world in various dimensions of international money, clearly behind the US dollar but well in advance of the Japanese yen. However, in spite of the jump in the size of the internal currency area, its external advantages compared to the Deutsche mark (the most important European currency on the international level before EMU) will be relatively limited at the start, because of the elimination of intra-EMU forex turnovers and the switching of intra-EMU trade and investment transactions as well as official reserve holdings to 'domestic' currency transactions and holdings. However, once the transitional period (stage IIIA), during which national denominations are still circulating on the local levels, is terminated, I consider it plausible that the euro will experience a gradual extension of its international role, which may be quicker in international investment than in international trade, in time closing at least part of the gap to the dollar.

While financial market forces may somewhat accelerate this euro expansion – compared to dollar expansion earlier this century, for example – I do not expect them to lead the euro to world leadership or to a balanced position with the dollar in the short or medium term, because European financial markets will not be as large, developed and integrated as US financial markets from the start of EMU. First, internal financial market integration – although of course strengthened through the elimination of exchange rate risk and more homogeneous monetary policy and money market arrangements – will be gradual, because historically developed national market and regulatory structures cannot be harmonized instantaneously. Secondly, some obstacles to European financial market growth and integration, such as the predominant role of universal banks in financial systems (although bank lending will certainly become less important compared to the status quo) and the relative importance of national budgetary policies (leading, for example, to credit risk differentials in bond yields) may turn out to be permanent.

It was also found that, in general, whether a particular non-core country joins EMU or not has only a limited impact on the internationalization potential of the euro. However, there is one notable exception to this rule – the UK. This is primarily due to the position of London as a, or even the, leading international financial centre, with extremely broad and liquid foreign exchange, stock, international bond, derivatives and commodities markets. In addition, the pound sterling still plays a larger role on the international level than many other industrial-country currencies. If the UK joined relatively soon after the first wave of member countries, it would strengthen the euro's international scope. If it stayed out forever, a considerable handicap for the euro, compared to the dollar or the yen, could remain.

World trade figures suggest that the euro's role would expand primarily in transactions with neighbouring countries, such as non-EMU European countries (including CEECs, as well as Southern and Eastern Mediterranean countries). In contrast to the Deutsche mark before

EMU, the euro might also gain some more importance in Asia. I expect euro growth to proceed mainly at the expense of the dollar. Trade figures and some other economic fundamentals also suggest that the Japanese yen could rise to a stronger international role within Asia. Whether this actually materializes will depend to a large extent on the restructuring of the Japanese banking system and on the exchange arrangements implemented in the aftermath of the current Asian crisis.

The theoretical arguments and empirical facts discussed imply that the following policies by European authorities could enhance the *potential* for euro internationalization. (1) A stability oriented monetary policy resulting in low inflation and low exchange rate variability; (2) avoidance of capital controls; (3) measures fostering further integration, deepening and broadening of European financial markets. (3) could include, for example, the harmonization of financial regulations on an incentive oriented level; safe but not over-priced large-value payment systems; some coordination of government securities features; market oriented remunerations of potential reserve requirements; and private initiatives for the harmonization of market conventions and the integration of securities settlement systems. A stronger centralization of budgetary policies could also foster government bond market integration, but obviously – as is also the case for some of the other measures – it could be in conflict with other objectives. In any case, it should be stressed that, in the presence of network externalities, inertia in currency structures and a strong role for financial market expectations, these policies would to some extent be necessary but not sufficient for the euro to become an important international currency.

By pointing to measures which could enhance the international scope of the euro, I do not wish to argue whether or not euro internationalization is desirable from the point of view of European or world economic welfare. Such a statement would require a different type of analysis, measuring the costs and benefits of euro internationalization for citizens of different countries, which is beyond the scope of this book.[52] Since currency internationalization is not part of the usual objectives of economic policies and without having done a thorough evaluation of the overall costs and benefits, Europe's authorities might be well advised neither to actively obstruct market forces for euro internationalization, if they emerge, nor to seek their currency's internationalization at any price.

---

[52] Alogoskoufis and Portes (1991); Emerson *et al.* (1991); and Portes *et al.* (1997) have begun to address this issue.

5 Trading volumes and transaction costs: from the short run to the long run

> When the relatively most saleable commodities have become 'money,' the event has in the first place the effect of substantially increasing their originally high saleableness.   *(Karl Menger, 1892)*

> Social institutions like money are public goods ... Another time-honoured observation is the analogy of money and language. Both are means of communication. The use of a particular language or a particular money by one individual increases its value to other actual or potential users ... The public good argument applies to acceptability as means of payment ... Indeed, there is, as the language analogy suggests, arbitrariness and circularity in acceptability ... Dollar bills and coins are acceptable because they are acceptable.   *(James Tobin, 1980)*

5.1   Introduction[1]

As has been argued in chapter 3 and in the theoretical survey of chapter 2, the relationship between the volume of payments in a currency and its transaction costs is an essential element in the internationalization of currencies. If this relationship is negative – i.e. the more a currency is used the more attractive it becomes to be used even more (economies of scale or network externalities) – there are some circular forces at work, which can, first, result in multiple equilibria and, secondly, prolong the position of a dominant international currency. In the present chapter several tests are performed to see whether this oft-presumed relationship is empirically valid. Since the foreign exchange (forex) market plays a pivotal role in the internationalization of currencies (see chapter 1, section 1.2), I employ forex bid–ask spreads, as a measure of transaction costs, and newly available forex trading volumes for the empirical analysis. The distinction between short-run and long run effects is essential. If the long-run relationship between forex volumes and spreads had turned out to be positive, the current theory of vehicle currencies would have had to have been rewritten.

[1] This chapter draws on Hartmann (1996a, 1997a, 1997b). Excepts from the *Journal of International Money and Finance* are reproduced with kind permission of Elsevier Science.

The question of the effect of forex trading volumes on spreads is, however, interesting for at least three further reasons. First, it can say something about whether more refined financial market micro-structure theories are valid in forex markets as well. Secondly, and related to this, it is important for the discussion about liquidity and market efficiency. Finally, the relationship between trading volumes and bid or ask prices may be relevant for (short-run) exchange rate forecasting. In this chapter I shall mainly focus on the micro-structure of forex markets and draw the conclusions for international currencies at the end.

Early time-series estimations on the short-term relation between transaction volumes and transaction costs in the forex market, as measured by bid–ask spreads, resulted in the finding that spreads increase with volume at constant volatility (Glassman, 1987).[2] Information cost models of dealer spreads, such as that of Copeland and Galai (1983) together with an assumption on the information content of volume, can provide a theoretical basis for this result. Is the view, taken in earlier chapters of this book, that larger markets have lower transaction costs mistaken? I shall argue in the present chapter that such a conclusion would be premature. Building on the notion put forward by Bessembinder (1994) that trading volume has two components, which may have a differential impact on spreads, I am going to argue that the long-run effect of volume is unambigously negative.

To reach this conclusion, we need to proceed in four steps. In section 5.2 I shall present a brief review of the theory of financial market spreads, refining the arguments of chapter 3, and I shall derive a synthetical model which will serve as a base line for empirical tests. Then, in section 5.3, another, more elaborate, survey is made of the previous empirical literature on forex bid–ask spreads, which – in my reading – has not been successful in giving a clear picture about the impact of trading volumes on spreads. Sections 5.4 and 5.5 present two very different types of estimates and tests of this relationship. I show, first, a daily Generalized Method of Moments (GMM) time-series estimation, focusing on the short run, and I then show a panel-data random-effects estimation, with emphasis on the long run. Both approaches lead to fully complementary results, suggesting that, even though information-related unpredictable volume can temporarily increase spreads, liquidity-enhancing predictable volume drives transaction costs down in the long run.

---

[2] In this book the 'short run' is defined to be at a *daily* frequency. 'Ultra short-run' estimations (i.e. *intra-daily* high-frequency estimations) are not undertaken.

5.2   Spread theory refined

Finance theory has identified three basic sources of bid–ask spreads: (1) order-processing costs, (2) inventory-holding costs and (3) information costs of market-making. Each one is influenced by trading volume in a particular manner. Order-processing-cost models often assume the existence of some fixed costs of market-making or of providing 'immediacy' for the exchange of ownership titles (Demsetz, 1968). These costs may come, for example, from the subscriptions to electronic information and trading systems (such as Reuters or Telerate in the forex market). They give rise to economies of scale of market-making. At a given spread, when a dealer expects that trading volume will increase in the next trading period, *ceteris paribus* his expected profit goes up as well. However, inter-dealer competition will force him to narrow his spread to avoid losing business to competitors under-cutting him. Hence *predictable volume* should reduce spreads through an order processing-cost effect (Stoll, 1978; Black, 1991, chapter 3).

In contrast, the effect of trading volume on inventory holding costs is ambiguous, depending, for example, on transaction sizes. Inventory cost models, like Stoll (1978), Ho and Stoll (1981) and others, view dealers not only as providers of liquidity services but also as optimizers of their own securities portfolio. In this framework they try to choose the return–risk efficient portfolio, which maximizes their (or their shareholders') utility. However, since providing 'immediacy' (standing ready to trade in a security at any time desired by customers) implies being pushed away from this portfolio, they announce bid and ask prices which assure that their positions are not too far from the optimal portfolio and provide revenues compensating for the remaining utility losses. On average, larger transactions will push the dealer 'further' away from his desired portfolio, such that *ceteris paribus* the larger the transaction sizes in the order flow expected, the larger the spreads.

However, if trading volume is expected to come in many small, statistically independent orders, then by the law of large numbers increased (predictable) volume could also decrease spreads through an opposite inventory cost effect. Since additionally larger volume is not necessarily driven by larger transaction sizes (dealers may decompose one large transaction into several smaller ones of 'standard' size, for example, or transaction frequency may increase) and Reuters quoted spreads are binding only up to a certain maximum transaction size, it is unlikely that inventory cost effects can be identified through aggregate volumes and spreads. As outlined in chapter 3 and in the inventory cost literature quoted above, they are better identifed through (predictable) *volatilities* and spreads.

Information-cost models suggest a relation between bid–ask spreads and information arrival or the presence of agents with better information than dealers in the market (Copeland and Galai, 1983; Glosten and Milgrom, 1985; Kyle, 1985). If new information has arrived, so that dealers risk getting into transactions with 'insiders', then they will widen spreads in order to deter some of the informed traders or to earn higher mark-ups from liquidity-motivated traders, whose demand elasticity is rather low. (When asked for a quote, dealers do not know whether the counterparty is an information or a liquidity trader.) Therefore, the more important the information arrival during a trading period, the higher the dealers' information costs, the larger their spreads. However, a major obstacle to the empirical implementation of these models is that the rate of information arrival or the share of information trading in overall trading is unobservable. The use of *unpredictable* forex volume as a solution to this observability problem is discussed further below.

There are two more arguments which may reinforce the point made by the order processing cost literature, suggesting a negative impact of predictable volume on bid–ask spreads. The first, advanced by Easley and O'Hara (1992b), again comes from the information-cost literature. Since market-makers gain from transactions with liquidity traders, spreads decrease with an increase in the expected (or 'normal') order flow from them. The second is a search cost argument. When the interbank market grows, and liquidity is not reduced by over-proportional increases in transactions sizes, then it becomes easier for the dealing banks to square undesired or take on desired positions. One might think though that the pure search-cost reductions in markets as liquid as those for forex are relatively small. Since both effects create scale economies in market-making, I shall refer to them below as 'order-processing effects' as well.

All the three types of spread models above also highlight the role of *expected* return volatility. Since my primary interest is in trading volume here, I do not dwell on this. Instead I note that most of these models predict that spreads widen with the volatility predicted for the coming trading period. Putting all the pieces together, one can then write the following model of forex dealer spreads

$$s = f(\sigma^p, x^p, I), \tag{5.1}$$

where s is the dealer spread, σ^p is the predictable volatility of the exchange rate, x^p the predictable component of trading volume, and I the flow of new information. Theory predicts that $\partial f/\partial \sigma^p > 0$ and $\partial f/\partial I > 0$. Strictly speaking the sign of $\partial f/\partial x^p$ is not determined, since when volume increases come in large blocks the economies of scale in market-making can be compensated for by a surge in inventory costs. As argued above this is very unlikely to happen and the sign is most likely to be negative.

Most of the models quoted above have been developed to analyse the behaviour of stock market specialists. Although there are differences between the micro-structure of stock and forex markets, attempts to explicitly model these differences have been scarce (Flood, 1991). Lyons (1995) highlights the additional tools of inventory control available for forex dealers as compared to stock market specialists.

Model (5.1) is not specified in a way that it can be estimated and tested directly. As noted before, the rate of new information arrival I is not observable. As pointed out by Bessembinder (1994) models of the mixture-of-distributions hypothesis (MDH) make a link between information flow, volume and volatility, which helps finding a testable specification. One MDH model, which elaborates on Clark (1973) and Epps and Epps (1976), is presented in Tauchen and Pitts (1983). In this model the joint distribution of (observable) daily price changes and transaction volumes of an asset is derived from a model of (unobservable) intra-day equilibrium price changes and intra-day volumes. New information during the day causes traders to update their reservation prices and demand or supply the respective asset until the average of their individual reservation prices clears the market again. If they disagree about the interpretation of the new information, then the respective equilibrium price change comes with high transaction volume, while relative unanimity results in a price change with little volume. More formally, Tauchen and Pitts find the following expression for daily trading volumes

$$v = \sum_{i=1}^{I} v_i = \mu_v I + \sigma_v \sqrt{I}\, n, \tag{5.2}$$

where I is a random variable measuring the number of intra-day equilibria (or, in other words, the daily information arrival rate),

$$v_i \sim \mathrm{N}\!\left(\mu_v, \sigma_v^2\right) \tag{5.3}$$

is the trading volume related to the ith intra-day information arrival and n a standard normal random variable. The mean μ_v and the standard deviation σ_v of intra-day volumes are both increasing functions in trader disagreement, as measured by the standard deviation of individual traders' reservation price update due to a new information arrival (see Tauchen and Pitts, 1983, formula 7).

Following Bessembinder (1994), it is assumed that the major part of this information-driven volume comes as a surprise to dealers. Then one can write *unpredictable volume* (x^u) as a function g of the information arrival rate,

$$x^u = g(I, \cdot) \tag{5.4}$$

(5.1) and (5.4) give the new spread equation (5.5) which contains only observable variables,

$$s = f(\sigma^p, x^p, g^{-1}(x^u)). \tag{5.5}$$

As a final remark, it is noted that the Tauchen–Pitts model implies an equation similar to (5.2) relating information arrival to unexpected volatility (σ^u). Hence x^u and σ^u are jointly driven by I and therefore strongly correlated. An econometric specification of the spread model should therefore include x^u alone and not σ^u (or vice versa). Even then x^u is clearly endogenous and thus has to be instrumented in the econometric implementation of (5.5). This fact was ignored in earlier studies.

5.3   A survey of spread estimations

Econometricians estimating the effect of trading volumes on bid–ask spreads in the forex market have used five different sources to measure trading activity. These are forex turnovers as collected by central banks in the main trading centres, forex futures turnovers at the Chicago International Monetary Market (IMM), Tokyo forex-broker turnovers, quoting frequencies on Reuters screens, and single banks' transaction volumes. Since volume data have until very recently been the 'bottleneck' in the type of analysis we are interested in, the empirical survey following now is organized around these volume sources, which mainly determine the econometric technique chosen.

BIS global volumes

In the early 1980s the Federal Reserve Bank of New York, the Bank of Canada, the Bank of England and the Bank of Japan began collecting forex turnovers as reported by most dealers (and brokers) in their respective markets for a particular month (usually April). Since 1989 the BIS has coordinated this survey for a much larger number of central banks (twenty-one in 1989 – excluding Germany's Bundesbank – and twenty-six in 1992 and 1995). BIS surveys offer different breakdowns of volumes, for example according to trading centres, currency pairs, counterparties (inter-dealer versus dealer–customer) and contract types (spot, forward etc.). Because of almost complete coverage in most markets local double counting, arising from the fact that each transaction is reported by two forex dealers, can be corrected for relatively precisely. However, since the national reports do not break down cross-border volume according to counterpart countries, imprecise corrections for cross-border double counting enter some errors. A second problem with BIS turnover surveys is their extremely low frequency. Since they are relatively costly for both private banks and central banks, they are undertaken only every three years, which precludes any time-series techniques. Finally, one might object that monthly market volumes do not correspond to the time horizon of dealers when they set spreads.

The branch of the volume-spread literature exploiting these three-yearly surveys was pioneered by Black (1991), who undertook a pooling regression of four annual observations (1980, 1983, 1986, 1989) for seven dollar markets. He finds a significantly positive sign for a composite variable, where exchange rate volatility enters in the numerator and trading volume in the denominator. A simple cross-section regression by Bingham (1991) with twenty observations from the 1989 BIS report resulted in a negative, but insignificant volume parameter. Because of their large coverage and relatively deep breakdowns I take the BIS volumes up again for the long-run analysis reported in section 5.5 below. However, several shortcomings of the previous papers are improved, in particular concerning the econometric model and theoretical underpinnings as well as the data (e.g. the number of observations, the measurement of spreads and volumes).

More precisely, I use a short panel of global spot inter-dealer turnovers for twenty-two currency pairs over April 1989 and thirty-three currency pairs over April 1992. This volume measure is more exact than those employed in the former studies with BIS data which take *total* volumes, containing also swap and forward as well as dealer–customer transactions. Each observation is adjusted for differences in the number of business days in financial centres and therefore reflects volume for a 'representative' business day for that month.[3] Part of the observations were taken directly from the BIS surveys (BIS, 1990, 1993), others are computed from the national surveys sent to me by central banks. In the latter case, global turnover of a currency pair was approximated by the sum of the *local* turnovers in each currency's domestic trading centre *plus* the higher one of

---

[3] Hence, even though daily representative volumes are used, they rather reflect *monthly* trading activity (see BIS, 1993).

Table 5.1   *The eight largest forex markets, April 1992*

Market	Volume[a]	Ticks[b]	Spread[c]	Volatility[d]
USD/DEM	87,938.5	112,184	4.562	31.85
USD/JPY	44,147.8	51,565	5.711	22.58
USD/GBP	22,876.0	39,979	4.624	28.08
USD/CHF	16,736.9	44,231	6.181	37.12
DEM/GBP	15,712.3	6,617	4.138	18.43
DEM/JPY	12,298.7	7,123	4.141	30.98
DEM/CHF	9,110.2	6,472	3.405	16.18
DEM/FRF	6,701.1	5,476	1.111	4.06

Notes:
[a] Business daily average of global spot transaction volume during April 1992 (mn USD).
[b] Number of Reuters quotes during April 1992.
[c] Monthly tick-by-tick average of relative Reuters spreads (in basis points, (5.6) multiplied by 10,000).
[d] Average of daily absolute middle-price changes during April 1992 (in basis points, derived from (5.8)).
Sources: BIS (1993), local central bank surveys, Olsen & Associates databank.

the two *cross-border* turnover numbers reported for each centre. (This convention may induce a downward bias in the measurement of those currencies' volumes, but since no major currency – which is traded in more than the two home financial centres – was concerned, this effect should be extremely small.) In a few cases the share of spot inter-dealer transactions in overall volume had to be approximated.

These volume data are matched with monthly aggregates of high-frequency spreads and volatilities from Reuters (described further below).[4] Table 5.1 reports the data for the eight largest markets in April 1992, in descending order of volume. Having found that a one-way random effects specification is most appropriate for this dataset, the hypothesis that the volume parameter is larger than or equal to zero can be rejected at the 5 per cent significance level.

IMM futures volumes

Daily currency futures volumes at the Chicago IMM are readily available since the number of traded contracts per day is reported by the market and the sizes of contracts are standardized. The obvious disadvantage of these data is that they represent only a small share (about 1 per cent) of

---

[4] The total number of fifty-five observations was limited by the number of rates quoted in Reuters with which the volume data had to be matched. Unfortunately, no Reuters data were available to extend the dataset to the April 1995 BIS turnover survey (BIS, 1996).

total as well as forward forex trading. While Bessembinder (1994) argues that the stock market experience shows that the correlation between spot and futures volumes is relatively high, it will be argued in section 5.4 that stochastic processes fitted on forex futures volumes are different from those fitted on forex spot volumes. Moreover, forex market spot turnover growth slowed down considerably in the late 1980s, while forward turnovers continued to grow forcefully (BIS, 1993). Dumas (1996) points out that the choice of futures volumes (from an organized market) to measure total volumes of a market working mostly over the counter (OTC), may also induce an omitted-variable problem in the estimations. Finally, while available time series are quite long, the IMM provides markets only for the six *major* currencies against the US dollar.

In her seminal paper Glassman (1987) matched these daily volumes with the corresponding futures price data. She estimated six spread equations with seemingly unrelated regression (SUR) for 1975–83. In three cases a *positive* impact of volume on spreads is significant at the 5 per cent (or lower) level, in two cases it is also positive but on a higher level of significance, and in the remaining case a negative coefficient is completely insignificant.

Bessembinder (1994) tested a model by Easley and O'Hara (1992b) with the futures data, suggesting that expected and unexpected volumes should have opposite effects on spreads. The former volume component should reduce spreads through the order processing-cost channel, while the latter should increase spreads through the information-cost channel. Bessembinder does feasible generalized least squares (FGLS) estimations for four dollar markets between January 1979 and December 1992. He fits a stochastic process on the volume series in order to distinguish between the 'expected' (or predictable) and the 'unexpected' (or unpredictable) component. The parameters estimated for 'expected' volumes are consistently negative, while those for 'unexpected' volume are always positive. However, the significance levels of these parameter estimates are sensitive to the currency regarded and to the convention on the measurement of spreads. In fact, the only cases where the hypothesis of the volume effect being zero can be rejected at a significance level of 5 per cent (or better) are for spreads quoted in European terms in the markets for dollar/pound and dollar/yen ('expected' volume), as well as dollar/mark ('unexpected' volume).

Jorion (1996), applying a similar decomposition as Bessembinder for seven years of daily dollar/mark futures volumes coupled with spot price data (1985–92), estimates (heteroscedasticity-consistent OLS) a negative coefficient for 'expected' volume (significance level 5 per cent) and an insignificant (positive) coefficient for 'unexpected' volume.

Tokyo broker volumes

A longer time series of *spot* forex volumes has now been discovered (Wei, 1994). These data are published by the financial newspaper *Nihon Keizai Shimbun*, exclusively for the dollar/yen market. In Tokyo all forex *brokers* have to report their volume of transactions in dollar/yen concluded between opening and 3.30 p.m. (local time) to the Bank of Japan. Although dollar/yen is traded world-wide, the Japanese part is a good proxy for global spot forex turnover in this currency pair.

Nevertheless, even this excellent time series may also have some drawbacks. It may be affected by changes in the share of brokered deals in total trading, as has been the case in Japan (Bank of Japan, 1993). It may also be argued that broker volumes may be slightly different from direct interdealer volumes – for example, containing larger single transaction sizes. However, in the Federal Reserve Bank of New York's (1992) survey, spot-broker volume did not show larger transaction sizes than direct interdealer volume on average. Since it appears to be the best forex turnover time series available at present, I shall make use of it in section 5.4.

Wei (1994), whose main interest is in volatilities and spreads, uses the Tokyo broker volumes in a univariate OLS regression with monthly data (only one trading day per month) between 1983 and 1990 in order to estimate the volume effect for dollar/yen alone. Like Glassman (1987), he finds the volume parameter to be positive, both in levels and in logs, although it is never more significant than 10 per cent.

In contrast to Wei, section 5.4 fully exploits the daily frequency of these data for the period of 1987–94 and further elaborates on Bessembinder's (1994) methodology. In particular, spreads and volatilities are derived from high-frequency data and the endogeneity of unpredictable turnover is accounted for by introducing unpredictable Reuters FXFX tick frequency (see pp. 142ff.) as an instrumental variable. With these improvements Bessembinder's qualitative results are confirmed, but the results turn out to be statistically much stronger, both for the negative 'expected' volume parameter (5 per cent significance) and the positive 'unexpected' volume parameter (1 per cent significance).

Do these findings imply that unpredictable volume is an omitted variable in the estimations of section 5.5, where plain 'monthly' volumes are used? The answer is no. In section 5.4 daily unpredictable volumes are modelled as the residuals of an ARIMA process, which by definition have zero mean. Apart from some unsystematic error they cancel out when aggregated over longer time periods, such as a month. BIS trading volumes therefore measure *predictable* (long-run) turnover alone, which in conjunction with the results of section 5.5, implies a strong prior in favour of a negative volume parameter in our panel estimations in section 5.5.

Reuters tick frequency

The use of quoting (tick) frequency as a proxy for trading volume (or market activity) was pioneered by Demos and Goodhart (1992) and Bollerslev and Domowitz (1993). In the interbank forex market practically all participants are connected with the Reuters information system, where dealing banks feed in their bid and ask rates. The quotes are continuous twenty-four hours a day, seven days a week. The obvious advantage of Reuters ticks is their extremely high frequency, which allows for measures of activity with time horizons much closer to those likely to predominate in the real market. Additionally, the quoting bank and its location can be identified from the respective Reuters page.

On the other hand, there are a number of disadvantages. First, the quoting frequency of dealers may not always be a precise measure of their trading activity.[5] It is not clear whether real transactions are done at the quoted prices and, if so, at which amounts. While in normal times it can be expected that quoting frequency exceeds transactions frequency, in hectic market situations it may be the other way round, because dealers are too busy to feed in new quotes.

Secondly, the huge amount of data which accumulates rapidly when the Reuters information is stored requires powerful computer facilities, including automatic filters to clean the data from outliers, for example wrongly fed quotes. This may be the main reason why Goodhart's dataset, used in the two studies quoted above, is limited to less than three months. The forex consulting firm Olsen & Associates (Zurich) has such facilities and stored Reuters quotes since the middle of the 1980s (see Dacorogna *et al.*, 1993).

Demos and Goodhart (1992) use plain tick frequency (on Reuters page FXFX) as a measure of half-hourly market activity in dollar/mark and dollar/yen between April and June 1989. However, with a trivariate Vector Autoregression (VAR) model (also including volatilities), they do not find any significant correlations between ticks and spreads. Bollerslev and Domowitz (1993) also exploit Goodhart's dataset, but – in order to

---

[5] As an extreme example, it happens sometimes that a major dealer in a small, relatively illiquid market quotes in short time intervals, quasi automatically twenty-four hours a day. Although it is Reuters' policy to prevent such behaviour, sometimes a bank trying to advertise its presence in this market succeeds in doing this for weeks. Such a case happened in the US dollar (USD)/Portuguese escudo (PTE) market in April 1992. In this particular case, almost all Reuters quotes came from the same bank.

correct for some of the problems mentioned above – simulate synthetic dollar/mark 'transaction frequencies', counting one transaction whenever two banks' spreads overlap within a five-minute time interval. A maximum-likelihood estimation of a GARCH model shows the impact of the length of time between two 'trades' on the spread to be significantly negative (the number of plain quote arrivals as another measure of market activity is clearly insignificant).[6] Davé (1993) – who has full access to the Olsen & Associates database – plots hourly dollar/mark Reuters spreads for January 1986–September 1993 against hourly quoting frequency and hourly price changes. In contrast to the former studies he shows a clear trade-off between spread size and 'market activity' *at constant volatility*.

In section 5.4 it is argued that tick frequency may be a measure of the rate of information arrival over the trading day, which is the mixing variable in models of the mixture-of-distributions hypothesis, such as Tauchen and Pitts (1983), driving unpredictable trading volume (see section 5.2, eqaution (5.2)). After decomposing daily ticks into a predictable and an unpredictable component, it is shown that the latter performs very well as an instrumental variable for *unpredictable* dollar/ yen spot turnover (see p. 141 above). In another high-frequency analysis Lyons (1996) finds that the informational content of transaction size is strong in times of high quoting frequency (in the Reuters 2000–1 system), while it is weak in times of low quoting frequency (see also p. 144). However, Goodhart *et al.* (1996), by comparing one day of Reuters FXFX tick frequencies with *transactions data* from the trading system Reuters D2000-2, have cast some doubt on the quality of the former as a proxy for trading activity in high-frequency analyses.

In section 5.5 below I also present panel estimates testing *monthly* tick frequencies as a measure of monthly (predictable) trading activities. All results closely resemble those found for the relationship between BIS volumes and spreads. The ticks parameter is negative in all specifications (including the one-way random effects model). It is even more significant (below the 1 per cent level) than that with BIS volumes.

Individual dealer transactions volumes

Since most banks are extremely concerned about revealing their forex positions to their competitors, access to real transaction order flows of

---

[6] It should be emphasized though that the GARCH model has not turned out to be a good econometric specification for *intra-day* foreign exchange data (Andersen and Bollerslev, 1994; Guillaume *et al.*, 1997). Also, given the imprecision in the timing of FXFX quotes, a five-minute sampling interval looks extremely short.

single dealers has been extremely rare.[7] Nevertheless, Lyons (1995, 1996) has been able to record five days of transactions data (Reuters 2000-1 system) for one US dealer and one US broker for dollar/mark in August 1992. The originality of Lyons' ultra-high-frequency analysis notwithstanding, his dataset has the problem of rather limited coverage, with both respect to time and to the number of dealers covered. For example, the week considered is in the run up to the 1992 EMS crisis, and the only market he studies is the one which stands out as the inter-vehicle currency market (dollar/mark).

Although Lyons (1995) focuses more on the explanation of intra-day volatility his econometric test of an extended version of Madhavan and Smidt's (1991) Bayesian pricing model also implies that – in line with information-cost theories – dealer spreads clearly widen with the *size* of single transactions. However, in a follow-up project with the same type of data (Lyons, 1996) evidence is provided that transaction size can be *less* informative when *transaction* frequency is high than when it is low. This contrasts with his result on quoting frequency as a measure of trading activity (referred to on p. 143). Finally, possible economies of scale in market-making through order-processing effects, suggesting a negative effect of transaction size on spread, are disregarded.

Measurement of bid–ask spreads

Bid and ask prices in the forex market also pose some measurement problems, which are often ignored. The main handicap is that most available data are *quoted* prices rather than real transaction prices. This is reflected in the spread–volume literature. Glassman (1987) uses daily quotes of a single Chicago futures dealer. Demos and Goodhart (1992), Bollerslev and Domowitz (1993), as well as Davé (1993) have access to continuous Reuters quotes (page FXFX). Bingham (1991), Bessembinder (1994), and Jorion (1996) use daily data from the DRI data bank, which are Reuters quotes of a 'representative' dealing bank at some time during the day (e.g. at London closing). Black (1991) exploits fixing rates in some European markets, as published by the Bundesbank.

In sections 5.4 and 5.5 I report spread estimations using averages – 'tick-by-tick' – of quoted relative Reuters spreads (pages FXFX and WXWY), as defined in (5.6)[8]

---

[7] Goodhart and Guigale (1988) have daily trading volumes from two London dealers. Unfortunately this dataset, which covered several months in 1986, seems to be lost.

[8] All exchange rate data used in sections 5.4 and 5.5 were kindly provided by Olsen & Associates (Zurich).

$$s_{ij} = 1/L \sum_{l=1}^{L} \left[\ln\left(e^a_{ij}\right)_l - \ln\left(e^b_{ij}\right)_l \right]. \tag{5.6}$$

L is the number of Reuters ticks during the measurement period (as determined by the volume data) for currency pair ij, which is one day in section 5.4 and one month in section 5.5. a and b indicate ask and bid prices. Since I found evidence that absolute spreads (ask *minus* bid) clearly move proportionately to the exchange rate, I report only the results for relative spreads (log ask *minus* log bid) below.[9]

These Reuters data have some peculiar features. First, quoted spreads are usually larger than traded spreads. (For example, it can be estimated from table 5.1 and Lyons, 1995, that USD/DEM quoted spreads are about two to three times larger.) Notice however, that these measurement errors should not bias the estimates, because spreads are the explained variable in the regressions we are interested in. Secondly, the distribution of absolute (difference between ask and bid rate) Reuters spreads is discrete, with most of the mass on only a few numbers, such as five, seven, and ten basis points for dollar/mark (Goodhart and Curcio, 1991; Bollerslev and Melvin, 1994), although with relative (or fractional) spreads this pattern becomes blurred. Both features indicate that the quoted spreads are less variable than the traded spreads and therefore suffer from lost information. However, Bollerslev and Melvin (1994) show that there still is a high degree of variability in continuously quoted absolute Reuters spreads. Thus, the averages of continuous quotes employed here (usually hundreds or even thousands over a day) will be much more informative than daily 'representative' spreads. (Absolute fixing quotes hardly move over time at all.) Overall, the shortcomings of quoted spreads (Goodhart et al., 1996) are much more severe for intra-day than for inter-day or even monthly estimations. For example, only at very high frequencies does it really matter whether transaction prices lie sometimes outside the FXFX spreads, because the latter are fed in the system relatively slowly.

5.4   Spreads and volumes in the short run: a time-series approach

In this section I present direct tests of the model derived in (5.1)–(5.5) with a time-series estimation using daily dollar/yen data from 1987–94 (see p. 141). I first describe how the explanatory variables – predictable and unpredictable volume as well as predictable volatility – are measured and then how one can tackle such a specification econometrically.

---

[9] See Glassman (1987) for a discussion of the choice between absolute and relative spreads.

Emphasis is given to an appropriate instrumental variable to account for the endogeneity of unpredictable volume. Finally, estimation results are presented.

The predictable and the unpredictable

In order to estimate (5.5) one has to decompose observed dollar/yen broker trading volumes into a predictable component (x^p) and an unpredictable component (x^u) measuring I. This can be done with an autoregressive integrated moving average model (ARIMA). On the basis of standard unit roots tests, Box–Jenkins diagnostic checks, the Akaike information criterion (Harvey, 1981) and (in-the-sample) forecasting performance (root-mean-square error and Theil's inequality coefficient; Theil, 1961), it can be found that an ARIMA(9,1,1) specification performed best (table 5.2).[10] The fitted log volumes are then taken to measure the predictable component $(x_t^p = E_{t-1}x_t)$ and the residuals to measure the unpredictable component $(x_t^u = x_t - E_{t-1}x_t)$. Bessembinder's (1994) specification for futures volumes – an ARIMA(10,1,0) – did not pass the diagnostic checks and produced worse forecasts for my spot volume data than the process in table 5.2. Jorion (1996) specified a transfer function model of a deterministic trend with ARMA(1,1) residuals, again for futures volumes. However, my dollar/yen spot volumes do not have a deterministic trend.

An additional finding of these estimates is the presence of conditionally heteroscedasticity in trading volumes. As reported in table 5.2 (last line), a Lagrange-multiplier test of conditional heteroscedasticity in the ARIMA-residuals rejects homoscedasticity against an ARCH(1). The theoretical model of Foster and Viswanathan (1995) can explain this phenomenon.

The third explanatory variable is predictable dollar/yen volatility. In contrast to trading volumes, the presence of autoregressive conditional heteroscedasticity (ARCH) in daily forex returns is a well known and often reported fact (Bollerslev *et al.*, 1992). This means that a good deal of daily volatility is also predictable. Baillie and Bollerslev (1989) make a convincing case in favour of a GARCH(1,1) to be a reasonably precise and parsimonious specification for forex returns. Therefore, I present GARCH(1,1)-forecasted volatilities from daily log returns to measure σ^p. In accordance with the volume measure, 'daily' is defined to mean from Tokyo opening until 3.30 p.m. Returns are computed from 'middle prices', defined as the arithmetic mean of log bids and log asks. Table 5.3

---

[10] All estimations in this book are run with TSP 4.2B.

Table 5.2   *ARIMA(9,1,1) model estimation for log volumes*

$$(1-\phi_1 L-\phi_2 L^2-\phi_3 L^3-\phi_4 L^4-\phi_5 L^5-\phi_6 L^6-\phi_7 L^7-\phi_8 L^8-\phi_9 L^9)\Delta x_t=(1-\theta_1 L)\varepsilon_t, \ \ \varepsilon \sim (0,\sigma_\varepsilon^2 \mathbf{I})$$

Parameter	ϕ_1	ϕ_2	ϕ_3	ϕ_4	ϕ_5	ϕ_6	ϕ_7	ϕ_8	ϕ_9	θ_1
Estimate	0.33	0.11	0.09	0.08	0.02	-0.02	0.01	-0.01	0.07	0.98
t-stat.	14.10	4.40	3.80	3.30	0.90	-0.60	0.30	-0.40	2.90	18.80

Test/ Stat.	adj. R^2: 0.31	Ljung–Box test:[a] $Q(20)=14.9$ [0.14]	ARCH test:[b] $\chi^2(1)=13.21$	Theil's inequality coefficient:[c] 0.04

Notes:
[a] Statistic for twenty lags, p-value in square brackets.
[b] Lagrange-multiplier test of ARCH(1) against ARCH(0) in ARIMA-residuals.
[c] Statistic between 0 (perfect fit) and 1 (Theil, 1961).
Conditional sum of squares estimation with 100 back-forecasted residuals, $T=1976$ observations. $\Delta = 1 - L$ is the difference operator.

Table 5.3   *GARCH(1,1) estimation for log returns*

$$\sigma_t = \sigma_0 + \varepsilon_t, \quad \varepsilon_t|\varepsilon_{t-1} \sim \mathbf{N}(0,h_t), \quad h_t = \alpha_0 + \alpha_1 \varepsilon_{t-1}^2 + \gamma_1 h_{t-1}$$

Parameter	σ_0	α_0	α_1	γ_1
Estimation	0.78	461.51	0.11	0.45
Asymptot t-stat.	1.03	9.14	5.88	9.31

Likel.-ratio tests of GARCH(1,1) against ARCH(0) and ARCH(1)	$\chi^2(2) = 94.69$ [00.00] $\chi^2(1) = 31.11$ [00.00]

Notes: Quasi-maximum-likelihood estimation, $T=1976$ observations, log returns multiplied by 10,000.

reports the estimation and a likelihood-ratio test rejecting conditional homoscedasticity and ARCH(1) against the GARCH(1,1).

Again, the error term ε_t from the GARCH(1,1) can be extracted to measure unpredictable volatility. As has been argued in the theoretical section, this variable could serve as an alternative measure of the rate of information arrival.

Another measure of predictable volatility has been proposed in the literature. Notably, Wei (1994) and Jorion (1996) extract daily expected exchange rate volatilities from forex option prices, as quoted at Chicago's IMM or the Philadelphia Exchange. Jorion (1995) argues that implied volatilities of forex options contain more information than predictions from backward-looking time-series models. However, volatility forecasts with options have their own problems, in particular when the horizon is as short as a day. In any case, the part not captured by time-series models is relatively small, and we intend to *control* only for volatility effects, since our main interest below is in volume effects.

Econometric Strategy

GMM estimation

Hansen's (1982) GMM estimator can be employed in order to estimate the following log-linear specification of model (5.5).

$$s_t = \beta_0 + \beta_1 \sigma_t^p + \beta_2 x_t^p + \beta_3 x_t^u + \varepsilon_t, \quad \varepsilon \sim (0, \Sigma), \quad t = 1, \dots, T. \quad (5.7)$$

For a given $(T \times l)$ instrument matrix Z this estimator finds the parameter vector $\hat{\beta}$ for which the (squared) moment functions $J(\hat{\beta}) = (T^{-1}Z'\varepsilon)' W^{-1} (T^{-1}Z'\varepsilon)$ are closest to zero. It is consistent and asymptotically normal under quite weak distributional assumptions. With the weighting matrix W equal to the covariance matrix of the moment functions $(Z'\varepsilon)$ it is also asymptotically efficient. GMM is most adequate for financial data, because, *inter alia*, it does not require knowledge of the likelihood function's form and residual covariance matrices robust against conditional heteroscedasticity and autocorrelation of any order are directly available (Andrews, 1991).

Under the hypothesis that Z and ε are orthogonal the asymptotic distribution of the (adjusted) objective function $TJ(\cdot)$ (a quadratic form) is $\chi^2(l - k)$, with degrees of freedom equal to the difference between the number of instruments (or orthogonality conditions) l and the number of explanatory variables k. In the case of over-identification $(l > k)$ this delivers a test of general model misspecification, the test of the over-identifying restrictions (TOR; Hansen, 1982). For more specific hypothesis testing, the GMM-analogue of the likelihood-ratio test outlined in Newey and West (1987b) can be used. The test statistic (M) is the difference of the objective functions of the restricted and the unrestricted model at convergence, $M = T[J(\beta_R) - J(\beta_U)]$, which follows itself a $\chi^2(r)$, with degrees of freedom equal to the number r of restrictions imposed. Newey and West show that this test, which can be called a moment-function difference test, is equivalent to Wald and Lagrange-multiplier tests, if the moment functions as well as the constraints are linear in the parameters, which will be the case below.

Instruments

Since GMM requires stationarity, the fitted ARIMA(9,1,1) volume series is differenced for the estimation of (5.7). Additionally, two dummy variables are introduced to account for weekends (dw_t) and holidays (dh_t). The choice of instruments (Z) involves a number of problems, which were avoided by Bessembinder (1994), who chose the explanatory variables as instruments and hence could not test for the over-identifying restrictions. First of all, the relation between unpredictable volume and information arrival sketched in section 5.2 is not deterministic, so that estimations without an instrument for x_t^u are biased. One can solve this problem by using daily dollar/yen quoting (tick) frequency on the Reuters FXFX page, here denoted q_t, as a measure of daily trading volume (see section 5.3, p. 143). Looking for an instrument for *unpredict-able* volume an ARIMA(11,1,1) can be fitted on ticks, applying the same techniques as for volumes, and the resulting ARIMA residuals can be used as the instrumental variable. To identify the model the remaining explanatory variables (including the constant and the dummies) are also chosen as instruments.

In order to test against possible remaining misspecifications additional instruments are needed. Unfortunately the residuals of (5.7) exhibit quite long autocorrelation, so that lagged values of the original instruments would be correlated with them and thus not useful to test for the over-identifying restrictions. Instead, the model has to be over-identified with the squares of predictable volatility, predictable volume and unpredictable ticks (or some higher moment). Notice that in the case of financial market data higher moments will usually contain additional information. Hence the χ^2-statistic of Hansen's TOR has three degrees of freedom.

Estimation results

Table 5.4 reports the results of two estimations. Line 1 contains a preliminary GMM estimation with the explanatory variables (including unpredictable *volume*) and their squares as instruments (GMM1). Line 2 contains the estimation, where unpredictable *ticks* replace unpredictable volumes in the instruments (GMM2). Asymptotic *t*-statistics (in parentheses) are computed from Gallant's (1987) conditional heteroscedasticity- and autocorrelation-consistent covariance matrix.[11] All estimations are undertaken for autocorrelation-corrections varying between ten and thirty lags. As the main results did not change during this sensitivity analysis, table 5.4 reports only those for twenty-lag autocorrelation correction. The TOR statistics are in column (7).

The first observation from table 5.4 is that the GMM1 specification is

---

[11] Andrews (1991) argues that Gallant's covariance matrix estimator, using the Parzen kernel to assure positive semidefiniteness, is superior to that of Newey and West (1987a), employing the Bartlett kernel, if both heteroscedasticity and autocorrelation are present.

Table 5.4   *Spread model estimations with decomposed volumes*

$$s_t = \beta_0 + \beta_1 h_t + \beta_2 \Delta E_{t-1} x_t + \beta_3 (x_t - E_{t-1} x_t) + \beta_4 dw_t + \beta_5 dh_t + \varepsilon_t, \quad \varepsilon \sim (0, \Sigma), \quad t = 1, \ldots, T$$

Estimation (1)	β_1 (2)	β_2 (3)	β_3 (4)	β_4 (5)	β_5 (6)	TOR[c] (7)
GMM1[a]	0.38	-3.82	7.08	0.01	0.02	$\chi^2(3) = 19.0$
	(3.23)	(-2.72)	(8.21)	(2.98)	(1.25)	[0.01]
GMM2[b]	0.52	-2.76	4.14	0.01	0.02	$\chi^2(3) = 4.4$
	(4.24)	(-2.01)	(3.15)	(3.19)	(1.43)	[0.22]

Moment-function difference test of $\beta_2 = \beta_3$:[d] $\quad \chi^2(1) = 9.1 \quad\quad$ Adj. R^2: 0.11
$\qquad\qquad\qquad\qquad\qquad\qquad\qquad\qquad\qquad$ [0.00]

Notes:
[a] Instruments: constant, $h_t, \Delta E_{t-1} x_t, x_t - E_{t-1} x_t, dw_t, dh_t, (h_t)^2, (\Delta E_{t-1} x_t)^2, (x_t - E_{t-1} x_t)^2$.
[b] Instruments: constant, $h_t, \Delta E_{t-1} q_t, q_t - E_{t-1} q_t, dw_t, dh_t, (h_t)^2, (\Delta E_{t-1} q_t)^2, (q_t - E_{t-1} q_t)^2$, with q_t daily log quoting frequency from Reuters FXFX.
[c] Test of the over-identifying restrictions (Hansen, 1982).
[d] Test from Newey and West (1987b), using the difference of the restricted and unrestricted GMM objective functions with constant weighting at convergence.
s_t is the daily average over relative Reuters' spreads, h_t is the one-step-ahead GARCH(1,1)-predicted log return variance (table 5.3 with $\sigma_0 = 0$), $\Delta E_{t-1} x_t$ is the first difference of the ARIMA(9,1,1)-fit of daily log volumes (table 5.2), $x_t - E_{t-1} x_t$ is the ARIMA(9,1,1)-residual of daily log volumes (table 5.2), dw_t and dh_t are weekend and holiday dummies respectively. Asymptotic (conditional) heteroscedasticity- and autocorrelation-consistent t-statistics (twenty lags; Gallant, 1987) in parentheses, p-values in square brackets, $T=1976$ observations.

strongly rejected by TOR while GMM2 is not. This indicates that unpredictable volumes are, in fact, correlated with GMM1-residuals and that spread estimations without an appropriate instrumentation for them are therefore biased. However, comparing the parameter estimates of both specifications, it turns out that there are no qualitative differences which would justify different interpretations. One implication is that Bessembinder's (1994) conclusions can be confirmed, although he did not instrument unpredictable volumes.

Summarizing GMM2, the signs of the parameters are consistent with the theories discussed in section 5.2. Predictable volume decreases spreads and unpredictable volume increases spreads. The former effect is significant at the 5 per cent level, while the latter is significant at the 1 per cent level. Again comparing GMM1 and GMM2, the misspecification of instruments results in an over-estimation of absolute volume parameter values by about one third. Asymptotic t-statistics of the volume parameters are also biased upwards. The volatility effect is positive and strongly significant.[12] Here the misspecification of GMM1 resulted in an under-estimation of the parameter value and the t-statistic. Moreover, dollar/yen forex spreads increase before weekends and – almost unnoticeably – before Japanese holidays, the former effect being significant at 1 per cent, the latter only at about 15 per cent. Intercepts are -7.4 in GMM1 as well as GMM2 (not reported in table 5.4, beause they have no economic interpretation). GMM2 can also be estimated allowing the structural parameters to vary over time, but this does not change any of the main results in table 5.4. Precisely the same results as for GMM2 occur when third moments of the instruments are used.

The negative impact of predictable volume on spreads suggests the presence of important order-processing-cost effects on forex spot spreads. This corresponds to research on stock market spreads, also finding an important order-processing-cost component (de Jong *et al.*, 1995). As might be expected, these order-processing-cost effects are not swamped by possible positive inventory-cost effects of block trading (see section 5.2). Furthermore, the strong effects of predictable volatility (positive) and unpredictable volume (new information arrival, positive) indicate the presence of important other inventory and information cost components. The statistical weakness of the 'holiday effect' compared to the 'weekend effect' on spreads can be explained by the fact that, in many cases, other large forex trading centres (for example, London or New York) remain open when there is a Japanese banking holiday (JP Morgan, 1994). In a companion project (Hartmann, 1997a), I have performed the same type of analysis replacing unpredictable volume as the measure of information arrival by unpredictable volatility. The results were analogous.

I also estimated restricted versions of GMM1 and GMM2, assuming that both volume components have the same effect on spreads, with similar results to the previous literature. However, the TOR rejects these specifications in general and Newey and West's (1987b) moment-functions difference test rejects the specific null of equality of β_2 and β_3 (table 5.4, last row). This should give a warning that predictable daily transaction volume should not be confused with information-related surprises in trading, because the former reduces transaction costs while the latter increases them.

---

[12] Similar volatility effects were also found by Agmon and Barnea (1977); Bingham (1991); Black (1991); Bessembinder (1994); Bollerslev and Melvin (1994); Boothe (1988); Glassman (1987); Jorion (1996).

5.5 Spreads and volumes in the long run: a panel-data approach

In section 5.4 a long daily time series for dollar/yen was used to estimate the differential impact of trading activity on bid–ask spreads in the short run. In the present section a completely different type of dataset is used to test whether, in the long run, only the negative impact of the predictable component in trading volumes survives. This second dataset has a large cross-sectional dimension over currency pairs, with only two observations in the time dimension which are three years apart. We start with a short discussion of monthly measurement of volumes and volatilities. Then the econometric panel techniques for such data are described, before I present the spread estimation results for BIS volumes as well as Reuters ticks.

Monthly measures of volumes and volatilities

The monthly measurement of continuously quoted spreads, the explanatory variable here, has been described in the empirical survey pp. 137–9 above. The empirical implementation of the volume decomposition undertaken in section 5.4 is important for the specification of the explanatory variables in the new econometric tests. The unpredictable parts of daily volumes and ticks were measured as the residuals of ARIMA models. These residuals have, by definition, an expected value of zero. Thus, *monthly aggregates* of volumes or ticks reflect only the *predictable* trading activity, since the unpredictable parts cancel out. Notice that the fact that the unpredictable component of trading volume can be neglected for longer time horizons implies that the theoretical-spread equation (3.5) in chapter 3 is a reasonable description of how transaction costs are determined in the foreign exchange (forex) market in the long run, which is more relevant for the phenomenon of vehicle currencies.

While in the time-series approach above unpredictable forex trading volumes were measured by unpredictable Tokyo-broker trading volumes and instrumented by unpredictable Reuters tick frequency, in the panel approach now following *predictable* (monthly) trading volumes are measured in two alternative ways. In a first estimation the plain forex turnovers from the three-yearly BIS surveys are the explanatory variable. In a second estimation plain monthly Reuters tick frequencies are tested as the explanatory variable. As will be seen below, both measures lead to very similar parameter estimates, although the statistical significance is stronger in the latter case.

The explanatory volatility variable employed in both estimations is the monthly average of daily absolute changes in Reuters middle rates,

$$\sigma_{ij} = \frac{1}{D-1} \sum_{d=1}^{D-1} \left| \left(e_{ij}^m \right)_{d+1} - \left(e_{ij}^m \right)_d \right|, \tag{5.8}$$

where

$$e_{ij}^m = \frac{\ln e_{ij}^a + \ln e_{ij}^b}{2} \tag{5.9}$$

is the middle rate and D is the total number of days for a month. Daily averages are chosen to make the measure compatible with BIS volume figures. As in the case of volumes, these monthly averages rather reflect, up to some unsystematic error, the aggregate of *predictable* price changes over shorter time intervals. Notice that option-implied volatilities (Wei, 1994; Jorion, 1995, 1996) cannot be used in our cross-section approach, because reliable option quotes for smaller markets are not available. The observed values of the volume, ticks, spread and volatility measures for the eight largest markets in April 1992 are reported in table 5.1.

Econometric strategy

The dataset used is an unbalanced panel with two periods, twenty-two observations in period 1 (April 1989) and thirty-three observations in period 2 (April 1992). In order to estimate the impact of trading volumes on bid–ask spreads standard panel techniques with relative spreads as the dependent variable and trading volumes/ticks as well as exchange rate volatilities as the independent variables are applied. Since the time dimension is short, the exposition focuses on the derivation of the one-way error components model.[13]

Let $i = 1, \ldots, N$ denote the index for currency pairs ($N = 33$) and ($t \le 2$). y_{it} is the log relative spread for currency pair i at time t, and y is the $[55 \times 1]$ vector of all spread observations. X is the $[55 \times 3]$ matrix of all observations of the independent variables in logs, including a vector of 1s in the first column. The first step is the OLS estimation of the *total* model with all observations pooled,

$$y = X\beta + \eta \qquad \eta \sim N(0, \sigma^2 I) \tag{5.10}$$

β is the $[3 \times 1]$ parameter vector and η the (non-spherical, normal) error vector.

Then the *between* model is to be estimated – i.e. an OLS regression is

---

[13] This means that I neglect potential time effects here. In Hartmann (1997b) I estimated more complex two-way error components models, comprising individual *and* time effects. Since time effects were comparatively weak, the results hardly differed from those presented further below.

undertaken with a cross-section where every observation is an arithmetic average over both periods,

$$y_B = X_B \beta_B + \eta_B \qquad \eta_B \sim N(0, \sigma_B^2 I), \tag{5.11}$$

where

$$y_{iB} = \begin{cases} 0.5(y_{i1} + y_{i2}) & \text{if } \exists t = 1 \text{ for } i, \\ y_{i2} & \text{otherwise.} \end{cases} \tag{5.12}$$

σ_B^2 can be useful for the tests and estimations explained further below.

Third, the *within* model is to be estimated – i.e. each variable is centred around the mean over both periods

$$y_W = X_W \beta_W + \eta_W \qquad \eta_W \sim N(0, \sigma_W^2 I), \tag{5.13}$$

where

$$y_{itW} = y_{it} - y_{iB}. \tag{5.14}$$

(Currency pairs with a single observation in time are dropped here.) With only two periods this is equivalent to taking the differences between both periods. The point in doing this is to remove any *individual effects* – i.e. differences in the intercepts between currency pairs which are constant over time. In fact, the within model also amounts to the same as introducing a dummy variable for every currency pair (for example, Greene, 1993).

However, simply 'filtering out' the possible individual effects comes at a high cost in terms of lost degrees of freedom. Therefore, a further step is to estimate a *random-effects* model allowing for unobservable individual effects (α_i) in the error term,

$$y = X \beta_R + \eta_R, \ \eta_{itR} = \alpha_i + \varepsilon_{it} \qquad \eta_R \sim N(0, I \otimes \Sigma_R), \tag{5.15}$$

where

$$\Sigma_R = \begin{cases} \begin{bmatrix} \sigma_\alpha^2 + \sigma_\varepsilon^2 & \sigma_\alpha^2 \\ \sigma_\alpha^2 & \sigma_\alpha^2 + \sigma_\varepsilon^2 \end{bmatrix} & \text{if } \exists t = 1 \text{ for } i, \\ \sigma_\alpha^2 + \sigma_\varepsilon^2 & \text{otherwise.} \end{cases} \tag{5.16}$$

$\sigma_\alpha^2 = \text{var}(\alpha_i) \ \forall i$ and $\sigma_\varepsilon^2 = \text{var}(\varepsilon_{it}) \ \forall it$. Since the α_i are a source of autocorrelation in the whole error term η_{itR}, (5.15) has to be estimated using feasible generalized least squares (FGLS). This amounts to the OLS estimation of the following weighted model (see, for example, Greene, 1993),

$$y^* = X^* \beta^* + \eta_R^* \qquad \eta_R^* \sim N(0, \sigma_{\eta^*}^2 I), \tag{5.17}$$

where

$$y_{it}^* = y_{it} - (1 - \theta_i)y_{iB}, \tag{5.18}$$

with

$$\theta_i^2 = \frac{\sigma_\varepsilon^2}{\sigma_\varepsilon^2 + T_i\sigma_\alpha^2} \tag{5.19}$$

and T_i the number of observations for currency pair i. θ_i^2 can be estimated from the within and the total model. In fact, it can be shown from (5.13) and (5.15) that

$$2E(\hat{\sigma}_W^2) = \sigma_\varepsilon^2. \tag{5.20}$$

Since the panel is unbalanced, the denominator of (5.19) cannot be estimated without bias from the between residual variance. Instead I estimate σ_α^2 indirectly from the residual variances of the total (5.10) and the within model (5.13) exploiting

$$\text{plim}_i(\hat{\sigma}^2) - 2E(\hat{\sigma}_W^2) = \sigma_\alpha^2. \tag{5.21}$$

Taylor (1980) finds the FGLS estimator for the random-effects model parameters to be more efficient than the OLS estimator in the fixed-effects (within) model, even for moderately sized samples such as the one available for this section. The snag in this specification is that if the random effects (α_i) are correlated with the (observable) explanatory variables, then $\hat{\beta}^*$ will be biased (Mundlak, 1978). Thus, it has to be tested for the absence of such a correlation between errors and regressors.

The preceding step, however, is to test for the *existence of individual effects*. Notice that for balanced panels

$$E(\hat{\sigma}_B^2) = \frac{\sigma_\varepsilon^2}{T} + \sigma_\alpha^2. \tag{5.22}$$

Thus for the subset of data with two observations in time one can exploit

$$E(\hat{\sigma}_B^2|_{T(i)=2}) = \frac{\sigma_\varepsilon^2}{2} + \sigma_\alpha^2. \tag{5.23}$$

Both estimators (5.20) and (5.23) follow a χ^2 distribution with degrees of freedom (df) corresponding to those of the within and the (adjusted) between (B') estimation. Therefore

$$\frac{\hat{\sigma}_B^2|_{T(i)=2}}{\hat{\sigma}_W^2} \sim F_{df\ B',df\ W} \tag{5.24}$$

is a statistic with which one can test the null of the *absence* of individual effects ($\sigma_\alpha^2 = 0$). If this hypothesis is rejected, then it has to be decided between the within and the random effects specification.

One can choose on the basis of two types of tests, a 'Mundlak test' and a Hausman (1978) test. To save space I describe only the specification of the 'Mundlak test' here, as depicted by Dormont (1989).[14] Under Mundlak's hypothesis $E(\alpha|X) \neq 0$ in the random-effects model (5.15), more precisely

$$\alpha_i = x'_{iB}\pi + \delta_i \qquad \delta_i \sim \text{iiN}(0, \sigma_\delta^2) \,\forall i. \tag{5.25}$$

By inserting (5.25) in (5.15) one can test the null hypothesis of the absence of a correlation bias with a simple F-test for the linear constraint $\pi = 0$. If the null cannot be rejected, then we can have confidence that, apart from possible other misspecifictions, an FGLS estimation of (5.15) is consistent and asymptotically efficient.

Estimation results

The results found when applying the panel estimation techniques described in the preceding subsection are summarized in tables 5.5–5.7. All results reported there are linear equations in logs, since Box–Cox transformations, not reported here, suggested that a log specification fitted the data better, and additionally Jarque–Bera normality tests showed the residuals in all specifications in levels to be non-normal. The explanation for this non-normality lies in the extreme skew observable in the distribution of intra-day forex spreads. It is in accord with the hypothesis that the relationship between volumes and spreads is of some non-linear form, as suggested by the dealer–spread model in chapter 3.

The separated regressions in the first two lines of table 5.5 indicate a standard error in 1992 about twice as large as that in 1989. This was confirmed by a Goldfeld–Quandt and a likelihood-ratio test for groupwise heteroscedasticity. The higher imprecision in 1992 could reflect the increased volatility of international financial markets. Statistically it might come from the higher correlation between volume and volatility observable for 1992 as compared to 1989. In contrast to former studies, all the following estimations are corrected for groupwise heteroscedasticity.

Another important observation is the apparent stability of parameter estimates, not only between different estimators but also over time. Estimates of the three structural parameters hardly differ in the two separate estimations for April 1989 and April 1992. A more formal covariance analysis to test for structural instabilities is reported in table 5.6 (upper row): A standard Chow test as well as tests on changes in a

---

[14] Strictly speaking, this test was not described in Mundlak's (1978) article. However, it follows directly from the specification chosen by him. For an exposition of the Hausman test see, for example, Greene (1993).

Table 5.5 *Panel estimations of the relationship between spreads, volumes and volatilities*

Estimation/ test	Intercept β_0 (t, t_{White})	Volume β_1 (t, t_{White})	Volatility β_2 (t, t_{White})	Adjusted R^2	Standard error of regression	White test [p-value]	Jarque–Bera normality test [p-value]
1989 (OLS)	1.817 (5.93, 9.34)	−0.034 (−1.21, −1.48)	0.415 (8.02, 15.24)	0.75	0.23	4.27 [0.51]	0.89 [0.64]
1992 (OLS)	1.810 (3.92, 4.86)	−0.031 (−0.81, −0.98)	0.414 (6.21, 6.67)	0.54	0.42	6.48 [0.26]	0.86 [0.65]
Total (OLS)	1.817 (7.35, 9.89)	−0.033 (−1.52, −1.72)	0.414 (10.53, 13.72)	0.94	0.97	5.53 [0.79]	0.22 [0.89]
Between (OLS)	1.789 (4.89, 6.77)	−0.039 (−1.23, −1.68)	0.430 (7.62, 9.23)	0.85	1.01	12.04 [0.21]	0.52 [0.77]
Within (OLS)	1.983 (4.47, 5.37)	−0.048 (−1.26, −0.96)	0.406 (4.88, 7.06)	0.99	0.33	13.79 [0.13]	1.18 [0.56]
Random effects model (FGLS)	1.834 (6.97, 8.50)	−0.038 (−1.68, −1.72)	0.420 (9.92, 12.26)	0.97	0.65	7.47 [0.59]	0.01 [1.00]
Test on indiv. effects [p-value]	$F_{19,19} = 3.156$ [0.01]						
Tests on corr. with expl.var. [p-values]	Mundlak test: $F_{3,49} = 0.018$ [1.00]		Hausman test: $\chi^2(3) = 0.342$ [0.95]				

Source: Reprinted from *Journal of International Money and Finance*, 17 (4), 'Do Reuters Spreads Reflect Currencies' Differences in Global Trading Activity?', table 2. © 1998, with permission of Elsevier Science.

single parameter, given that the others are constant over time, cannot reject the null hypothesis of structural stability. The extreme stability of parameters over the different panel techniques is particularly reassuring because of the limited size of the sample.

The third main result visible in table 5.5 is that the F-test on the absence of individual effects strongly rejects the null hypothesis ($F_{19,19} = 3.16$, level of significance below 1 per cent). Hence, one has to account for the fact that the intercepts for different currency pairs are different. Sources of this additional cross-sectional variation of bid–ask spreads could be omitted explanatory variables. For example, the predominance of conventional widths for absolute spreads in the Reuters system might explain part of this phenomenon. Complementary explanations may be related to different exchange rate regimes, the existence of capital controls, differences in the intensity of competition and the micro-structures in bilateral markets (unrelated to volumes and volatilities) or to measurement errors in (expected) volumes and volatilities. In any case, the presence of individual effects could cast some further doubt on former studies with a cross-section dimension, where they have been disregarded.

In order to decide whether one can work with the random-effects model, which leaves more degrees of freedom than the fixed-effects model, the Mundlak test is applied. A Fischer statistic of 0.18 leads us not to reject the null hypothesis, such that we can continue to work under the assumption that the individual effects are exogenous and apply the random-effects model. (The Hausman test supports this conclusion.) Furthermore, the result could indicate that the ignorance of individual effects in former studies might not have caused biases in parameter values but 'only' in standard errors and inference.

Now that we have found the right econometric specification we can focus on the estimated parameters. The first observation, already found in section 5.4 and in numerous earlier studies, is that the impact of exchange rate volatility on forex spreads is positive and strongly significant (significance level below 1 per cent). As expected, the volume parameter is negative, although at a lower level of significance. The two-tailed t-test of the hypothesis that it is equal to zero rejects the null at a significance level just below 10 per cent with usual or heteroscedasticity-consistent (White) standard errors. (In any case, neither a White nor a Breusch–Pagan heteroscedasticity test comes close to rejecting the null hypothesis of homoscedastic residuals.) However, since section 5.4, in conjunction with theoretical considerations, implies a strong prior in favour of a negative volume effect in this specification, a one-tailed t-test of the null that the volume parameter is greater than or equal to

Table 5.6 *Analysis of covariance for spread estimations*

Model	Chow test [*p*-value]	Test on const. intercept, other parameters const. [*p*-value]	Test on const. volume/ ticks parameter, other parameters const. [*p*-value]	Test on const. volatility parameter, other parameters const. [*p*-value]
Random effects model with volumes	$F_{3,49} = 0.017$ [1.00]	$F_{1,51} = 0.044$ [0.83]	$F_{1,51} = 0.048$ [0.83]	$F_{1,51} = 0.036$ [0.85]
Random effects model with ticks	$F_{3,46} = 0.083$ [0.97]	$F_{1,48} = 0.005$ [0.94]	$F_{1,48} = 0.001$ [0.98]	$F_{1,48} = 0.002$ [0.97]

Source: Reprinted from *Journal of International Money and Finance*, 17 (4), 'Do Reuters Spreads Reflect Currencies' Differences in Global Trading Activity?', table 3. © 1998, with permission of Elsevier Science.

zero may be considered more appropriate. This test rejects at 5 per cent significance.

In order to elaborate further on the source of the individual effects which emerged so strongly from the previous regressions, two other explanatory variables can be introduced, a dummy for fixed exchange rate regimes prevailing in bilateral markets and another dummy for the presence of capital controls for at least one of the currencies in a bilateral market.[15] With these extensions the broad picture still remains the same as before, in particular concerning the adequacy of the random effects specification. The absence of individual effects was still rejected, although – indeed – at a reduced level of significance. As might be expected, the exchange regime parameter had a negative and the capital control parameter a positive sign, but since both were clearly insignificant in the final specification and also produced multicollinearity problems we abstain from reporting further details here.[16]

In a final step we can extend the analysis to our second measure of trading volumes, Reuters FXFX and WXWY tick frequencies. Bollerslev and Domowitz (1993) conclude their paper by stressing 'the potential importance of extending existing literature to replace volume by quote generation activity in order to explain the theoretical link between market activity and the bid–ask spread'. However, Goodhart *et al.* (1996) have thrown some doubt on this claim by comparing half-hourly Reuters FXFX *quoted* data with half-hourly Reuters D2000-2 quoted and *transaction* data for dollar/mark over one day. They discover that D2000-2 *quotes* are a good predictor for D2000-2 *transaction frequency*. However, *FXFX* quotes are a poor predictor for *D2000-2* quoting frequency. From the discussion of tick frequencies in section 5.3 this result is not very surprising. But I conjecture that, although tick frequencies might not perform very well for ultra-high-frequency (intra-day) estimations, such as Bollerslev and Domowitz (1993) and Goodhart *et al.* (1996), it might still be a useful measure for longer time horizons. For example, in section 5.4 daily *unpredictable* quoting frequency was successfully used as an instrumental variable for unpredictable yen/dollar trading volume, and in the present panel dataset BIS volumes and Reuters ticks are strongly correlated.

Table 5.7 reports the main results of the same spread estimations as those shown in table 5.5, except that tick frequencies are now the measure of trading activity (or volume). Three observations had to be

---

[15] The relevant information can be extracted from the International Monetary Fund's report on exchange arrangements and exchange restrictions (IMF, 1990, 1993).

[16] For example, fixed exchange rate regimes will usually result in lower exchange rate volatility or smaller currencies are more likely to have capital controls.

Table 5.7 *Panel estimations of the relationship between spreads, ticks and volatilities*

Estimation/ test	Intercept β_0 (t, t_{White})	Ticks β_1 (t, t_{White})	Volatility β_2 (t, t_{White})	Adjusted R^2	Standard error of regression	White test [p-value]	Jarque–Bera normality test [p-value]
1989 (OLS)	1.784 (6.22, 11.27)	−0.032 (−1.40, −2.06)	0.427 (7.88, 13.84)	0.76	0.23	6.74 [0.24]	0.93 [0.63]
1992 (OLS)	1.774 (3.75, 5.10)	−0.031 (−0.52, −0.76)	0.427 (5.80, 5.85)	0.56	0.40	5.91 [0.32]	1.76 [0.41]
Total (OLS)	1.782 (7.84, 10.73)	−0.032 (−1.54, −2.19)	0.427 (10.29, 12.82)	0.94	0.97	4.49 [0.88]	0.27 [0.87]
Between (OLS)	1.792 (5.24, 7.00)	−0.041 (−1.39, −2.37)	0.438 (7.35, 8.72)	0.86	1.05	6.38 [0.70]	0.46 [0.80]
Within (OLS)	1.827 (4.49, 10.38)	−0.043 (−1.85, −3.06)	0.448 (5.22, 8.15)	0.99	0.30	9.55 [0.39]	0.43 [0.81]
Random effects model (FGLS)	1.805 (7.42, 12.10)	−0.039 (−1.99, −2.85)	0.434 (9.60, 15.66)	0.97	0.61	6.56 [0.68]	0.69 [0.71]

Test on indiv. effects [p-value]: $F_{16,16} = 2.892$ [0.02]

Tests on corr. with expl.var. [p-values]: Mundlak test: $F_{3,46} = 0.059$ [0.98]   Hausman test: $\chi^2(3)=1.201$ [0.75] removed from the original dataset, because they showed extremely large residuals in preliminary estimations: For example, the tick frequencies for USD/PTE (Portuguese *escudo*) and USD/SKE (Swedish *kroner*) in April 1992 were clearly erratic. In the former case one bank was quoting steadily in very short time intervals, in the latter case two banks seem to have entered a 'quoting war'; in both cases quoting was obviously unrelated to trading activity. Similar problems appeared for USD/MYR (Malaysian *ringgit*) in April 1989. Fifty-two observations remain, twenty-one for April 1989 and thirty-one for April 1992.

The results are extremely similar to those with BIS volumes and, therefore, confirm both the findings in the preceding spread estimations as well as the usefulness of Reuters ticks as a measure of trading volumes for longer time horizons. Increases in (expected) tick frequencies reduce forex spreads, an effect which seems to be quite significant from table 5.7. As one can see from the bottom row of table 5.6, the structural parameters are, again, stable over time.

The main conclusion from this section is that the long-run effect of market size on bid–ask spreads in the forex market seems to be negative. This is exactly what one should have expected from the short-run time-series regressions in section 5.4.

5.6   Conclusions

The main aim of this chapter has been to test whether one of the crucial elements of the theory of (national and) international money is empirically valid. As discussed *in extenso* in chapters 2 and 3, and as applied to international currency competition in chapter 4, a key theoretical hypothesis is that there are economies of scale or network externalities in the use of media of exchange. This presumption can hold only if increased trading volume of a currency leads to a reduction in its exchange costs in the long run. The empirical test was performed by various estimates of the relationship between trading volumes and bid–ask spreads in the forex market, and with this approach substantial evidence in favour of the network externality hypothesis was found.

Another aim of the chapter has been to test the implications of the three main financial market micro-structure theories – order-processing cost models, inventory-cost models and information-cost models – for the determination of forex bid–ask spreads and, related to the network externality hypothesis, by these means to solve the puzzle of the spread–volume relationship in empirical financial market micro-structure analysis. Building on the idea of Bessembinder (1994) that trading volume may have a differential impact on spreads in the short run, section 5.2 argued that unpredictable volume or volatility should increase spreads, owing to information-cost effects, and predictable volume should decrease spreads, owing to order-processing-cost effects. Inventory-cost effects imply a positive relationship between predictable volatility and spreads.

After a survey of the previous empirical spread literature and of sources for trading volumes in section 5.3, considerable evidence for the presence of all three effects could be provided with a unique eight-year-long time series of dollar/yen spot forex data and a short panel of forex data for many currency pairs. In particular, the short-term differential effect of trading volumes on spreads in the time series could be reconciled with an unambiguously negative effect of trading volumes on spreads in the long run (confirming network effects in currency uses). Moreover, unpredictable and predictable Reuters quoting ('tick') frequencies turned out to be good measures of the rate of information arrival at a daily time horizon and of (predictable) trading volume at a monthly time horizon. This contrasts with the high-frequency literature, which has questioned the usefulness of Reuters ticks.

6   General conclusions

> A remarkable movement is going on in the world towards a uniformity
> of coinage between different nations ... Ultimately the world will see
> one *code de commerce*, and one money as the symbol of it. We are, as
> yet, very distant from so perfect an age.   *(Walter Bagehot, 1868)*

In this volume I have studied the phenomenon of international currencies
from two different angles. First I explained some key elements of this
phenomenon, mostly with the means of financial market micro-structure
analysis, both theoretically and empirically (analytical chapters 3 and 5).
Secondly, I brought this approach together with the more traditional
macroeconomic analyses of international currencies and institutional
considerations in order to examine what might be the effect of European
Economic and Monetary Union (EMU) on the international use of the
three main currencies – the dollar, the yen and the euro (the successor to
the mark, chapter 4). Chapter 1 explained the choice of subject matter
with academic reasons (understanding better an under-researched area),
political reasons (the implications of the internationalization of the euro
for international monetary and financial policy coordination) and also
business reasons (the importance of euro internationalization for many
banks and other financial firms). Chapter 2 surveyed the research field of
international money and the previous theoretical, historical and empirical literature.

   In this short concluding chapter I shall briefly summarize the main
results of the book and draw some tentative conclusions leading to more
far-reaching issues which had to be left outside the primary scope of the
present study. I have organized this final summary and outlook in three
sections. Section 6.1 will summarize the results on international currency
use after EMU and will draw some policy conclusions. Section 6.2
sketches the main findings for the theory of international money in
general and section 6.3 those for foreign exchange (forex) market micro-
structure analysis. In both these sections conclusions are drawn about

the areas in which the results, in my view, make additional future research efforts desirable.

6.1   International monetary and financial policies

The main findings and predictions from the discussion of EMU's impact on international currency uses are: (1) The euro is extremely likely to jump virtually immediately (no later than the end of EMU stage IIIA) to no. 2 in the international 'order' of currencies on practically all dimensions of international money, starting at least slightly above the current level of the Deutsche mark (in relative terms). It will be in advance of the Japanese yen but still well behind the US dollar. (2) After this small initial jump (from the mark to the euro) the single currency will experience a gradual extension of its role closing part of the gap to the dollar, but from the analysis undertaken above it appears very unlikely that it can fully catch up with, or even overtake, the US currency's present dominant role at any time in the near future (say, during the first decade of the new millenium). (3) In international financial markets this expansionary path can be quicker than in foreign trade invoicing, for example. But given the still relatively segmented state of European financial markets and the prospects for their further integration and development after the currency changeover, it does not appear likely that they can reach the depth and breadth of US securities markets in the immediate future. (4) This argument would gain strength if the United Kingdom decided definitely to stay out of monetary union. In fact, the UK seems to be the only non-core country whose participation, or not, in EMU would make an important difference for the euro, not only because of London's role as a leading international financial centre but also because the pound sterling is still one of the most used currencies in international trade and investment after the dollar, the mark and, perhaps, the yen. (5) With or without the UK, most early external euro growth will take place in the neighbouring non-EMU European countries, including Central and Eastern Europe (CEE), and in the Southern and Eastern part of the Mediterranean. This trend will be strengthened if these countries gear their exchange rate arrangements towards the euro. Some euro expansion can also be expected in trade and investment with Asia. (6) Whereas most euro growth is likely to occur at the expense of the US dollar, the prospects for the yen to develop a stronger international role (apart from the arithmetic relative gain through EMU) are not very strong. However, if the Asian crises, including Japan's considerable problems in the banking sector, can be overcome relatively rapidly and if Asian policy-makers decide in the aftermath of these crises to establish new exchange arrangements away from the dollar towards a strong pegging role for the yen, the Japanese currency could at least develop a stronger regional role than has been the case so far. At least for a quite significant period of time after EMU, international currency structures will still remain hierarchical, although less so than previously.

One implication of the *gradual* expansion of the euro predicted above is that, *ceteris paribus*, a monetary targeting strategy by the European Central Bank (ECB), if considered desirable for reasons outside the scope of this book, need not be rendered impossible through international influences on the intermediate targets shortly after the changeover. However, given the growing international attractiveness of European financial markets over time, even though gradual, the EMI/ECB will be well advised to also prepare the option of inflation targeting in order to be able to switch to this approach when euro internationalization is further advanced and monetary targets become more volatile.

Another implication of the path predicted for the euro is that fundamental adjustments of the international monetary and financial policy coordination and of the refinancing and governance structures of the International Monetary Fund (IMF) may, perhaps, be politically justified by the enhanced domestic monetary habitat of the euro and by the special structure of intra-EMU monetary and fiscal policy-making institutions, but not necessarily immediately through a dominant role for the euro in world trade and financial markets. This fact, together with obstacles of a political nature, may rather lead to transitory interim arrangements for the first years after January 1999, instead of a full-scale reform of international monetary policy coordination. The same principle could apply to the current arrangements for banking and financial market supervision and crisis management.

However, as the recent Asian crises have underlined and as Europe's larger Continental banks grow more hungry for external markets, this latter fact may already be more problematic, in the short run. Although somewhat independent of monetary union in Europe, the current Asian crises have provoked much criticism of current multilateral arrangements for surveillance and international policy coordination. Asian policy-makers have expressed their desire for more regional arrangements of surveillance and, if necessary, emergency lending, for example; this factor could lead to a weakening of the coordinating bodies on the global level, although it is much too early to make any predictions. The undoubtedly increased world influence of the EU through monetary union and subsequent euro internationalization is likely to advance in smaller steps, not in a sudden and major leap forward.

6.2   Theory of international money

The theory developed in chapter 3 dwelt on forex vehicle currencies, not only a pivotal function of international money but also the only case of a strictly market-based emergence of media of exchange on a large scale in modern times. Within the framework chosen it turned out that: (1) Currencies with high (predictable) trading volume and low (predictable) short-term exchange rate volatilities are most likely to emerge as media of exchange (vehicles) in the spot forex market. Hence, countries which maintain a dominant role in international trade and investment (which often is, but need not be, congruent with domestic size) are also likely to experience the internationalization of their currencies, as long as their exchange rates are not excessively volatile. The important role of risk, in the form of volatility, has been widely disregarded in most of the theoretical literature on international currencies. (2) The negative long-run volume effect on spreads results in network externalities (or economies of scale) in vehicle use and, therefore, in an element of circularity in the currency exchange structure. (3) With some imperfection in inter-dealer competition, there can be multiple equilibria for the same set of exogenous variables or multiple vehicle currencies in equilibrium, which can exhibit the hierarchical relationships observed in history. (4) Uniformly high exchange rate volatility can lead to a forex 'barter' equilibrium, without any exchange medium at all. (5) Depending on the size and nature of shocks hitting the international monetary system, regime shifts from one dominant international currency to another, for example, can be both gradual or 'catastrophic', and once-dominant currencies can maintain their position, although the respective country's role in international trade and investment may have ceased.

The present theory has explained the internationalization of currencies through the interaction of size (volume) and risk, in the form of exchange rate volatility, the two main determinants of transaction costs in the forex market. Although not explicitly derived through a formal model on this occasion, very similar factors play an analogous role for other international money functions, such as for foreign trade vehicles. As discussed in chapter 2, investment-currency theory enters another dimension of risk, namely correlation. My theory (in conjunction with the empirical results on the spread–volume relationship) favours concentration of currency use through network externalities, and potential countervailing forces through volatility are relatively weak. The decentralizing forces could be strengthened through the introduction of investors ('speculators'), who can put their money in several currencies at the same time. To the extent that exchange rate correlations are smaller than 1, this could lead to diversification, a more decentralized structure of currency uses, partly feeding back into forex turnovers.

Having said this, I consider it desirable if international currency theory in the future integrated these two approaches in a single model. Such a model could show the potential friction between the medium-of-exchange function and the store-of-value function which can emerge through currency competition, described intuitively in chapter 2, section 2.2, in a more rigorous way. It may well turn out that such an approach would identify another source of bias in international portfolio investment, in addition to the well known home-currency bias.

Another area of international currency theory, which is in my view in urgent need of further analysis, has to do with the welfare effects of currency internationalization. In particular, a major source of international 'seigniorage' may be related to investment currency use. The more foreign investors demand one country's bonds, so goes the argument, the lower the domestic interest rates will be, stimulating domestic investment and growth. Is this effect robust in a general framework? Is it empirically important, as compared to the often highlighted transaction-cost effects of more liquid domestic financial markets? Can the welfare effects of the frequently mentioned constraints on domestic macroeconomic policies through currency internationalization be theoretically clarified and measured?

6.3   Forex market micro-structure analysis

This book has added a financial market micro-structure perspective to the study of international currencies. By tackling different points of interest for the mechanisms of currency internationalization, I had to go deeper into forex micro-structure analysis, which I did to a large extent empirically.

The most important result of this book for market micro-structure analysis is, perhaps, a reconciliation of the contradictory or inconclusive results in the previous literature on the volume-spread relationship. It can be shown that the effect of daily predictable trading volumes on spreads is strongly negative, while the effect of daily unpredictable volumes is strongly positive. The former effect results from the order-processing costs of market-making, whereas the latter effect results from information-cost effects. However, when volume data are aggregated over a longer time horizon, such as a month, the unpredictable component cancels out and only the negative long-run 'liquidity' effect of trading volume remains. In order to find statistically significant results on these effects, it was necesary to scrutinize thoroughly the available data on volumes, and also on spreads. One important finding from this scrutiny and subsequent estimates was that Reuters quoting (tick) frequency is a surprisingly well performing measure for daily or monthly forex trading activity. Another finding is an intertemporal clustering phenomenon in the variability of daily trading volumes similar to that observable for daily price returns (conditional heteroscedasticity).

This latter result leads immediately to the suggestion to test Reuters ticks as a proxy for trading volumes in intra-day analyses of the volume–spread and the volume–volatility relationships. In particular, since unpredictable ticks performed extremely well as a measure of the daily rate of information flow, it might be worthwhile linking this with explicit news items on the Reuters screens. While ticks will be inappropriate for ultra-short-term horizons, such as several minutes (Goodhart *et al.*, 1996), it could perform well for an hourly or two-hourly frequency, even more so with Reuters' introduction of RICS, where more banks feed in more quotes more quickly.

A second area for future micro-structure research emerges from the theoretical study of currency exchange structures in chapter 3 and the ample evidence provided for them in chapter 4 section 4.2. In particular, these exchange structures can be used to enhance our understanding of the information transmission through financial market prices. For example, when there are three currencies A, B and C, and C is known to be a vehicle currency, then – depending on the type of shock/information arrival – changes in the AC and BC exchange rates can be expected to lead the changes in the cross-rate AB (de Jong *et al.*, 1996, advanced a first interesting econometric study along these lines). Needless to say, tests of this particular and other hypotheses are even more promising with real transactions data, along the lines of Lyons' (1995, 1996) work, in particular if broader data sets could be collected.

Finally, in the last couple of years considerable changes in the trading infrastructure of forex markets have taken place. The changes mainly relate to the adoption of electronic trading systems, in particular continuous auction automated brokering services, through which significant volumes are now channelled (BIS, 1996). These new techniques affect the micro-structure of forex markets and their impact also deserves further scrutiny. All these efforts can be seen in the light of the long-term aim to finally find more satisfactory explanations for the causes and amplitude of exchange rate fluctuations.

Bibliography

Adler, M., Dumas, B. (1983). 'International portfolio choice and corporation finance: a synthesis', *Journal of Finance*, 38, 925–84

Agmon, T. and Barnea, A. (1977). 'Transaction costs and marketability services in the eurocurrency money market', *Journal of Monetary Economics*, 3(3), 359–66

Alchian, A. (1977). 'Why money?', *Journal of Money, Credit, and Banking*, 9(1), 133–40

Aliber, R. (1966). *The Future of the Dollar as an International Currency* (New York: Praeger)

(ed.), (1969). *The International Market for Foreign Exchange* (New York: Praeger)

Allen, P. (1986). 'The ecu: birth of a new currency', *Group of Thirty Occasional Papers*, 20 (New York)

(1993). 'Transactions use of the ecu in the transition to EMU: a model of network externalities', *Récherches Economiques de Louvain*, 59(1–2), 155–76

Allen, W. (1977). 'A note on uncertainty, transaction costs and interest parity', *Journal of Monetary Economics*, 3(3), 367–73

Alogoskoufis, G. and Portes, R. (1991). 'International costs and benefits from EMU', *European Economy*, Special edition, 1, 231–45

(1992). 'European monetary union and international currencies in a tripolar world', in Canzoneri, M., Grilli, V. and Masson, P. (eds.), *Establishing a Central Bank – Issues in Europe and Lessons from the US* (Cambridge: Cambridge University Press), 273–301

(1997). 'The euro, the dollar and the international monetary system', paper presented at the IMF Conference 'EMU and the International Monetary System' (Washington, DC) (17–18 March)

Amihud, Y. and Mendelson, H. (1982). 'Asset price behavior in a dealership market', *Financial Analysts Journal* (May–June), 50–9

Andersen, B. (1992). 'Survey of the Danish foreign-exchange market, April 1992', *Danmarks Nationalbank Monetary Review* (November), 14–19

Andersen, T. (1994). 'Stochastic autoregressive volatility: a framework for volatility modeling', *Mathematical Finance*, 4, 75–102

Andersen, T. and Bollerslev, T. (1994). 'Intra-day seasonality and volatility persistence in foreign exchange and equity markets', Northwestern University, Kellogg Graduate School of Management, mimeo

Andrews, D. (1991). 'Heteroskedasticity and autocorrelation consistent covariance matrix estimation', *Econometrica*, 59(3), 817–58

Arrowsmith, J. (1996). 'Pitfalls on the path to a single European currency', *EUI Working Paper*, 96/21, European University Institute (Florence) (May)

Bagehot, W. (1868). 'A universal money', in Bagehot, W. and St John-Stevas, N. *The Collected Works of Walter Bagehot* (London: The Economist, 1978), 57–104

Bagehot, W. (pseud., 1971). 'The only game in town', *Financial Analysts Journal*, 27(2), 12–14, 22

Bagehot, W. and St. John-Stevas, N. (1978). *The Collected Works of Walter Bagehot: The Economic Essays*, vol. 9–11 (London: The Economist)

Bahrain Monetary Agency (1992). 'Foreign exchange trading in Bahrain' (Manama)

Baillie, R. and Bollerslev, T. (1989). 'The message in daily exchange rates: a conditional variance tail', *Journal of Business and Economic Statistics*, 7(3), 297–305

Banca d'Italia (1990). 'Turnover on the foreign exchange market', *Economic Bulletin*, 10 (February), 51–5

(1993). 'Turnover on the foreign exchange market', *Economic Bulletin*, 16, (February), 65–9

Bank for International Settlements (BIS) (1990). *Survey of Foreign Exchange Market Activity* (Basle) (February)

(1993). *Central Bank Survey of Foreign Exchange Market Activity in April 1992* (Basle) (March)

(1996). *Central Bank Survey of Foreign Exchange and Derivatives Market Activity 1995* (Basle) (May)

(1997a). *67th Annual Report (Basle) (June)*

(1997b). *International Banking and Financial Market Developments (Basle) (August)*

Bank of Japan (1989). 'Summary of results of the Tokyo foreign exchange market turnover survey conducted in April 1989 by the Bank of Japan', press release (14 September) (Tokyo)

(1993). 'Summary of results of the Tokyo foreign exchange market turnover survey', *Bank of Japan Quarterly Bulletin* (February), 37–45

Banque de France (1989). 'Enquète sur le marché des changes de Paris', press release 89–23 (6 November) (Paris)

Baron, D. (1976). 'Fluctuating exchange rates and the pricing of exports', *Economic Inquiry*, 14, 425–38

Baumol, W. (1952). 'The transaction demand for money: an inventory theoretic approach', *Quarterly Journal of Economics*, 66, 545–56

Baumol, W., Panzer, J. and Willig, R. (1982). *Contestable Markets* (New York: Harcourt Brace Jovanovich)

Bénassy, A. and Deusy-Fournier, P. (1994). 'La concurrence pour le statut de monnaie internationale', *Economie Internationale*, 59(3), 107–44

Bénassy, A., Italianer, A. and Pisani-Ferry, J. (1994). 'The external implications of the single currency', *Economie et Statistique*, Special issue, 9–22

Bénassy-Quéré, A. (1996). 'Potentialities and opportunities of the euro as an international currency', *Document du Travail*, Centre d'Etudes Prospectives et d'Informations Internationales, 96–09 (Paris) (August)

Bénassy-Quéré, A., Mojon, B. and Pisani-Ferry, J. (1997). 'The euro and exchange rate stability', paper presented at the IMF Conference 'EMU and the International Monetary System' (Washington, DC) (17–18 March)

Bera, A. and Jarque, C. (1980). 'Efficient tests for normality, heteroscedasticity, and serial independence of regression residuals', *Economics Letters*, 6, 255–9

Bergquist, R. (1990). 'Foreign exchange markets in April 1989 – a global study', *Quarterly Review*, Sveriges Riksbank, 1, 24–31

(1993). 'The foreign exchange market in April 1992', *Quarterly Review*, Sveriges Riksbank, 4, 5–12

Bergsten, F. (1997). 'The impact of the euro on exchange rates and international policy cooperation', paper presented at the IMF Conference 'EMU and the International Monetary System' (Washington, DC) (17–18 March)

Bergsten, F. and Henning, R. (1996). 'Global economic leadership and the Group of Seven', Institute for International Economics (Washington) (June)

Bessembinder, H. (1994). 'Bid–ask spreads in the interbank foreign exchange markets', *Journal of Financial Economics*, 35(3), 317–48

Bilson, J. (1983). 'The choice of an invoice currency in international transactions', in Bhandari, J. and Putnam, B. (eds.), *Economic Interdependence and Flexible Exchange Rates* (Cambridge, MA: MIT Press), 384–401

Bingham, G. (1991). 'Foreign exchange markets: structure, intervention and liquidity', *de Pecunia*, 3(2), 85–121

(1992). 'Foreign exchange markets', in Newman, P. *et al.* (eds.), *The New Palgrave Dictionary of Money and Finance*, vol. 2 (New York: Stockton Press), 155–57

Black, S. (1985). 'International money and international monetary arrangements', in Kenen, P. and Jones, R. (eds.), *Handbook of International Economics*, vol. 2 (Amsterdam: North-Holland), 1153–93

(1990). 'The international use of currencies', in Suzuki, Y., Miyake, J. and Okabe, M. (eds.), *The Evolution of the International Monetary System* (Tokyo: University of Tokyo Press), 175–94

(1991). 'Transactions costs and vehicle currencies', *Journal of International Money and Finance*, 10(4), 512–27

Bloch, M. (1954). *Esquisse d'une Histoire Monétaire de l'Europe* (Paris: A. Colin)

Bloomberg News (1997). 'Japan in Asian talks to raise yen's status', *International Herald Tribune* (October 16, 1997)

Bollerslev, T. (1986). 'Generalized autoregressive conditional heteroscedasticity', *Journal of Econometrics*, 31, 307–27

Bollerslev, T., Chou, R. and Kroner, K. (1992). 'ARCH modeling in finance – a review of the theory and empirical evidence', *Journal of Econometrics*, 52, 5–59

Bollerslev, T. and Domowitz, I. (1993). 'Trading patterns and prices in the interbank foreign exchange market', *Journal of Finance*, 48(4), 1421–43

Bollerslev, T. and Melvin, M. (1994). 'Bid–ask spreads and volatility in the foreign exchange market: an empirical analysis', *Journal of International Economics*, 36(3–4), 355–72

Booth, L. (1984). 'Bid–ask spreads in the market for forward exchange', *Journal of International Money and Finance*, 3(2), 209–22

Boothe, P. (1988). 'Exchange rate risk and the bid–ask spread: a seven-country comparison', *Economic Inquiry*, 26(3), 485–92

Bourguinat, H. (1985). 'La concurrence des monnaies véhiculaires – vers le polycentrisme monétaire?', in *Croissance, échange et monnaie en économie internationale – Mélanges en l'honneur de Monsieur le Professeur Jean Weiller* (Paris: Economica), 434–64

Brand, D. (1993). 'Currency substitution in developing countries: theory and empirical analysis for Latin America and Eastern Europe', Ifo Institute for Economic Research (Munich)

Branson, W. and Hendersen, D. (1984). 'The specification and influence of asset markets', in Jones, R. and Kenen, P. (eds.), *Handbook of International Economics*, vol. 2 (Amsterdam: North-Holland), 749–805

Brunner, K. and Meltzer, A. (1971). 'The uses of money: money in the theory of an exchange economy', *American Economic Review*, 61, 784–805

Buerkle, T. (1996). 'EU agrees to form new currency grid and cements EMU', *International Herald Tribune* (April 15) 13, 15

Bufman, G. and Leiderman, L. (1992). 'Simulating an optimizing model of currency substitution', *Revista de Analisis Economico*, 7, 109–24

Calvo, G. and Végh, C. (1992). 'Currency substitution in developing countries: an introduction', *Revista de Analisis Economico*, Special issue, 7(1), 3–28

Campbell, J. and Perron, P. (1991). 'Pitfalls and opportunities: what macroeconomists should know about unit roots', *NBER Macroeconomics Annual* (Cambridge, MA: NBER)

Canto, V. and Nickelsburg, G. (1987). *Currency Substitution – Theory and Evidence from Latin America* (Dordrecht: Kluwer Academic)

Carse, S. and Wood, G. (1979). 'Currency of invoicing and forward covering: risk-reducing techniques in British foreign trade', in Martin, J. and Smith, A. (eds.), *Trade and Payments Adjustments under Flexible Exchange Rates* (London: Macmillan), 174–96

Chrystal, A. (1977). 'Demand for international media of exchange', *American Economic Review*, 67(5), 840–50

(1979). 'Some evidence in defense of the vehicle currency hypothesis', *Economics Letters*, 3, 267–70

(1984). 'On the theory of international money', Black, J. and Dorrance, G. (eds.), *Problems of International Finance* (New York: St Martin's Press,) 77–92

Cipolla, C. (1956). *Money, Prices, and Civilization in the Mediterranean World* (London)

Clark, P. (1973). 'A subordinated stochastic process model with finite variance for speculative prices', *Econometrica*, 41(1), 135–55

Close, N. and Duenwald, C. (1992). 'Survey of the Canadian foreign exchange market', *Bank of Canada Review* (October) 23–35

Clower, R. (1968). 'A reconsideration of the microfoundations of monetary theory', *Western Economic Journal*, 6(1), 1–8

Cohen, B. (1971). *The Future of Sterling as an International Currency* (London: Macmillan)

(1992). 'Sterling area', in Newman, P. *et al.* (eds.), *The New Palgrave Dictionary of Money and Finance*, vol. 3 (New York: Stockton Press), 554–5

(1993). 'Beyond EMU: the problem of sustainability', *Economics and Politics*, 5(2), 187–203

(1994). 'The geography of money – currency relations among sovereign states', *Document de travail de l'OFCE*, 94–07 (Paris: OECD)

Cohen, D. (1997). 'How will the euro behave?', *CEPR Discussion Paper*, 1673 (July)

Cooper, R. (1972). 'Eurodollars, reserve dollars, and asymmetries in the international monetary system', *Journal of International Economics*, 2(4), 325–44

Copeland, T. and Galai, D. (1983). 'Information effects on the bid–ask spread', *Journal of Finance*, 38(5), 1457–69

Cuddington, J. (1983). 'Currency substitutability, capital mobility, and money demand', *Journal of International Money and Finance*, 2, 111–33

Dacorogna, M., Müller, U., Nagler, R., Olsen, R. and Pictet, O. (1993). 'A geographical model for the daily and weekly seasonal volatility in the foreign exchange market', *Journal of International Money and Finance*, 12, 413–38

Davé, R. (1993). 'Statistical correlation of data frequency, price change, and spread', Olsen & Associates, Internal Document, RDD.1993–04–26 (Zurich) (April)

Dawkins, W. (1996). 'The yen in Asia: a currency for business', *Financial Times* (23 March 1996), III

de Boissieu, C. (1988). 'Concurrence entre monnaies et polycentrisme monétaire', in Fair, D. and de Boissieu, C. (eds.), *International Monetary and Financial Integration: The European Dimension* (Dordrecht: Kluwer Academic), 187–208

de Grauwe, P. (1989). *International Money: Post-war Trends and Theories* (Oxford: Oxford University Press)

de Jong, F., Nijman, T. and Röell, A. (1995). 'A comparison of the cost of trading French shares on the Paris Bourse and on SEAQ International', *European Economic Review*, 39(7), 1277–1301

de Jong, F., Mahieu, R. and Schotman, P. (1996). 'Price discovery in the foreign exchange market: an empirical analysis of the yen/Dmark rate', *LIFE Working Paper*, WP-96–38, University of Limburg, Maastricht (August)

de Macedo, J., Goldstein, J. and Meerschwam, D. (1984). 'International portfolio diversification: short-term assets and gold', in Bilson, J. and Marston, R. (eds.), *Exchange Rate Theory and Practice* (Chicago: Chicago University Press), 199–238

Demos, A. and Goodhart, C. (1992). 'The interaction between the frequency of market quotations, spread, and volatility in the foreign exchange market', London School of Economics, *Financial Markets Group Discussion Papers*, 152 (October)

Demsetz, H. (1960). 'The problem of social cost', *Journal of Law and Economics*, 3, 1–4

(1968). 'The cost of transacting', *Quarterly Journal of Economics*, 82(1), 33–53

de Nederlandsche Bank (1989). 'Survey of turnover in the foreign exchange market of banks in the Netherlands', press release (Amsterdam) (13 September)

(1992). 'Survey of turnover in the foreign exchange market of banks in the Netherlands in April 1992', press release (Amsterdam) (24 September)

Dennert, J. (1993). 'Price competition between market makers', *Review of Economic Studies*, 60(3), 735–51

Denton, N. (1996). 'Banks plan clearing house for trade in emerging market debt', *Financial Times* (10 July), 20

Despres, E., Kindleberger, C. and Salant, W. (1966). 'The dollar and world liquidity: a minority view' (Washington, DC); reprinted in Kindleberger, C. (1981) *International Money – A Collection of Essays* (London: Allen & Unwin), 42–52

Deusy-Fournier, P. (1995). 'L'UEM et la cohérence du polycentrisme monétaire', unpublished doctoral thesis, Université de Paris X–Nanterre (Paris)

Deutsche Bundesbank (1991). 'The significance of the Deutsche mark as an invoicing currency in foreign trade', *Monthly Report*, 43(11), 40–4

  (1997). 'The role of the Deutsche mark as an international investment and reserve currency', *Monthly Report*, 49(4), 17–30

Diamond, P. (1982). 'Aggregate demand management in search equilibrium', *Journal of Political Economy*, 90, 881–94

Dolado, J., Jenkinson, T. and Sosvilla-Rivero, S. (1990). 'Cointegraton and unit roots', *Journal of Economic Surveys*, 4(3), 249–73

Dominguez, K. (1997). 'The dollar exposure of Japanese companies', University of Michigan, mimeo

Dominguez, K. and J. Frankel (1993) 'Does foreign exchange intervention work?' (Washington, DC: Institute for International Economics) (September)

Dooley, M., Lizondo, J. and Mathieson, D. (1989). 'The currency composition of foreign exchange reserves', *IMF Staff Papers*, 36, 385–434

Dormont, B. (1989). 'Introduction à l'économétrie des données de panel', *Monographies d'économétrie*, Centre National de la Recherche Scientifique (Paris)

Dornbusch, R. (1983). 'Real interest rates, home goods, and optimal external borrowing', *Journal of Political Economy*, 91, 141–53

Dowd, K. and Greenaway, D. (1993). 'Currency competition, network externalities and switching costs: towards an alternative view of optimum currency areas', *Economic Journal*, 103, 1180–89

Dumas, B. (1984). 'Comment', in Bilson, J. and Marston, R. (eds.), *Exchange Rate Theory and Practice* (Chicago: Chicago University Press), 232–6

  (1994). 'Partial equilibrium versus general equilibrium models of the international capital markets', in van der Ploeg, F. (ed.), *The Handbook of International Macroeconomics* (Oxford: Blackwell), 301–47

  (1996). 'Comment on Philippe Jorion's "Risk and turnover in the foreign exchange market"', in Frankel, J., Galli, G. and Giovannini, A., *The Microstructure of Foreign Exchange Markets* (Chicago: University of Chicago Press), 37–40

Easley, D. and O'Hara, M. (1992a). 'Adverse selection and large trade volume: the implications for market efficiency', *Journal of Financial and Quantitative Analysis*, 27(2), 185–208

  (1992b). 'Time and the process of security price adjustment', *Journal of Finance*, 47(2), 577–605

ECU Institute (ed.) (1995). 'International currency competition and the future role of the single European currency', final report of the working group 'European Monetary Union – International Monetary System' (London: Kluwer Law International)

Eichengreen, B. (1987) 'Hegemonic stability theories in the international monetary system', *Brookings Discussion Paper in International Economics*, 54 (Washington, DC) (February)

  (1997). 'The euro as a reserve currency', University of California at Berkeley, mimeo

Eichengreen, B. and Bayoumi, T. (1996). 'Is Asia an optimum currency area? Can it become one? Regional, global and historical perspectives on Asian monetary relations', University of California at Berkeley, Center for International and Development Studies, *Working Paper*, C96–081 (December)

Eichengreen, B. and Frankel, J. (1996). 'The SDR, reserve currencies, and the future of the international monetary system', in Mussa, M. *et al.* (eds.), *The Future of the SDR in the Light of Changes in the International Financial System* (Washington, DC: International Monetary Fund), 337–78

Einzig, P. (1970). *The History of Foreign Exchange*, 2nd edn (London: Macmillan)

Eldor, R., Pines, D. and Schwartz, A. (1988). 'Home asset preferences and productivity shocks', *Journal of International Economics*, 25, 165–76

Emerson, M., Gros, D., Italianer, A., Pisani-Ferry, J. and Reichenbach, H. (1991). *One Market, One Money* (Oxford: Oxford University Press)

Emerson, M. and Huhne, C. (1993). *L'ecu* (Paris: Economica)

Epps, T. and Epps, M. (1976). 'The stochastic dependence of securities market price changes and transaction volume: implications for the mixture-of-distributions hypothesis', *Econometrica*, 44, 305–21

Errunza, V. and Losq, E. (1989). 'Capital flow controls, international asset pricing, and investors' welfare: a multi-country framework', *Journal of Finance*, 44, 1025–37

European Commission (1997). 'The impact of the introduction of the euro on capital markets ('Giovannini Report') (Brussels) (July)

European Council (1992). 'Treaty on European Union ('Maastricht Treaty')' (Brussels)

  (1995). 'Conclusions of the Spanish presidency' (Brussels) (December)

European Monetary Institute (EMI) (1997). 'The single monetary policy in stage three: specification of the operational framework' (Frankfurt) (January)

Fama, E. (1980). 'Banking in the theory of finance', *Journal of Monetary Economics*, 6, 39–57

Farrel, J. and Saloner, G. (1986). 'Installed base and compatibility: innovation, product preannouncments and predation', *American Economic Review*, 76, 940–55

Federal Reserve Bank of New York (1989). 'Summary of results of the US foreign exchange market survey conducted in April 1989', press release (New York) (13 September)

  (1992). 'Summary of results of the US foreign exchange market turnover survey conducted in April 1992 by the Federal Reserve Bank of New York' (New York)

Feenstra, R. (1986). 'Functional equivalence between liquidity costs and the utility of money', *Journal of Monetary Economics*, 17, 271–91

Filosa, R. (1995). 'Money demand stability and currency substitution in six European countries (1980–1992)', *BIS Working Paper*, 30 (Basle) (November)

Fischer, S. (1974). 'Money and the production function', *Economic Inquiry*, 12(4), 517–33

Fisher, D. (1989). 'The market in foreign exchange in London', *Bank of England Quarterly Bulletin* (November) 531–5

Flandreau, M. (1995). *L'or du monde – La France et la stabilité du système monétaire international 1848–1873* (Paris: L'Harmattan)

Fleming, M. (1997). 'The round-the-clock market for US treasury securities', *Federal Reserve Bank of New York Economic Policy Review* (July), 9–32

Flood, M. (1991). 'Microstructure theory and the foreign exchange market', *Federal Reserve Bank of St Louis Economic Review* (November/December), 52–70

Folkerts-Landau, D. and Garber, P. (1992). 'The European Central Bank: a bank or a monetary policy rule?', in Canzoneri, M., Grilli, V. and Masson, P. (eds.), *Establishing a Central Bank: Issues in Europe and Lessons from the US* (Cambridge: Cambridge University Press), 86–110

Folkerts-Landau, D., Garber, P. and Schoenmaker, D. (1996). 'The reform of wholesale payment systems and its impact on financial markets', *Group of Thirty Occasional Paper*, 51 (Washington, DC)

Fosgard, H. (1989). 'Turnover in the foreign-exchange market', *Danmarks Nationalbank Monetary Review* (November) 8–11

Foster, D. and Vishwanathan, S. (1995). 'Can speculative trading explain the volume–volatility relation?', *Journal of Business and Economic Statistics*, 13(4), 379–96

Frankel, J. (1992). 'Dollar', in Newman, P. *et al.* (eds.), *The New Palgrave Dictionary of Money and Finance*, vol. 1 (New York: Stockton Press), 696–702

(1993). 'Is Japan creating a yen bloc in East Asia and the Pacific?', in Frankel, J. and Kahler, M. (eds.), *Regionalism and Rivalry, Japan and the United States in Pacific Asia* (Chicago: University of Chicago Press), 53–85

(1995). 'Still the lingua franca: the exaggerated death of the dollar', *Foreign Affairs*, 74(4), 9–16

(1996). 'Exchange rates and the single currency', in Steil, B. (ed.), *The European Equity Markets: The State of the Union and an Agenda for the Millenium* (London: The Royal Institute for International Affairs), 355–99

Frankel, J. and Froot, K. (1990). 'Chartists, fundamentalists, and trading in the foreign exchange market', *American Economic Review (Papers and Proceedings)*, 80(2), 181–5

Frankel, J., Galli, G. and Giovannini, A. (eds.) (1996). *The Microstructure of Foreign Exchange Markets* (Chicago: University of Chicago Press)

Frankel, J. and Wei, S.-J. (1994). 'Yen bloc or dollar bloc? Exchange rate policies of the East Asian economies', in Ito, T. and Krueger, A. (eds.), *Macroeconomic Linkages: Savings, Exchange Rates, and Capital-Flows* (Chicago: University of Chicago Press), 295–329

Fratianni, M. (1982). 'The dollar and the ecu', in Dreyer, J., Haberler, G. and Willett, T. (eds.), *The International Monetary System: A Time of Turbulence* (Washington, DC: American Enterprise Institute for Public Policy Research)

(1992). 'Dominant and dependent currencies', in Newman, P. *et al.* (eds.), *The New Palgrave Dictionary of Money and Finance*, vol. 1 (New York: Stockton Press), 702–4

French, K. and Poterba, J. (1991). 'International diversification and international equity markets', *American Economic Review*, 81, 222–6

Friedman, M. (1971). 'A theoretical framework for monetary analysis', *NBER Occasional Paper*, 112 (New York)

Funke, N. and Kennedy, M. (1997). 'International implications of European Economic and Monetary Union', *OECD Economics Department Working Paper*, OCDE/GD(97)61 (Paris)

Gallant, A. (1987). *Nonlinear Statistical Models* (New York: Wiley)

Garber, P. (1996). 'The use of the yen as a reserve currency', *Monetary and Economic Studies*, 14(2), 1–21

Giavazzi, F. and Giovannini, A. (1989). *Limiting Exchange Rate Flexibility – The European Monetary System* (Cambridge: Cambridge University Press)

Giddy, I, Saunders, A. and Walter, I. (1996). 'Clearing and settlement', in Steil, B. (ed.), *The European Equity Markets: The State of the Union and an Agenda for the Millenium*, (London: The Royal Institute for International Affairs), 321–50

Giovannini, A. and Turtelboom, B. (1994). 'Currency substitution', in van der Ploeg, F. (ed.), *The Handbook of International Macroeconomics* (Oxford: Blackwell), 390–436

Glassman, D. (1987). 'Exchange rate risk and transaction costs: evidence from bid–ask spreads', *Journal of International Money and Finance*, 6(4), 481–90

Glosten, L. and Milgrom, P. (1985). 'Bid, ask and transaction prices in a specialist market with heterogeneously informed traders', *Journal of Financial Economics*, 14, 71–100

Goeltz, K. (1980). 'Comment', in Levich, R. and Wihlborg, C. (eds.), *Exchange Risk and Exposure: Current Developments in International Financial Management* (Lexington, MA: Lexington Books), 81–6

Goldstein, M., Folkerts-Landau, D., Garber, P., Rojas-Suárez, L. and Spencer, M. (1993). *International Capital Markets. Part I: Exchange Rate Management and International Capital Flows* (Washington, DC: International Monetary Fund)

Goodhart, C. (1988). 'The foreign exchange market: a random walk with a dragging anchor', *Economica*, 55, 437–60

(1993). 'The external dimension of EMU', *Recherches Economiques de Louvain*, 59(1–2), 65–80

(1996). 'The transition to EMU', Second Annual Lecture delivered at the Scottish Economic Society/Royal Bank of Scotland (January)

(1997). 'Two concepts of money and the future of Europe', London School of Economics, *Financial Markets Group Special Paper*, 96 (June)

Goodhart, C. and Curcio, R. (1991). 'The clustering of bid/ask prices and the spread in the foreign exchange market', London School of Economics, *Financial Markets Group Discussion Papers*, 110 (January)

Goodhart, C. and Giugale, M. (1988). 'Some evidence on daily trading activity in the London forex market', London School of Economics, *Financial Markets Group Discussion Papers*, 34 (September)

Goodhart, C. and Lemmen, J. (1997). 'Credit risks and European government bond markets: a panel data analysis', London School of Economics, mimeo (September)

Goodhart, C. and O'Hara, M. (1998). 'High-frequency data in financial markets: issues and applications', *Journal of Empirical Finance*, 4(2–3), 73–114

Goodhart, C. and Schoenmaker, D. (1995). 'Should the functions of monetary policy and banking supervision be separated', *Oxford Economic Papers*, 47, 539–60

Goodhart, C., Ito, T. and Payne, R. (1996). 'One day in June 1993: a study of the working of Reuters 2000–2 electronic foreign exchange trading system', in Frankel, J. *et al.* (eds.), *The Microstructure of Foreign Exchange Markets* (Chicago: University of Chicago Press), 107–79

Goodhart, C., Hartmann, P., Llewellyn, D., Rojas-Suárez, L. and Weisbrod, S. (1998). 'Financial regulation: why, how and where now?', monograph prepared for the 1997 Bank of England Central Bank Governors' Symposium (London: Routledge)

Grassman, S. (1973). 'A fundamental symmetry in international payments patterns', *Journal of International Economics*, 3, 105–16

(1976). 'Currency distribution and forward cover in foreign trade', *Journal of International Economics*, 6, 215–21

Greene, J. and Heller, W. (1981). 'Mathematical analysis and convexity with applications to economics', in Arrow, K. and Intriligator, M. (eds.), *Handbook of Mathematical Economics*, vol. 1 (Amsterdam: North-Holland), 15–52

Greene, W. (1993). *Econometric Analysis*, 2nd edn (New York: Macmillan)

Gros, D. (1996). 'Towards Economic and Monetary Union: Problems and prospects', *CEPS Paper*, 65, Centre for European Policy Studies (Brussels)

Gros, D. and Thygesen, N. (1992). 'European monetary integration: from the European Monetary System to European Monetary Union' (London)

Group of Ten (1993). 'International capital movements and foreign exchange markets – a report to the Ministers and Governors by the Group of Deputies' (Rome) (April)

Group of Thirty (1980). 'The foreign exchange markets under floating rates – a study in international finance by the Exchange Markets Participants' Group' (Washington, DC)

(1982). 'How central banks manage their reserves' (New York)

Guillaume, D., Dacorogna, M., Davé, R., Müller, U., Olsen, R. and Pictet, O. (1997). 'From the bird's eye to the microscope: a survey of new stylized facts of the intra-daily foreign exchange markets, *Finance and Stochastics*, 1, 95–129

Hakkio, C. (1993). 'The dollar's international role', *Contemporary Policy Issues*, 11, 62–75

Hansen, L. (1982). 'Large sample properties of generalized method of moments estimators', *Econometrica*, 50(4), 1029–54

Harrod, R. (1952). 'The pound sterling', *Essays in International Finance*, 13 (Princeton University)

Hartmann, P. (1994). 'Vehicle currencies in the foreign exchange market', *DELTA Discussion Paper*, 94–13 (Paris) (June)

(1996a). 'Trading volumes and transaction costs in the foreign exchange market – evidence from daily dollar–yen spot data,' London School of Economics, *Financial Markets Group Discussion Papers*, 232 (January)

(1996b). 'The future of the euro as an international currency: a transactions perspective', *CEPS Research Report*, 20, Centre for European Policy Studies (Brussels) (December) (subsequently also issued as London School of Economics *Financial Markets Group Special Paper*, 91)

(1997a). 'Foreign exchange vehicles before and after EMU: from dollar/mark to dollar/euro?', in Welfens, P. (ed.), *European Monetary Union – Transition, International Impact and Policy Options* (Berlin: Springer Verlag), 133–55

(1997b). 'Do Reuters spreads reflect currencies' differences in global trading activity?', London School of Economics, *Financial Markets Group Discussion Paper*, 265 (April) (also *Journal of International Money and Finance*, 17(4), 1988)

(1997c). 'The currency denomination of world trade after European Monetary Union', London School of Economics, mimeo (September)

Harvey, A. (1981). *Time Series Models* (Oxford: Philip Allan)

Hausman, J. (1978). 'Specification tests in econometrics', *Econometrica*, 46(6), 1251–71

Healey, J. (1992). 'The foreign exchange market in London', *Bank of England Quarterly Bulletin*, 32(4) (November) 408–17

Heller, R. and Knight, M. (1978). 'Reserve currency preferences of central banks', *Essays in International Finance*, 131, Princeton University (December)

Henning, R. (1997). 'Cooperating with Europe's Monetary Union', *Policy Analysis in International Economics*, 49 (Washington, DC: Institute for International Economics)

Ho, T. and Stoll, H. (1981). 'Optimal dealer pricing under transactions and return uncertainty', *Journal of Financial Economics*, 9, 47–73

Hsiao, C. (1986). *Analysis of Panel Data* (Cambridge: Cambridge University Press)

International Monetary Fund (IMF) (1990). 'Annual report on exchange arrangements and exchange restrictions' (Washington, DC)

(1993). 'Annual report on exchange arrangements and exchange restrictions' (Washington, DC)

(1994). 'Annual report on exchange arrangements and exchange restrictions' (Washington, DC)

(1995). *Annual Report* (Washington, DC) (April)

(1996a). *Annual Report* (Washington, DC) (April)

(1996b). *International Financial Statistics Yearbook* (Washington, DC)

(1997a). *Annual Report* (Washington, DC) (April)

(1997b). *World Economic Outlook* (advance copy) (Washington, DC) (September)

Iwami, T. (1994). 'The internationalization of yen and key currency questions', *IMF Working Paper*, WP/94/41 (April)

Jevons, W. (1875). *Money and the Mechanism of Exchange* (London)

Jobert, T. (1992). 'Test de racine unitaire: une stratégie et sa mise en oeuvre', *Cahiers de Recherche Economie, Mathématiques et Applications*, 92.44 (Université de Paris I – Panthéon-Sorbonne)

Jones, C., Kaul, G. and Lipson, M. (1994). 'Transactions, volume, and volatility', *Review of Financial Studies*, 7(4), 631–51

Jones, R. (1976). 'The origin and development of media of exchange', *Journal of Political Economy*, 84(4), 757–75

Jorion, P. (1995). 'Predicting volatility in the foreign exchange market', *Journal of Finance*, 50(2), 507–28

(1996). 'Risk and turnover in the foreign exchange market', in Frankel, J. *et al.* (eds.), *The Microstructure of Foreign Exchange Markets* (Chicago: University of Chicago Press), 19–37

JP Morgan (1994). 'World holiday and time guide' (New York)

Karpoff, J. (1987). 'The relation between price changes and trading volume: a survey', *Journal of Financial and Quantitative Analysis*, 22(1), 109–26

Katz, M. and Shapiro, C. (1986). 'Technology adoption in the presence of network externalities', *Journal of Political Economy*, 94(4), 822–41

Kenen, P. (1983). 'The role of the dollar as an international currency', *Group of Thirty Occasional Papers*, 13 (New York)

(1995). *Economic and Monetary Union in Europe* (Cambridge: Cambridge University Press)

Kim, K. and Schmidt, P. (1993). 'Unit root tests with conditional heteroscedasticity', *Journal of Econometrics*, 59(3), 287–300

Kindleberger, C. (1966). 'Balance of payments deficits and the international market for liquidity', in Kindleberger, C. (ed.), *Europe and the Dollar* (Cambridge, MA: MIT Press), 1–26

(1967). 'The politics of international money and world language', *Essays in International Finance*, 61 (Princeton University)

(1972). 'The benefits of international money', *Journal of International Economics*, 2, 425–42

(1973a). *The World in Depression, 1929–1939* (Berkeley, CA: University of California Press)

(1973b). 'Standards as public, collective and private goods', *Kyklos*, 36(3), 377–96

(1981). *International Money – A Collection of Essays* (London: Allen & Unwin)

(1986). 'International public goods without international government', *American Economic Review*, 76(1), 1–13

(1993). *A Financial History of Western Europe*, 2nd edn (Oxford: Oxford University Press)

Kiyotaki, N. and Wright, R. (1989). 'On money as a medium of exchange', *Journal of Political Economy*, 97(4), 927–54

Klein, B. (1974). 'The competitive supply of money', *Journal of Money, Credit, and Banking*, 51, 423–53

Klein, B. and Melvin, M. (1982). 'Competing international moneys and international monetary arrangements', in Connolly, M. (ed.), *The International Monetary System: Choices for the Future* (New York: Praeger), 199–225

Klopstock, F. (1957). 'The international status of the dollar', *Essays in International Finance*, 28 (Princeton University)

Klump, R. (1986). *Entstehung und Verwendung internationaler Schlüsselwährungen* (Hamburg: Verlag Weltarchiv)

(1989). 'Der Dollar als internationale Schlüsselwährung – Ursachen und Perspektiven', *Kredit und Kapital*, 22(3), 375–400

Knapp, G. (1905). *Staatliche Theorie des Geldes* (Leipzig)

Kono, M., Low, P., Luanga, M., Mattoo, A., Oshikawa, M. and Schuknecht, L. (1997). 'Opening financial services and the role of the GATS', *WTO Special Study* (Geneva) (September)

Kouri, P. and de Macedo, J. (1978). 'Exchange rates and the international adjustment process', *Brookings Papers on Economic Activity*, 1, 111–50

Krugman, P. (1980). 'Vehicle currencies and the structure of international exchange', *Journal of Money, Credit, and Banking*, 12(3), 503–26

(1984). 'The international role of the dollar: theory and prospect', in Bilson, J. and Marston, R. (eds.), *Exchange Rate Theory and Practice* (Chicago: University of Chicago Press), 261–78

(1991). 'History versus expectations', *Quarterly Journal of Economics*, 106(2), 651–67

Kubarych, R. (1978). 'Foreign exchange markets in the United States', Federal Reserve Bank of New York (New York)

Kunieda, Y. (1994). 'Progress in the internationalization of the yen', *Tokyo Financial Review*, Bank of Tokyo, 19(2), 1–9

Kwan, C. (1994). *Economic Interdependence in the Asia-Pacific Region: Towards a Yen Bloc* (London: Routledge)

Kyle, A. (1985). 'Continuous auctions and insider trading', *Econometrica*, 53(6), 1315–35

Laidler, D. (1969). 'The definition of money', *Journal of Money, Credit, and Banking*, 1(1), 508–25

Leahy, M. (1996). 'The dollar as an official reserve currency under EMU', *Open Economies Review*, 7, 371–90

Lewis, K. (1995). 'Puzzles in international financial markets', in Grossman, G. and Rogoff, K. (eds.), *Handbook of International Economics* (Amsterdam: North-Holland), 1913–71

Lindert, P. (1969). 'Key currencies and gold 1900–1913', *Princeton Studies in International Finance*, 24 (Princeton University) (August)

Lopez, R. (1951). 'The dollar of the middle ages', *Journal of Economic History*, 10(3), 209–34

Lucas, R. (1982). 'Interest rates and currency prices in a two-country world', *Journal of Monetary Economics*, 10, 335–60

Lyons, R. (1995). 'Tests of microstructural hypotheses in the foreign exchange market', *Journal of Financial Economics*, 39, 321–51

(1996). 'Foreign exchange volume: sound and fury signifying nothing?', in Frankel, J. *et al.* (eds.), *The Microstructure of Foreign Exchange Markets* (Chicago: Chicago University Press), 183–205

(1997). 'A simultaneous trade model of the foreign exchange hot potato', *Journal of International Economics*, 42, 257–98

Maddala, G. (ed.) (1993). *The Econometrics of Panel Data*, 2 vols (Aldershot: Edward Elgar)

Madhavan, A. and Smidt, S. (1991). 'A Bayesian model of intraday specialist pricing', *Journal of Financial Economics*, 30, 99–134

Maehara, Y. (1993). 'The internationalization of the yen and its role as a key currency', *Journal of Asian Economics*, 4(1), 153–70

Magee, S. (1974). 'US import prices in the currency-contract period', *Brookings Papers on Economic Activity*, 1, 117–68

Magee, S. and Rao, K. (1980). 'Vehicle and nonvehicle currencies in international trade', *American Economic Review (Papers and Proceedings)*, 70(2), 368–73

Markowitz, H. (1952). 'Portfolio selection', *Journal of Finance*, 7, 77–91

Martin, P. (1997). 'The exchange rate policy of the euro: a matter of size?', *CEPR Discussion Paper*, 1646 (December)

Masson, P. and Taylor, M. (1992). 'Common currency areas and currency unions: an analysis of the issues', *CEPR Discussion Paper*, 617 (February)

Masson, P. and Turtelboom, B. (1997). 'Characteristics of the euro, the demand for reserves and policy coordination under EMU', *IMF Working Paper*, WP/97/58 (Washington, DC: IMF) (May)

Mastropasqua, C., Micossi, S. and Rinaldi, R. (1988). 'Interventions, sterilization and monetary policy in European Monetary System countries, 1979–1987', in Giavazzi, F., Micossi, S. and Miller, M. (eds.), *The European Monetary System* (Cambridge: Cambridge University Press) 252–91

Matsuyama, K., Kiyotaki, N. and Matsui, A. (1993). 'Toward a theory of international currency', *Review of Economic Studies*, 60(2), 283–320

McCallum, B. (1989). *Monetary Economics – Theory and Policy* (New York: Macmillan)

McCauley, R. (1997). 'The euro and the dollar', forthcoming as *BIS Working Paper* (Basle)

McCauley, R. and White, W. (1997). 'The euro and European financial markets', *BIS Working Paper*, 41 (Basle) (May)

McKinnon, R. (1969). 'Private and official international money: the case of the dollar', *Essays in International Finance*, 74 (Princeton University)

(1979) *Money in International Exchange* (New York: Oxford University Press)

(1982). 'Currency substitution and instability in the world dollar standard', *American Economic Review*, 72, 320–33

(1985). 'Two concepts of international currency substitution', in Connolly, M. and McDermott, J. (eds.), *The Economics of the Caribbean Basin* (New York: Praeger), 101–13

Meese, R. and Rogoff, K. (1983). 'Empirical exchange rate models of the seventies – do they fit out of sample?', *Journal of International Economics*, 12(1,2), 3–24

Menger, K. (1892). 'On the origins of money', *Economic Journal*, 2, 239–55

Menkhoff, L. (1995). 'Zur deutschen Position im internationalen Devisenhandel: Starke Währung, schwacher Standort', *Kredit und Kapital*, 28(3), 431–52

Müller, U. A. (1986). 'Transaction volume estimation in the currency spot market using spread and volatility', Olsen & Associates, *Internal Document*, UAM.1986-11-03 (Zürich) (March)

Mundlak, Y. (1978). 'On the pooling of time series and cross section data', *Econometrica*, 46(1), 69–85

Mussa, M. (1981). 'The role of official intervention', *Group of Thirty Occasional Papers*, 6 (New York)

Mussa, M., Boughton, J. and Isard, P. (1996). *The Future of the SDR in the Light of Changes in the International Financial System* (Washington, DC: International Monetary Fund)

Neal, L. (1990). *The Rise of Financial Capitalism: International Capital Markets in the Age of Reason* (New York: Cambridge University Press)

Newey, W. (1985). 'Generalized method of moments specification testing', *Journal of Econometrics*, 29(3), 229–56

Newey, W. and West, K. (1987a). 'A simple positive semi-definite, heteroske-dasticity and autocorrelation consistent covariance matrix', *Econometrica*, 55, 703–08

(1987b). 'Hypothesis testing with efficient method of moments estimation', *International Economic Review*, 28(3), 777–87

Niehans, J. (1969). 'Money in a static theory of optimal payment arrange-ments', *Journal of Money, Credit, and Banking*, 1(4), 707–26

(1971). 'Money and barter in general equilibrium with transaction costs', *American Economic Review*, 61, 773–83

(1978). *The Theory of Money* (Baltimore: Johns Hopkins University Press)

(1984). *International Monetary Economics* (Baltimore: Johns Hopkins University Press)

Obstfeld, M. and Rogoff, K. (1996). *Foundations of International Macroeco-nomics* (Cambridge, MA: MIT Press)

Oh, S. (1989). 'A theory of a generally acceptable medium of exchange and barter', *Journal of Monetary Economics*, 23, 101–19

Organization for Economic Cooperation and Development (OECD) (1997). *OECD Financial Statistics Part I* (Paris) (September)

Osborne, D. (1984). 'Ten approaches to the definition of money', *Economic Review*, Federal Reserve Bank of Dallas (March) 1–23

(1985). 'What is money today?', *Economic Review*, Federal Reserve Bank of Dallas (January) 1–15

Ostroy, J. and Starr, R. (1974). 'Money and the decentralization of exchange', *Econometrica*, 42, 1093–1113

(1990). 'The transactions role of money', in Friedman, B. and Hahn, F. (eds.), *Handbook of Monetary Economics*, vol. 1 (Amsterdam: North-Holland), 3–62

Pagano (1989). 'Endogenous market thinness and stock price volatility', *Review of Economic Studies*, 56, 269–88

Page, S. (1977). 'Currency invoicing in merchandise trade', *National Institute Economic Review*, 81(3), 77–81

(1981). 'The choice of invoicing currency in merchandise trade', *National Institute Economic Review*, 98(4), 60–72

Petersen, M. and Fialkowski, D. (1994). 'Posted versus effective spreads: good prices or bad quotes?', *Journal of Financial Economics*, 35(3), 269–92

Phillips, P. (1987). 'Asymptotic expansions in non-stationary vector autoregres-sions', *Econometric Theory*, 3(1), 45–68

Phillips, P. and Perron, P. (1988). 'Testing for a unit root in time series regressions', *Biometrika*, 75(2), 335–46

Pickering, G. and Sawchuk, C. (1989). 'Survey of the Canadian foreign exchange market,' *Bank of Canada Review* (October), 3–18

Pineau, G. (1993). 'Activité du marché des changes de Paris. Principales tendances', *Bulletin Mensuel de la Banque de France* (September), 109–16

Polak, J. (1992). 'Reserve currency', in Newman, P. *et al.* (eds.), *The New Palgrave Dictionary of Money and Finance*, vol. 3 (New York: Stockton Press), 339–42

(1997). 'The IMF and its EMU members', paper presented at the IMF Conference 'EMU and the International Monetary System' (Washington, DC) (17–18 March)

Pollin, J.-P. and Ullmo Y. (1992). 'Réseaux et finance', in Curien, N. (ed.), *Economie et Management des Entreprises de Réseau* (Paris: Economica)

Poloz, S. (1984). 'The transactions demand for money in a two-currency economy', *Journal of Monetary Economics*, 14, 241–50

Portes, R. (1993). 'EMS and EMU after the fall', *The World Economy*, 16, 9–15

Portes, R., Rey, H. and Alogoskoufis, G. (1997). 'The emergence of the euro as an international currency', *CEPR Discussion Paper*, 1741 (London) (October)

Prati, A. and Schinasi, G. (1997). 'European monetary union and international capital markets: structural implications and risks', *IMF Working Paper*, WP/97/62 (Washington, DC: IMF) (May)

Pryor, F. (1977). 'The origins of money', *Journal of Money, Credit, and Banking*, 9, 391–409

Rao, R. and Magee, S. (1980). 'The currency of denomination of international trade contracts', in Levich, R. and Wihlborg, C. (eds.), *Exchange Risk and Exposure: Current Developments in International Financial Management* (Lexington: Lexington Books), 61–80

Rey, H. (1997). 'International trade and currency exchange', London School of Economics, *Centre for Economic Performance Discussion Paper*, 322, (February)

Rogoff, K (1997). 'Foreign and underground demand for euro notes: blessing or curse?', paper presented at the 26th Economic Policy Panel Meeting hosted by the Centre for European Economic Integration (Bonn) (17–18 October)

Rohlfs, J. (1974). 'A theory of interdependent demand for a communications service', *Bell Journal of Economics and Management Science*, 5(1), 16–37

Roll, R. (1984). 'A simple implicit measure of the effective bid–ask spread in an efficient market', *Journal of Finance*, 39(4), 1127–39

Romer, P. (1986). 'Increasing returns and long-run growth', *Journal of Political Economy*, 94, 1002–37

Roosa, R. (1965). *Monetary Reform for the World Economy* (New York: Praeger)

Roosa, R. and Hirsch, F. (1966). 'Reserves, reserve currencies, and vehicle currencies: an argument', *Essays in International Finance*, 54 (Princeton University)

Rother, P. (1994). 'Currency substitution – a survey', International Monetary

Fund, Monetary and Exchange Affairs Department (Washington, DC: IMF), mimeo

Saville, I. (1992). 'Foreign exchange reserves', in Newman, P. *et al.* (eds.), *The New Palgrave Dictionary of Money and Finance*, vol. 2 (New York: Stockton Press), 161–4

Scharrer, H. (1981). 'Currency diversification in international trade and payments: empirical evidence', in Sargent, J. (ed.), *Europe and the Dollar in the World-wide Disequilibrium* (Rockville: Sijthoff and Noordhoff), 225–41

Schlesinger, H., Gros, D. and Lannoo, K. (1996). 'The passage to the euro', *CEPS Working Party Report*, 16, Centre for European Policy Studies (Brussels) (December)

Schoenmaker, D. (1995). 'Banking supervision in stage three of EMU', London School of Economics, *Financial Markets Group Special Paper*, 72 (June)

Shubik, M. (1990). 'A game theoretic approach to the theory of money and financial institutions', in Friedman, B. and Hahn, F. (eds.), *Handbook of Monetary Economics*, vol. 1 (Amsterdam: North-Holland), 171–219

Sidrauski, M. (1967). 'Rational choice and patterns of growth in a monetary economy', *American Economic Review*, 57, 534–44

Siglienti, S. (1981). 'The future of the dollar as a reserve asset', in Sargent, J. (ed.), *Europe and the Dollar in the World-wide Disequilibrium* (Rockville: Sijthoff and Noordhoff), 184–223

Smith, A. (1776). *An Inquiry into the Nature and Causes of the Wealth of Nations* (Harmondsworth: Penguin, 1970)

Solnik, B. (1974). 'An equilibrium model of the international capital markets', *Journal of Economic Theory*, 8, 500–24

Sorin, S. (1994). 'Strategic market games with exchange rates', Université de Paris X–Nanterre, *Document de travail du THEMA*, 9411 (September)

South African Reserve Bank (1993). 'Average daily turnover on the South African foreign exchange market', *Quarterly Bulletin*, B137–B138

Starr, R. and Stinchcombe, M. (1993). 'Exchange in a network of trading posts', University of California–San Diego, mimeo; forthcoming in Chichilnisky, G. (ed.), *Markets, Information and Uncertainty, Essays in Economic Theory in Honor of Kenneth Arrow* (New York: Cambridge University Press)

Steil, B. (ed.) (1996). 'The European equity markets: the state of the union and an agenda for the millenium' (London: The Royal Institute for International Affairs)

Stockman, A. and Dellas, H. (1989). 'International portfolio non-diversification and exchange rate variability', *Journal of International Economics*, 26, 271–89

Stoll, H. (1978). 'The supply of dealer services in securities markets', *Journal of Finance*, 33(4), 1133–51

Stulz, R. (1981). 'On the effects of barriers to international investment', *Journal of Finance*, 36, 923–34

Suvanto, A. (1993). 'Foreign exchange dealing – essays on the microstructure of the foreign exchange market', The Research Institute of the Finnish Economy (ETLA) (Helsinki)

Swoboda, A. (1968). 'The Euro-dollar market: an interpretation', *Essays in International Finance*, 64 (Princeton University)

(1969). 'Vehicle currencies and the foreign exchange market: the case of the dollar', in Aliber, R. (ed.), *The International Market for Foreign Exchange* (New York: Praeger), 30–40

Taguchi, H. (1982). 'A survey of the international use of the yen', *BIS Working Papers*, 6 (Basle) (July)

Tauchen, G. and Pitts, M. (1983), 'The price variability–volume relationship on speculative markets', *Econometrica*, 51, 485–505

Tavlas, G. (1991). 'On the international use of currencies: the case of the Deutsche mark', *Essays in International Finance*, 181 (Princeton University)

(1992). 'Vehicle currencies', in Newman, P. *et al.* (eds.), *The New Palgrave Dictionary of Money and Finance*, vol. 3 (New York: Stockton Press), 754–7

Tavlas, G. and Ozeki, Y. (1992). 'The internationalization of currencies: an appraisal of the Japanese yen', *IMF Occasional Paper*, 90 (Washington, DC: IMF)

Taylor, W. (1980). 'Small sample considerations in estimation from panel data', *Journal of Econometrics*, 13(2), 203–23

Tesar, L. and Werner, I. (1992). 'Home bias and the globalization of securities markets', *NBER Working Paper*, 4218 (Cambridge, MA)

Theil, H. (1961). *Economic Forecasts and Policy* (Amsterdam: North-Holland)

Thomas, S. and Wickens, M. (1991). 'Currency substitution and vehicle currencies: tests of alternative hypotheses for the dollar, DM and yen', *CEPR Discussion Paper*, 507 (London)

Thygesen, N. (1997). 'Relations among the IMF, the ECB and Fund/EMU members', paper presented at the IMF Conference 'EMU and the International Monetary System' (Washington, DC) (17–18 March)

Tinic, S. (1972). 'The economics of liquidity services', *Quarterly Journal of Economics*, 86, 79–93

Tobin, J. (1956). 'The interest-elasticity of transactions demand for cash', *Review of Economics and Statistics*, 38(3), 241–7

(1958). 'Liquidity preference as behavior towards risk', *Review of Economic Studies*, 25, 65–86

(1980). 'Discussion', in Kareken, J. and Wallace, N. (eds.), *Models of Monetary Economies* (Minneapolis: Federal Reserve Bank of Minneapolis), 83–90

Triffin, R. (1964). 'The evolution of the international monetary system: historical reappraisal and future perspectives', *Princeton Studies in International Finance*, 12 (Princeton University)

Tygier, C. (1983). *Basic Handbook of Foreign Exchange – A Guide to Foreign Exchange Dealing* (London: Euromoney)

United Nations (UN) (1994). *Statistical Yearbook 1992* (New York)

(1995). *Statistical Yearbook 1993* (New York)

(1996). *Statistical Yearbook 1994* (New York)

United Nations Development Programme (UNDP) (1994). *United Nations Common Coding System* (New York) (March)

United States Federal Reserve Board (1996). *Federal Reserve Bulletin* (Washington, DC) (January)

van de Koolwijk, P. (1994). 'The international use of main currencies: a statistical overview of recent developments', report prepared for the Directorate General for Economic and Financial Affairs of the European Commission (Tilburg) (July)

Vaubel, R. (1978).   *Strategies for Currency Unification: The Economics of Currency Competition and the Case for a European Parallel Currency* (Tübingen: Mohr)

(1984).   'The government's money monopoly: externalities or natural monopoly', *Kyklos*, 37(1), 27–58

(1986).   'Currency competition versus government money monopolies', *Cato Journal*, 5(3), 937–42

Viaene, J.-M. and Vries, C. de (1992).   'On the design of invoicing practices in international trade', *Open Economies Review*, 3, 133–42

Vizy, M. (1989).   *La zone franc* (Paris: Centre des Hautes Etudes sur l'Afrique et l'Asie Modernes)

Vogler, K. (1993).   'Inter-dealer trading', London School of Economics, *Financial Markets Group Discussion Papers*, 174 (November)

von Hayek, F. (1977).   *Entnationalisierung des Geldes – Eine Analyse der Theorie und Praxis konkurrierender Umlaufsmittel* (Tübingen: Mohr)

Walters, A. (1992).   'Sterling', in Newman, P. *et al.* (eds.), *The New Palgrave Dictionary of Money and Finance*, vol. 3 (New York: Stockton Press) 549–54

Wei, S.-J. (1994).   'Anticipations of foreign exchange volatility and bid–ask spreads', *NBER Working Paper*, 4737 (Cambridge, MA) (May)

White, H. (1980).   'A heteroscedasticity-consistent covariance matrix estimator and a direct test for heteroscedasticity', *Econometrica*, 48, 817–38

(1982).   'Maximum likelihood estimation of misspecified models', *Econometrica*, 50, 817–38

Whitman, M. von (1974).   'The current and future role of the dollar: how much symmetry?', *Brookings Papers on Economic Activity*, 3, 539–83

Williams, D. (1968).   'The evolution of the sterling system', in Whittlesey, C. and Wilson, J. (eds.), *Essays in Money and Banking in Honour of R.S. Sayers* (Oxford: Clarendon Press), 266–97

Williamson, J. (1971).   'The choice of a pivot for parities', *Essays in International Finance*, 90 (Princeton University)

(1982).   'A survey of the literature on the optimal peg', *Journal of Development Economics*, 11, 39–61

(1996).   'The case for a common basket peg for East Asian countries', Institute for International Economics (Washington, DC), mimeo

World Bank (1997).   *World Development Indicators* (CD ROM) (Washington, DC: World Bank)

World Trade Organization (WTO) (1996).   *Annual Report (volume II)* (Geneva)

Wyplosz, C. (1997).   'An International role for the euro?', University of Geneva, mimeo (August)

Yeager, L. (1968).   'Essential properties of the medium of exchange', *Kyklos*, 21(1), 45–69

(1976).   *International Monetary Relations: Theory, History, and Policy* (New York: Harper & Row)

Index

n.1 is a note to the text discussion, n.a is a note to a table in the text.